STUDIES IN
COLOSSIANS
AND
PHILEMON

BOOKS BY W. H. GRIFFITH THOMAS

Genesis: A Devotional Commentary
Through the Pentateuch Chapter by Chapter
Outline Studies in the Gospel of Matthew
Outline Studies in the Acts of the Apostles
St. Paul's Epistle to the Romans: A Devotional Commentary
The Apostle John
The Apostle Peter
Hebrews: A Devotional Commentary
The Holy Spirit of God
Ministerial Life and Work

STUDIES IN
COLOSSIANS
AND
PHILEMON

W.H. GRIFFITH THOMAS, D.D.

Edited by His Daughter

Baker Book House
Grand Rapids, Michigan

PHOTOLITHOPRINTED BY CUSHING - MALLOY, INC.
ANN ARBOR, MICHIGAN, UNITED STATES OF AMERICA
1973

In loving memory of

ELMER HALLOWELL GILLESPIE

(1898-1970)

for whom to live was Christ
and to die was gain

PREFACE

The major portion of this volume, or Part I, is a revision of my father's book entitled *Christ Pre-eminent: Studies in the Epistle to the Colossians,* which was published in 1923 by the Bible Institute Colportage Association (now Moody Press), and which has been out of print for many years. The outline used is mentioned briefly near the end of the original volume and was found in expanded form among my father's lecture notes. It bears clear indications of having been developed and presented after the book had appeared. This is in line with his practice of never giving in public a series of addresses based entirely on already published material. This fresh analysis of the Epistle to the Colossians appeals to me as more mature, cohesive, and spiritually suggestive than the headings used in the first edition, so that I have enjoyed not only expanding the text by including in it other material on the subject, but also meeting the challenge of fitting the whole acceptably into the later form. In particular, I have drawn on unpublished sermon notes left by my father and also from some printed material of his, as follows: excerpts from two out-of-print books, *Life Abiding and Abounding* (London: Marshall Bros., 1909), and *The Prayers of St. Paul* (Edinburgh: T. and T. Clark, 1914); and articles from the following periodicals: *The Sunday School Times, Daily Bible,* and *Moody Bible Institute Monthly* (now *Moody Monthly*).

The second and shorter section of the present volume, dealing with the Epistle to Philemon, represents my first attempt at connected composition based on my father's unpublished outline notes. This was done in order to enlarge the book and to make the material thus utilized consistent in form with that concerning the Epistle to the Colossians.

In this entire effort I have been aided by reference to a notebook of my father's on "The Prison Epistles of St. Paul," based largely on his study of Bishop Lightfoot's great classic, *The Epistles of St. Paul to the Colossians and Philemon,* and some other commentaries. When uncertain of how to interpret my father's Greek references, I have consulted Kenneth S. Wuest's *An Expanded Translation of the Greek New Testament* (Grand Rapids: Wm. B. Eerdmans Publishing Company, 1956, 3 vols.).

On the advice of Professor S. Lewis Johnson, Chairman of the Department of New Testament Literature and Exegesis at Dallas Theological Seminary, who had found great value in the original volume, I have added as appendices to the present one, first, an article on the life and work of the apostle Paul that was entitled "Saul Who Is Also Called Paul: An Outline Study" (*The Sunday School Times,* June 18, 1921), and, second, some unpublished notes on "A General Survey of St. Paul's Epistles."

It remains only to express deep appreciation to all persons represented by these sources of help and for the unfailing cooperation of my late husband, the Rev. Elmer H. Gillespie, who liked to call our work together for Christ "The W. H. Griffith Thomas Memorial in Louisiana." It is my fervent hope that we have acceptably reproduced the scholarly material represented in this volume, in particular for the edification and use of new generations of Bible students.

Lafayette, Louisiana   Winifred G. T. Gillespie
June 1973

Lord, pardon what I have been;
sanctify what I am;
order what I shall be;
that Thine may be the glory
and mine the eternal salvation.
For Christ's sake.

*—Written on the flyleaf of the author's
first Bible after his conversion.*

CONTENTS

CONTENTS

PART TWO

THE EPISTLE OF
ST. PAUL, THE APOSTLE,
TO PHILEMON

PART ONE

THE EPISTLE OF
ST. PAUL, THE APOSTLE,
TO THE
COLOSSIANS

1 INTRODUCTION

Each Epistle of St. Paul has its own special characteristics, and when they are combined they sum up completely the teaching of the great apostle's life.[1] Dr. Agar Beet, treating these Epistles in their generally accepted chronological order, from Thessalonians to Titus, says that they exhibit the springtime (I and II Thessalonians), summer (Galatians, I and II Corinthians, Romans), autumn (Ephesians, Philippians, Colossians, Philemon), and winter (the Pastoral Epistles) of the great apostle's year. They have also been described under the figure of a day in his life, as the Epistles of the morning, noon, afternoon, and evening. Bishop Lightfoot tabulates them in this way: (a) The Epistles of the Second Missionary Journey (I and II Thessalonians), as the Epistles of the Tribunal, or Christ the Judge; (b) The Epistles of the Third Missionary Journey (I and II Corinthians, Galatians, Romans), as the Epistles of the Cross, or Christ the Redeemer; (c) The Epistles of the First Captivity (Philippians, Ephesians, Colossians, Philemon), as The Epistles of the Throne, or Christ the Word; (d) The Epistles of the Release and Second Captivity (I Timothy, Titus, II Timothy), as the Epistles of the Congregation, or Church Organization (Lightfoot, *Biblical Essays,* p. 224).

It is not too much to say that Ephesians and Colossians together represent the highest, fullest concept of Christianity. Just as Romans tells

---

[1] See also Appendix 2.

us how to enter into fellowship with Christ through the gospel, so Ephesians and Colossians tell us how to abide therein. First we come out of bondage and then we are brought into the banqueting-house.

THE PLACE

Colosse was in Asia Minor and was reached from the sea at Miletus up the rivers Maeander and Lycus. There were three cities near one another: Laodicea, Hierapolis, and Colosse. St. Paul does not seem to have visited Colosse (2:1), but Epaphras, one of his converts at Ephesus during the three years there (Acts 19:10-26), evidently was instrumental in founding the Colossian Church and was its evangelist (Col. 1:4, 9; 4:12, 13; Philem. 23). The Epistle addressed to this Church was written during St. Paul's first imprisonment in Rome (Acts 28:30, 31), about A.D. 62 or 63.

THE PURPOSE

This Epistle was written primarily because in Colosse there was real danger from false teaching, a mixture of Judaism and Orientalism (2:16-18). This took the form, first, of an exclusive intellectualism, almost entirely connected with speculation, and then, on the practical side, the tendency was in either of two opposite directions, that of asceticism or that of sensualism. In what is called the Colossian heresy the fundamental idea was the evil nature of matter, and this suggested two questions: (1) How could God have created matter or even come into contact with it? This problem was solved by an assumed hierarchy of angelic beings, each grade containing less of the divine nature than the one above, until one was deemed low enough to be held responsible for that which is essentially evil, i.e., matter. (2) What, then, is redemption? This, it was said, must consist in liberation from matter, and it was to be secured by a rigid asceticism.

Just as in writing Galatians and Romans the apostle had waged constant warfare against everything legalistic and materialistic that might be placed as a stumbling block to those who desired to know and accept the gospel, so here he contends earnestly against theories that would minister to intellectual pride and exclusiveness.

In further consideration of the apostle's purpose in writing, it is especially interesting to notice the relation of this Epistle to that addressed to the Ephesian Christians, because the likeness between them is so striking. As one writer puts it: "Out of 95 verses in Colossians, 78 have a marked resemblance to Ephesians, while, out of the 155 verses in Ephesians, 78 resemble Colossians." But the particular character of this resemblance is even more striking. The same topics are treated in each, though with a very significant difference in application. In Colossians we are shown Christ in the Church, while in Ephesians the Church is seen to be in Christ. One writer has thus stated this comparison: "In the Ephesians the Church is the primary object, and the thought passes upward to Christ as the Head of the Church. In the Colossians Christ is the primary object, and the thought passes downward to the Church as the Body of Christ."

The more this contrast is studied the more remarkable it will appear. In Colossians the apostle gives a careful and thorough statement concerning the person and work of Christ, while in Ephesians the main topic is our Lord's relation to the Church. In Colossians there is no such emphasis on the Church and its privileges, but only on the great realities concerning its head, since nothing can be allowed for one moment to come between the soul and God. Further, the same obligations are emphasized in each Epistle, but with this different bearing: our life, as stated in Colossians, is to be lived in relation to Christ, while many of the moral applications in Ephesians are related to the Church and to the duties of one member of it to another.

Doubtless because of this very emphasis on the divine person and work of Christ, Colossians was intended for reading by other churches as well (4:16). The secret of purity, whether of doctrine or of life, and the assurance of protection against error are both found in the revelation of Jesus Christ as the Son of God and Savior of the world.

THE PLAN

The general structure of this Epistle is much the same as that of Paul's other Epistles, opening with a personal element (1:1-8), developing into a doctrinal section (1:9—2:23) that has a practical application (3:1—4:6), and closing with another personal section (4:7-18).

The author knows of many attempts to analyze this Epistle in detail, and in his opinion, two of them seem worthy of special attention. One of these was by Professor E. C. Caldwell[2] of Richmond, Virginia, who remarked that many writers seem to think that there is no organic structure in Colossians. Dr. Caldwell, on the contrary, maintained that there is a true literary arrangement and that every section, paragraph, and sentence has its proper place and function. This is how he set out his detailed plan of the Epistle:

---

[2]*The Princeton Theological Review,* October 1918 (pp. 559-71).

1. *Introduction* (1:1-14). This includes the salutation, the thanksgiving, and the opening prayer
2. *Part 1* (1:15-23). The preeminence of Christ over creation, providence, and redemption
3. *Part 2* (1:24 to 4:6). The practical effects of the preeminence of Christ:
   a. On Paul himself (1:24 to 2:7)
   b. On a false philosophy of the Christian life (2:8-23)
   c. On the true doctrine of the Christian life (3:1 to 4:6)

In this section there are five fruits of the Christian life, all proceeding from the union with Christ stated in 3:1-4. The first fruit is the death of the "old man" (3:5-9). The second fruit is the putting on of the "new man" (3:10, 11). The third fruit is the clothing of the new man with the garments of holiness (3:12-14). The fourth fruit is the transformation of relationships (3:18 to 4:1). The fifth fruit is a life of prayer and activity (4:2-6).

4. *Conclusion* (4:2-6).

This is only a bare outline of a most suggestive and valuable study. The other notable analysis is found in Dr. E. W. Bullinger's stimulating book *The Church Epistles* (p. 176), and it is particularly interesting to compare this outline with the former one and to see the points of agreement as well as of difference.

1. Opening salutation (1:1, 2)
2. Mutual reports and messages by Epaphras (1:3-8)
3. St. Paul's solicitude for the Colossian saints and his prayer for them (1:9 to 2:7)
4. Doctrinal correction, with special reference to union with Christ in His death (2:8-23)
5. Doctrinal correction, with special reference to union with Christ in His resurrection (3:1 to 4:1)
6. St. Paul's solicitude for the Colossian saints and their prayers for him (4:2-6)
7. Mutual reports and messages by Tychicus and Onesimus (4:7-9)
8. Closing salutation (4:10-18)

It will be noticed that in this outline there is an introversion, Section 1 corresponding to Section 8, 2 with 7, 3 with 6, and 4 with 5.

As we shall see in the following section, the special emphasis of the present volume suggests the submission of still another outline:

1. The Preliminary Greetings (1:1-8)
2. The Prayer of the Apostle (1:9-13)
3. The Person and Work of Christ (1:14-23)
4. The Presentation of the Christian Ministry (1:24-29)

5. The Power of Christ (2:1-23)
6. The Practice of the Christian Life (3:1-17)
7. The Proof of the Christian Life (3:18 to 4:6)
8. The Personal Conclusion (4:7-18)

THE PRINCIPLE

There seems no doubt that the dominating thought of this Epistle is the all-sufficiency of Christ. Dr. Caldwell believes that the well-known lines of Charles Wesley's great hymn express the central idea:

> Thou, O Christ, art all I want,
> More than all in Thee I find.

And he adds that whenever he reads Colossians he is reminded of the familiar passage by Robert Browning:

> I say, the acknowledgment of God in Christ
> Accepted by thy reason, solves for thee
> All questions in the earth and out of it,
> And has so far advanced thee to be wise.
> —from *A Death in the Desert*

Three great phrases in the Epistle sum up this truth: "That in all things he might have the preeminence" (1:18); "In him dwelleth all the fulness of the Godhead bodily" (2:9); "Christ is all, and in all" (3:11). The failure of the Colossians was at this very point, "not holding the Head" (2:19).

The story is told of the celebrated German sculptor J. H. von Dannecker that when he was asked by Napoleon Bonaparte to make a statue of Venus for the gallery of the Louvre he declined. An enormous sum was then offered him, but still he refused. When the Emperor angrily demanded the reason why, the sculptor answered: "Sir, I have made a statue of Jesus Christ, and I can never lower my chisel to carve an inferior subject." It is also said of Dannecker that the first time he modeled Christ he uncovered the finished statue, after years of hard work, in the presence of a little girl. When he asked her, "Who is that?" she clapped her hands in surprise and admiration, crying, "It is certainly a great man!" This disappointed the sculptor so much that soon the statue was broken up beyond repair; he felt he had failed since the child had not recognized his intention to represent our Lord. Dannecker went to work again and prayed much as he toiled; and when he invited the little girl into his studio a second time there was no expression of childish delight. Instead, the little one stole quietly up to the great figure as though it were alive, and murmured in awe, "He is the One who said, 'Suffer the little children to come unto Me'!" This typifies the dominant note of Colossians: the secret of true spiritual life is a deep consciousness of the reality and power of Christ.

The Epistle to the Colossians, moreover, has a direct bearing on the various heresies of our day, because it is concerned with the positive presentation of the antidote to every form of intellectual poison. As Bishop Handley Moule truly and forcibly said, "No surer test, according to the Holy Scriptures, can be applied to anything claiming to be Christian teaching than this, Where does it put Jesus Christ? What does it make of Jesus Christ? Is He something in it, or is He all?" (Moule, *Colossians Studies,* p. 15). Another writer, Bishop W. R. Nicholson, points out that the Colossian heresy was no vulgar falsehood, because at the bottom of it there was an intense yearning for something that could not be satisfied in teaching the mediation of angels and the consequent removal of God from all contact with matter. This attitude claimed to honor Him, and at the same time to show its own humility, amid human and earthly evils, in shrinking from any direct fellowship with Him. In its asceticism, meanwhile, it ministered to human pride and self-righteousness. "It was human nature," writes Bishop Nicholson, "as essentially displayed everywhere, and in all ages; the circumstances and particular tenets ever changing, but the affectation of humility, and the proud, self-righteous spirit ever remaining the same. And thus it is that the Colossian heresy was the anticipation of the errors of today, and that the Apostle's confutation of it supplies the needed instruction for ourselves" (Nicholson, *Oneness with Christ,* pp. 19, 20).

Writing many years ago, Dr. H. Sinclair Paterson reviewed the Epistle to the Colossians in words that are just as applicable to our own day:

> The main purpose of the Epistle . . . is strongly to set forth the supremacy and sufficiency of Christ, the Head of the body. Our knowledge, our growth, our obedience, are entirely dependent on our vital, continuous communion with Christ; through its fellowship with Him alone the Church is perfected in the whole will of God. There is no greater danger threatening us at the present time than the danger of interrupted or limited communication between the Head and the members. Where this communion is marred or lessened, feebleness must follow. In our own day many are permitting unbridled reason to lead them as far astray as these false speculations and philosophies led the Church at Colosse in the first century. And others are interposing, between the saint and his Saviour, mediators, whether heavenly or earthly, whether saints in the glory or priests here on earth. In any case they are separating from the Head; and, separate from the Head, there can only be

weakness and want. Our privilege is to enjoy personally the whole fulness of God in Christ, and that fulness is designed for our own individual completeness. And if it be our desire to walk worthy of the Lord unto all pleasing we must unhesitatingly reject any doctrine which limits or lessens a continuous, unintermitting fellowship with the Lord.

Our power for service, no less than our peace with God, depends on our abiding in Him, rooted and grounded in the Faith.[3]

Thus the real safeguard is a personal experience of Jesus Christ. As we consider our own circumstances today when faced with such cults as Unitarianism, Spiritism, Occultism, Russellism, Eddyism, and their various successors, as well as with Modernism or Liberalism within the professing churches, the one decisive test is His own question of the disciples, "What think ye of Christ?" Whenever we can ascertain where either men or systems put the divine person and atoning work of the Lord Jesus Christ, we can decide at once whether this or that is Christian or not.

This emphasis on a personal conviction and consciousness of Christ has a similar bearing on the serious lack of certitude that marks so much of church life today. As a thoughtful writer has said, "Men are casting about them on either side for some standing ground. They have no strong convictions. . . . Our present distress is ultimately due to theological unsettlement." Another writer has contrasted the remarkable certitude of the Old Testament prophet as he said with conviction, courage, and even alacrity, "Here am I," and the uncertainty and vague hopelessness with which many in the present day are asking, "*Where* am I?" But those who know by personal experience the Lord Jesus Christ have no doubt as to where they stand, since they are able to say with the apostle, "I know whom I have believed, and am persuaded that he is able . . ." (II Tim. 1:12).

> Whoso hath felt the Spirit of the Highest
> Cannot confound, nor doubt Him, nor deny.
> Yes, with one voice, O world, though thou deniest,
> Stand thou on that side, for on this am I.
> —H. W. H. Meyer: *St. Paul*

---

[3] *Word and Work,* October 12, 1882, p. 664.

2 THE PRELIMINARY GREETINGS

The personal openings of St. Paul's Epistles almost invariably contain revelations of the writer's Christian character; and at the same time they suggest elements that should mark our life in Christ today.

THE SALUTATION (vv. 1, 2)

1. The Authority. St. Paul describes himself as "an apostle of Christ Jesus through the will of God" (v. 1, *A.S.V.*), and the term *apostle* indicates here, as elsewhere, the thought of commission (cf. Matt. 10:2, 5). He fully realizes that he has been sent by Christ to do His work; and his reference to "the will of God" is a further reminder of apostolic authority as divinely derived and as independent of man. The phrase also suggests the truth of the title of Horace Bushnell's famous sermon, "Every Man's Life a Plan of God." Yet the apostle, while insisting upon the divine source and authority of his work, nevertheless showed himself to be truly humble, for he was not only independent of man but also, in a sense, independent even of himself, so submissive was he to God's will.

2. The Fellowship. The association of himself with "Timothy our brother" (v. 1, *A.S.V.*) is another indication of St. Paul's humility. Although he is going to have much to say that is deep and important, his naming of Timothy proves that he is ready, by connecting his young colleague with this revelation of Christian truth, to provide his readers through a twofold relationship with a twofold blessing. The word "brother" is of special interest because, according to Bishop Westcott (*Epistles of St. John*, p. 55), the term in the New Testament always signifies the Christian relationship, and is never to be enlarged and dissipated into the modern concept of the brotherhood of humanity as a whole.

3. The Destination. The Epistle is addressed to "the saints and faithful brethren in Christ that are at Colosse" (v. 2, *A.S.V.*). The word "saints" means "consecrated ones" and is a title applied to all Christians without exception. It is particularly important to realize that in the New Testament it never refers to spiritual condition, but only to spiritual position. Nowadays the term *saint* is often used as indicative of pretensions to special merit or holiness, and sometimes it is even employed cynically or scornfully by those who do not believe in the reality of Christian profession. The Bible view of a saint, however, is simply one who belongs to God; but it is not known why the apostle addresses his later Epistles to Christians instead of to a church as a whole, the change being marked by the writing of the Epistle to the Romans. These Colossian saints are described as "faithful brethren" (v. 2), implying steadfastness and trustworthiness both in their attitude to God and in their relationship with those around them, so that possibly it is a reminder of some members of the church who were not "faithful." The further twofold designation of the recipients of this letter as "in Christ" and "at Colosse" is a beautiful reminder of what has often been pointed out as the two spheres of the Christian life, the heavenly and the earthly. Notwithstanding the sinful atmosphere and all the danger involved in their living "at Colosse," these believers were safe and strong, and could feel truly satisfied, because they were also "in Christ." Our Lord similarly described the twofold environment of the Christian when He said He had spoken certain things "—that in me ye might have peace. In the world ye shall have tribulation" (John 16:33). Happy is the believer who realizes in his experience the relationship of these two spheres and who lives for Christ in his particular "Colosse."

4. The Character. The apostle, as usual, except in the Pastoral Epistles, greets his readers with "grace to you and peace" (v. 2, *A.S.V.*). The grace of God is the source of which the peace of God is the result; the one is the cause, the other the effect. These two words are also descriptive respectively of the Greek and the Hebrew salutations. But, beyond this, "grace" is the great Bible word expressive of God's undeserved and positive favor to the sinner, while "peace" is the outcome of that grace in the experience of the one who receives it. It is somewhat strange that, in the original, this grace and peace are limited here to "God our Father," because, as a rule, "the Lord Jesus Christ" (Rom. 1:7, et al.) is associated in this salutation.

This is more difficult to understand because in this Epistle the apostle has so much to say about the divine nature of our Lord. Yet the two words "God" and "Father" are helpfully expressive of the two divine aspects of power and love. The Hebrew term for God invariably means strength, while the thought of Him as our Father necessarily indicates His loving interest in us as His children through His Son our Lord.

THE THANKSGIVING (vv. 3-5a)

1. The Fact. With the one exception of the Epistle to the Galatians, St. Paul's letters always commence with thanksgiving and this seems to indicate a prominent feature of his religious life. He rejoiced to see every sign of the work of grace in the various communities of Christians, and he had equal joy in acknowledging this in thanksgiving to God. It would indeed be well for all believers if the note of gratitude were made more definitely a part of their spiritual life.

2. The Direction. The recipient of the thanksgiving of Paul is, of course, "God the Father of our Lord Jesus Christ" (v. 3, *A.S.V.*). The apostle was deeply conscious of the reality of God, and this relationship of the Father to the Son is of particular interest (cf. Rom 15:6; II Cor. 1:3; 11:31; Eph. 1:3; I Peter 1:3). God's Fatherhood in relation to Christ is one of the three aspects of the divine Paternity found in the New Testament and, of course, refers to the unique connection between the first and second persons of the Trinity. The other two aspects, include the general idea of God as "the Father, of whom are all things" (I Cor. 8:6; cf. Eph. 4:6), although there is actually no clear statement of the divine Fatherhood by creation; but then, and chiefly, there is the more specific sense in which He is our Father in Christ and by the Holy Spirit (cf. John 1:12; Rom. 8:14-17). There is no warrant, either in the words of our Lord or in the writings of His apostles, for the modern idea of a universal Fatherhood and brotherhood. In another passage we have the Father described by a corresponding and complementary phrase, "the God of our Lord Jesus Christ" (Eph. 1:17).

3. The Association. With thanksgiving came prayer, and here we note an instance of this important combination in the apostle's life. Like the two wings of a bird which are required to enable it to soar into the sky, St. Paul felt the need of both petition and acknowledgment as wings for his soul in its ascent to God's presence. Both of these are expressions of faith, prayer being the faith that asks, and thanksgiving implying the faith that accepts.

4. The Occasion. Three reasons are assigned for the thanksgiving and prayer of the apostle. Although he had not been to Colosse nor had come into contact with the Christians there, he had heard of their progress from his friend Epaphras, who had been the means of leading them to Christ (vv. 7, 8).

a. Paul rejoiced in their faith in Christ. This is naturally the first element of the Christian life, because it brings the soul into contact with our Lord. Three Greek prepositions are found in connection with faith. In some passages Christ is the object (*eis*) of faith; in others He is the foundation (*epi*) of faith; while yet again, as here, He is the sphere (*en*) of faith.

b. Paul also rejoiced in their love for all their fellow-Christians. This naturally sprang out of their faith in Christ because "faith . . . worketh by love" (Gal. 5:6), and those who are spiritually related to Christ are of necessity related to those who also belong to Him. The universality of the apostle's reference to love is noteworthy, for it is said to have been directed "toward all the saints." This essential unity of the Christian community is similarly emphasized in the companion Epistle to the Ephesians, as it speaks of the necessity of association with "all the saints" for the purpose of apprehending Christ's love (Eph. 3:18), and of the equal necessity of intercessory prayer for all God's people (Eph. 6:18). There is scarcely any way in which we can more definitely show our faith and love than by this interest in "all the saints."

c. Paul further mentions the hope laid up in the heavens. It is a little difficult to be certain of the precise connection here, for the apostle uses a different expression—"because of the hope. . . ." Some scholars believe that the thought harks back to his thanksgiving and prayer, which would thus have hope as well as faith and love for their object. Others favor the idea that the "faith" and the "love" are based on the "hope," thus explaining the change of expression. While the latter is more naturally grammatical, it is thought to be somewhat strange theologically, although in reality there does not seem to be any insuperable difficulty in thinking of the faith and love of these believers as springing from the absolute certainty of the great and glorious future that was theirs in Christ through the gospel. In either case, however, we have the three Christian graces of faith, love, and hope. Faith rests on the past, love works in the present, and hope presses toward the future; or, faith looks backward and upward, love looks outward, and hope looks forward. These three constitute the true, complete Christian life and not one of them should be omitted or slighted. We are only too apt to emphasize faith and love and forget hope but, inasmuch as hope is invariably connected with the coming of the Lord, "that blessed hope" (Titus 2:13), it is a vital part of our Christian life. Faith accepts, hope expects; faith appropriates, hope anticipates; faith receives, hope realizes; faith is always and only concerned with the past and present, hope is always and only concerned with the future. We know that faith comes by hearing; we shall find that hope comes by experience. Faith is concerned with a person who promises, hope with the thing promised; and faith is the root of which hope is a fruit.

This hope is said by St. Paul to be "laid up" for believers "in the heavens," and the verb is particularly worthy of notice because of its use elsewhere. Thus, a crown of righteousness is said to be "laid up" for those who love Christ's appearing (II Tim. 4:8, *A.S.V.*), while it is also recorded that it was "laid up" for men once to die (Heb. 9:27). Another solemn contrast is drawn in our Lord's parable of the pounds, where the unfaithful servant "laid up" his master's gift instead of using it (Luke 19:20). In two Old Testament passages, moreover, it is declared that the Lord has "laid up" His goodness for those who fear Him (Ps. 31:19) and "sound wisdom for the righteous" (Prov. 2:7). No Christian life, then, is complete which does not include in it this forward look of joyous certitude toward a bright future, for hope as a grace is not a mere spirit of what we call hopefulness, or a natural buoyancy of temperament. It is a distinctly Christian virtue, the result of union with God in Christ; and it has for its immediate object the Lord Jesus at His glorious appearing, and for its ultimate, eternal and exhaustless substance the glories of heaven and God as our all in all.

At this point in our study, we may profitably observe three elements of the Christian life that were prominent in the apostle's experience and that should also characterize ours:

1. Consciousness of Relationship to God. The apostle had no doubt as to what he was and where he stood. As a servant of Christ, he was fully assured of the will of God and of the grace that was continually coming from God. This "blessed assurance" is one of the essential secrets of true, vigorous, buoyant Christian living.

2. Concern for the Christian Life of Others. The apostle exercised not only faith in Christ, but also love toward Christ's followers; and this again is one of the fundamental realities of true Christianity. It is impossible for anyone to possess spiritual life without showing an interest in other believers, for, as St. John reminds us so frequently, the man who claims to love God without loving those who belong to God contradicts the very elements of the Christian faith (cf. I John 3:14-19; 4:7, 8, 11, 12, 20, 21; 5:2).

3. Completeness of Christian Character. In the threefold reference to faith, love, and hope, the apostle shows the necessity of a full-orbed Christian life. In St. John's word-picture of the Holy City, we are told that the length, breadth, and height of it are equal (Rev. 21:16), and this, as Phillips Brooks pointed out in one of his great sermons, suggests the necessity of a true proportion in the Christian life. Some people emphasize depth without breadth; others are concerned with breadth while failing in depth. The true believer, however, will aim at being both deep and broad, lest his depth alone should tend toward narrowness, or his breadth alone lead to shallowness. Every strong Christian character will possess the two elements of intensity and extensiveness, and these will be blended by its reach toward the height, to "seek those things which are above" (3:1). Thus faith, love, and hope in their proportion and balance will be at once the proof and the guarantee of a life that will constantly glorify God.

THE PERSONAL MESSAGE (1:5b-8)

One great thought is usually prominent, if not predominant, with St. Paul and is never far away from his mind—the nature and extension of the gospel, "the word" (v. 5b). It comes out again and again in his Epistles, and in unexpected ways, but here it arises quite naturally out of the salutation and the thanksgiving, and becomes to us a test of our spiritual experience.

1. The Word Revealed. The phrase employed is a striking one—"the word of the truth of the gospel which is come unto you" (vv. 5b, 6a). Christianity stands for reality as the revelation of truth that comes from above. It is also a "gospel," a message of good news, particularly because of the hope it brings of a bright future in Christ. This message is at once genuine and trustworthy and, as such, is incapable of alteration (cf. Gal. 2:5-14).

2. The Word Received. This gospel had been both heard and heeded, because the Colossian Christians had not only listened to it (v. 5), but they had welcomed it and had made it part of their personal experience. The preaching of the gospel calls for attention on the part of those to whom it is sent; and whenever it is thoughtfully and earnestly considered it will produce its blessed effects on mind, heart, and life. These hearers realized that it was "the grace of God in truth" (v. 6). Again, therefore, the idea of "truth" is made prominent, since the essence of good news is that which is true, while the value attaching to "grace," undeserved favor, is that it must be both real and effective. Then, not only had the gospel been assimilated in Colosse, but it had actually gone much farther, so that the apostle could speak of it having reached "all the world" (v. 6). This statement, in view of the early date of writing, is very significant in that it demonstrates the universality of the gospel (cf. Rom. 1:8; I Thess. 1:8) as the power of God unto salvation to all who believed (cf. Rom. 1:16).

3. The Word Reproduced. Another test of the gospel is fruitfulness, for whenever its message is heard and the grace of God known thereby in personal experience, this proof of "bearing fruit and increasing" (v. 6, *A.S.V.*) will be seen everywhere (cf. Matt. 7:20). Not only reception of the gospel but reproduction will always be the outcome of the hearing and learning of "the word of truth," the inevitable result of the gospel as a divine and living seed (cf. Matt. 13:18-23). This fruit was at once continuous and increasing, showing both inward and outward vigor (cf. Eph. 2:21; 4:15); and it is always an essential feature and a strong proof of the gospel that these results should be both constant and progressive.

Another point of importance is that this outcome marked the whole range of the Colossians' Christian life, "since the day" they first "heard . . . and knew the grace of God in truth" (v. 6; cf. Phil. 1:5). It does not take long for the gospel to work; indeed, the moment it is received into the heart it begins to bear fruit. Further, the use of the word "knew" is of special importance, because it is one of the marks of these Epistles of the Captivity in Rome, indicating a full and mature knowledge (e.g., Eph. 1:17, 18; 4:13). This word always includes a personal experience as well as an intellectual apprehension, part of that knowledge of God which is "life eternal" (John 17:3).

4. The Word Related (vv. 7, 8). It was the same message that Epaphras, the evangelist at Colosse (4:12; Philem. 23) had proclaimed to these people. Here he is described as Paul's "beloved fellow-servant" (v. 7, *A.S.V.*), as "a faithful minister of Christ" (v. 7), and as the one who had also "declared" to the apostle the Colossians' "love in the Spirit" (v. 8). Through the effectual ministry of Epaphras, they evidently were realizing the grace of God in such a way as to reproduce it in a love that came directly from the Holy Spirit of God. It is worthwhile noticing in this passage, moreover, a significant and suggestive implication of what is now known to the Christian Church as the doctrine of the Trinity (vv. 6-8). It is in such ways as this that the three persons of the Godhead—Father, Son, and Holy Spirit—are most definitely and effectually shown in their divine influence on the spiritual life of believers.

This consideration of God's Word illustrates very clearly a well-known statement of the apostle, namely, that the gospel is "the power of God unto salvation to every one that believeth" (Rom. 1:16).

a. The gospel as God's power. This word *power*, from the original of which comes our word *dynamic*, shows what Christianity was intended to be in heart and life; and the reality of it is abundantly evident in the way in which these Colossian Christians experienced "the grace of God in truth" (v. 6). This was the "dynamic" in their lives.

b. The gospel as God's power unto salvation. Salvation is one of the great words of the New Testament, covering past, present, and future. The acceptance of the gospel clearly resulted in the continuous work of salvation in these believers, as they allowed the grace of God to operate in their lives.

c. The gospel as God's power unto salvation for all. The universality of the gospel is evident here, as elsewhere. It had come to others besides those in Colosse, of course, and was bearing fruit "in all the world" (v. 6). Perhaps there is nothing more impressive than the adaptability of Christianity to the varied types, capacities, and circumstances of human life all over the world. This is one of the strongest evidences that it comes from God. Other and human religions are only partial and local, and so they make no universal appeal. Christianity, on the contrary, because its source is divine, is equally suited to all races of mankind.

d. The gospel as God's power unto salvation for all through believing. The emphasis is placed here on the way in which these people in Colosse first heard, then learned, then believed, and then came to know "the word of the truth of the gospel" (v. 5). This shows clearly that the message about Christ is intended to be received by simple trust. When it is thus accepted it soon vindicates itself in various ways in heart and life.

e. The gospel as God's power unto salvation for all believers to be proclaimed everywhere. This, too, is implied and suggested throughout this passage in Colossians. When the gospel is received it is to be passed on, for it is impossible to keep it locked up in the believing heart. As we have seen, when Epaphras received the message from St. Paul he, as a "faithful minister of Christ" (v. 7), quickly communicated it to others; and then the gospel bore fruit in them, whereby still others, in turn, were made acquainted with it. This is the supreme proof of the reality of our Christian life, viz., the proclamation of the gospel to others. Gratitude impels, for there is nothing else like it; and obedience compels, for so very many souls have not yet heard it.

3 THE PRAYER OF THE APOSTLE[1]

It has been truly said that if only we could hear a man's private prayers we could obtain an infallible guide to his spiritual life; and the prayers of St. Paul are a case in point. Moreover, those in Philippians, Ephesians, and Colossians, the Epistles of the First Captivity, are of particular interest because they express so fully his deeper experiences. On this account they are of great importance in revealing some of the most mature developments in the apostle's spiritual life; and they thus afford believers a valuable opportunity for testing and directing their own lives. What he prayed for others suggests what was essential for them and therefore for us. This, the first of the prayers in Colossians, also deserves special attention from the standpoint of Christian experience because it incorporates and introduces the great central theme of the Epistle.

THE REASON FOR THE PRAYER, (v. 9a)

Since St. Paul had neither founded nor even visited the Colossian Church, the information he had about its growing faith and love had come from Epaphras (vv. 7, 8); and ever since these tidings had arrived the

---

[1]Much of this section is taken from the author's small volume entitled *The Prayers of St. Paul* (Edinburgh: T. & T. Clark, and New York: Chas. Scribner's Sons, 1914), long out of print.

apostle had not only thanked God, as we have seen (vv. 3, 4), but also had unceasingly offered this prayer because of his deep interest in the spiritual well-being of the Christians in Colosse. Prayerful concern for the experiences of those to whom he was writing was one of the prominent marks of St. Paul's character. His was no self-centered life but one ever keenly alert to appreciate the indications of grace in others. Such interest in the spiritual life and progress of a believer's fellows is a real sign of divine grace, for it prevents him from being self-centered. How unlike we often are to a Christian of the type of Barnabas, of whom we read: "Who, when he came, and had seen the grace of God, was glad" (Acts 11:23)! This is only possible by having "a heart at leisure from itself"; and, when we are thus deeply interested in the manifestations of the divine working in the lives of other people, we shall not only praise God for them but also, like the apostle here, pray fervently for them. Thus will the blessing extend and deepen.

THE OBJECT OF THE PRAYER (vv. 9b-12a)

The substance of Paul's petition was twofold:

1. The Will of God To Be Understood (v. 9b). This is seen in the words "we . . . make request for you, that ye may be filled with the knowledge of his will in all spiritual wisdom and understanding" (*A. S. V.*). The will of God known and done is the keynote of all true Christian living, as it was of our blessed Lord's own earthly life. He came expressly to do the will of His Father, and in one of the deepest experiences of His human existence He said humbly, "Not my will, but thine, be done" (Luke 22:42). He told His disciples that His very meat was to do the will of Him who had sent Him (John 4:34); and He taught them to pray, "Thy will be done in earth, as it is in heaven" (Matt. 6:10). The will of God is, of course, the substance of revelation, for what is Scripture, from beginning to end, but the revelation of God's will for man? Perhaps the most all-embracing prayer is, "Teach me to do thy will" (Ps. 143:10); and certainly the ideal Christian life is summed up in the phrase, "He that doeth the will of God abideth for ever" (I John 2:17). Since this divine will is to dominate everything, well might the apostle pray for these believers of Colosse to be filled with the knowledge of it.

The word rendered "knowledge" means "mature spiritual experience," and it is one of the characteristic words of these four Epistles written from Rome (cf. Eph. 1:17; Phil. 1:9; Philem. 6; see p. 156). The apostle evidently regarded such mature knowledge, or deep spiritual experience, as the preeminent mark of a ripening Christian. In this respect St. John bears the same testimony in his reference to the three stages of the Christian life represented by "little children," "young men," and "fathers" (I John 2:12-14): the little children *have;* the young men *are;* the fathers *know.* This spiritual knowledge or experience is the great safeguard against error, in that it gives power to distinguish between good and evil, between truth and falsehood.

The measure of this knowledge is to be carefully noted—*"filled* with the knowledge of his will" (v. 9b). This word indicates a constant experience— a fulness that is to be realized continually. It is not a bare knowledge, but a complete one, a permanent and practical awareness of what is right and true. When the soul experiences this, it is provided not only with the greatest safeguard against danger but also with the secret of a strong, full, growing, powerful Christian life.

The characteristics of this knowledge should be shown "in all wisdom and spiritual understanding." "Wisdom" is a general term which implies the power of spiritual perception, the capacity for adapting the best means to bring about the best ends in the things of the spirit. At the same time, "spiritual understanding" is a definite application of wisdom to particular cases, the specific relation of principles to each other by which right action is taken. It really means "putting two and two together," as we say today, comparing ideas and opinions for the purpose of adopting the best in any given situation and, in general, apprehending the bearing of truth on life. Of the importance and necessity of this wisdom and this spiritual understanding scarcely anything need be said. Such Christian sensitivity and perception in the thousand-and-one crises of life is surely one of our greatest potential blessings. How many errors would be avoided, how many wanderings checked, by means of this spiritual discernment! Still more, how much joy would be experienced and how much genuine service rendered if we were always saying and doing the right thing, at the right time, and in the right way!

The difficulty with so many people today is that they are superficial in their knowledge and shallow in their experience, and so are a prey to various errors, "carried about with every wind of doctrine" (Eph. 4:14). We may safely aver, then, that to be "filled with the knowledge of his will in all wisdom and spiritual understanding" means for its complete realization a constant touch with those writings which present the clearly expressed plan of God. The divine will is in that Book, and when it, the Word of God, is illuminated by the Spirit of God we, His children, come to know His will concerning us. Indeed, no one will ever have the full knowledge of that will, no one can possibly be mature in Christian experience, if the Word of God is not his daily, definite, direct study and meditation. It purifies the perceptive faculties by its cleansing power; it illuminates the moral faculties with its enlightening power; it controls the emotional faculties with its protective power; and it energizes the volitional faculties with its stimulating power. Thus, in the constant, continuous use of the Word of God in personal practice, with reverent meditation and earnest prayer, we shall indeed, to paraphrase the apostle's words, "become filled with the full knowledge of His will in every avenue of perception and in their spiritual applications."

2. The Walk for God Is To Be Undertaken (vv. 10-12a). Knowledge, however, is never an end in itself, but always the means to an end; and so the apostle states the purpose for which he asks this knowledge of God's will. It is intended to lead to a corresponding practical living—"that ye may . . . walk worthily of the Lord unto all pleasing" (vv. 9-10, *A.S.V.*). Yes, knowledge is to be translated into practice. Christianity was often spoken of as "the Way" (Acts 19:9, 23; 22:4, *A.S.V.*), and "walking" is a word frequently found in Scripture, descriptive of the outward and visible expression in conduct of the inward life of faith. As the word presupposes life, aliveness, so it stands also for energy, movement, progress, conduct. How can a man walk unless he knows why he moves and whither he goes? Thus the knowledge of God's will is that which gives point and purpose to all Christian activity.

Walking "worthily of the Lord" is a profound and searching thought. Surely this is impossible; yet these are the plain words of the inspired writer and may well be compared with other passages of similar meaning. The apostle seems fond of the word "worthy": we are to walk worthy of our Christian calling (Eph. 4:1) and even worthy of God (I Thess. 2:12); and our conduct is to be worthy of the gospel (Phil. 1:27) just as the Christians in Rome were to receive a sister in Christ in a manner worthy of saints (Rom. 16:2). These are some of the glorious possibilities of grace, for we may be perfectly sure that St. Paul would not have placed such an ideal before us if it could not be realized. God's commands always imply the means of obedience and the promise of power.

The phrase "unto all pleasing" is particularly interesting. Bishop Moule felicitously renders it "to all meeting of His wishes, so as not only to obey explicit precepts but as it were to anticipate in everything" His will.[2] This reminds us of the Prayer Book version of Psalm 143:10: "Teach me to do the thing that pleaseth Thee." What a glorious ideal! We are so to walk as to please God in everything. But this may be accomplished only by living in such close touch with Him that we come instinctively to know what will please Him. These words sound a depth of the spiritual life with which comparatively few are familiar; and yet here they are, facing us quite incontrovertibly, with their call to a realization of that which God has

---

[2]Moule, *Colossians Studies,* p. 49.

placed before us. The word here rendered "pleasing" is not found elsewhere in the New Testament, but it is used in classical Greek to mean a preference of the will of others before one's own. The apostle, however, was strongly opposed to what he called "men-pleasing" (3:22; cf. Gal. 1:10; Eph. 6:6; I Thess. 2:4), as altogether incompatible with being a follower of the Lord. While, of course, he could be, and was, "all things to all men" (I Cor. 9:22), and could urge the duty of one's pleasing "his neighbour for his good, resulting in edification" (Rom. 15:2, Gr.), yet such an attitude must be subordinated to pleasing God, and this is meant to be continual—"*all* pleasing."

Again we may be sure that God does not mock us by setting up a standard to which we cannot attain. Scripture tells us that it has been realized, by Christ our example (cf. Matt. 3:17; John 8:29; Rom. 15:3), and by the patriarch Enoch (cf. Heb. 11:5; note perfect tense); and this is one of the "ambitions" of St. Paul (II Cor. 5:9) that we may safely assume he attained. From various other passages we, too, may learn the secret of being made pleasing to God. On our part, there must first be faith (Heb. 11:6), and then surrender (II Tim. 2:4), followed by obedience (I John 3:22). From God Himself will come indwelling power (Phil. 2:3) that will lead through experience to progress (I Thess. 4:1) and to the ultimate perfection of being "well pleasing in his sight" (Heb. 13:20, 21).

Returning to this worthy Christian walk, we note that there follow some specific details of it in four striking phrases marked by participles in conjunction with various prepositions:

We are to be "fruitful *in* every good work" (v. 10). Our Christian life is to be characterized by good works, and in every one of these we are to manifest the ripeness and, if it may be so put, the beauty and lusciousness associated with fruit. Mark, also, that our fruitfulness is to be "*in* every good work," that is, in the process of doing the work, and not merely as the outcome of it. The very working itself is intended to be fruitful apart from particular results. There may indeed be very few results of our service for God, but the service itself may and should be "fruitful."

Then we are to be "increasing *by*" (*A.S.V.,* marg., rather than "*in*" *K.J.V.*) "the knowledge of God" (v. 10). This knowledge is to grow, as knowledge always will, by accessions, and the more we know of God the more fruitful will be our life and the greater the increase of Christian graces. The context suggests, moreover, that the path toward the knowledge of God is not that of mere speculation, or even of devotional contemplation but is the way of definite, genuine, whole-hearted practice. We are to be "filled with the knowledge of his will" (v. 9) that we may be "fruitful" and thus be "increasing in the knowledge of God" (v. 10). In brief, we are to *know* in order that we may *do* in order that we may know

35

still more; so that we not only discover His will but actually get to know *Him* (cf. John 17:3; Phil. 3:10; I John 2:13).

A further outcome will be strength "*in* all power, according to the might (or manifestation) of his glory (or, His glorious power), *with a view to* all patience and longsuffering *with* joy" (v. 11, *A.S.V.*, Gr.). Every word calls for careful consideration since the apostle's thought is simply pouring itself out in such fashion that it almost seems as though he felt incapable of adequate expression for the very potentialities about which he prays. The divinely empowered strength that is to be ours is obviously a spiritual one, intended to lead to patience, longsuffering, and joy; or, in other words, an inward vigor of character is to manifest itself in a quiet, consistent endurance, humility, and cheerfulness. The man of the world might see in this phrase an anticlimax, for it is stated that the end of strength is patience and longsuffering rather than action of some kind; and yet Christianity finds its ideal both in energy expressed through character and, paradoxically, in activity often manifesting itself by passivity and in what may be called might in meekness. Notice, too, the suggestive addition, "with joyfulness." Patience and longsuffering without joy are apt to be cold and unattractive. There is a stern, stoical endurance of suffering that, while it may be admired sometimes, tends to repel. Even a merely resigned attitude, and still less a sullen one, will bring no glory to God. But when patience and longsuffering are permeated by joyfulness, the very life of Christ is lived over again in His followers. We hear far too much of resignation, which is only partially a Christian virtue, and far too little of an active delight in God's will.

Thus the three words "patience and longsuffering with joyfulness" are in their combination very challenging. "Patience" means a deliberate endurance rather than a mere passive acceptance of a given situation. It is the word used of Job (cf. Jas. 5:11) and, as we know, his attitude was not merely that of resignation, but of determined and persistent endurance in the face of trial. With this "patience" comes "longsuffering," which is to be understood as implying the temper of gentleness and loving-kindness. It is one thing to endure suffering; it is another to be kind with it (I Cor. 13:4). With this quiet, steady, beautiful life of endurance and love should indeed come "joyfulness"; and in many New Testament passages this spirit is exhibited in the life of Christ and the teaching of His apostles (e.g., Matt. 5:10-12; Heb. 12:2; I Peter 4:13; Phil. 1:17-19). Thus, as has been usefully pointed out, these three words form a climax: "patience" struggles and endures; "longsuffering" endures without a struggle; "joyfulness" endures and actually glories in suffering.

The crowning grace for which St. Paul prays is that of thankfulness— "giving thanks *unto* the Father" (v. 12a). How much it means! It is the heart being full of gladness and gratitude for all that God is, moment by moment, to the soul, the life full of brightness and buoyancy, and the character full of vitality and vigor. The apostle has already expressed his own thanksgiving (v. 3), and now he urges the same welcome grace upon his readers as that which, in a special way, gives force, tone, and character to the entire Christian life. Thanksgiving will always manifest itself in "thanks-living," and this will be of a definite sort; it will be the expression of our gratitude for the actual participation in the divine "inheritance" or economy. This is not something future and problematical but present and actual. The joy of the Lord is indeed the strength of His people (Neh. 8:10).

THE EMPHASIS OF THE PRAYER (vv. 12b, 13)

It is somewhat surprising that so little mention is made of God the Father in the lives and prayers of many Christian people, while there is an almost constant reference to "the Lord," by which title is usually understood our Lord Jesus Christ. This practice has given rise to some severe criticism of Evangelicalism as favoring what has been called a "Jesus-religion." While it is not a fair criticism, there is sufficient justification for it to make us give careful attention to the matter. It cannot be doubted, for instance, that many of our hymns, perhaps too many, are addressed to our Lord instead of to God the Father, which helps in the same direction, to concentrate attention on the second person of the Trinity to the frequent virtual forgetfulness of the first. The New Testament, on the other hand, invariably sets before us God the Father as both the primary source and the ultimate goal of the believer's life. He is revealed in the Son as the holy image of the Godhead inviting men to become like Him (cf. Matt. 5:48), and in the Spirit as the divine power making them like Him (cf. II Cor. 3:18).

The title "Father" is particularly noteworthy because of its frequency on the lips of our Lord. The Old Testament has comparatively little to say about the Fatherhood of God, and even when it does mention it the association is almost entirely with Israel and the Covenant. In the New Testament, however, the divine Fatherhood appears with remarkable fulness, mainly because it was, beyond all others, the name used by our Lord to express His own relationship to God. It has been computed that He spoke of the Father and used this title some 150 times, and it is to be noted how singularly infrequent was His use of the more general term "God." This emphasis on the Almighty not only as Christ's Father but as the Father of all believers (cf. John 1:12; Gal. 3:26) is of vital importance in regard to things spiritual; and the apostle in these verses of his Colossian

Epistle provides a valuable opportunity of seeing this truth for ourselves. Three great subjects are definitely associated with God the Father as the ground of the thankfulness just enjoined:

1. The Inheritance (v. 12). When St. Paul speaks in this verse of "the inheritance," he seems to be giving a Christian interpretation to a well-known Old Testament word (cf. Deut. 32:9; Job 31:2; Ps. 47:4); and from the thought of an earthly Canaan or other material possession to be inherited, he leads up to the truth of the spiritual inheritance of believers. This has been assigned to God's people and is the outcome of their new birth (I Peter 1:3, 4). It is of special importance, however, to remember that the terms and ideas associated with the New Testament words "heir" and "inheritance" are to be carefully distinguished from our modern use of the same words. Today the "heir" is one who has not yet come into his "inheritance" but has to wait until the death of the present possessor. In the New Testament, however, the believer's heritage is something present and actual, being enjoyed here and now. The Christian life may be usefully summed up in just six words, covering the whole from beginning to end. It starts with sonship; it proceeds to discipleship; it calls for stewardship; it is expressed in worship; it rejoices in fellowship; and it culminates in heirship (Rom. 8:17).

From this it may be realized that the spiritual counterpart of Canaan is not heaven but the life of spiritual privilege at the present time. It is, therefore, unfortunate that so many of our hymns connect Canaan with heaven. The old words,

> Could we but stand where Moses stood
> And view the landscape o'er,
> Not Jordan's stream nor death's cold flood
> Could fright us from the shore,

give a wrong impression of the New Testament teaching concerning the Promised Land (cf. Heb. 3:7 - 4:11). It may be questioned also whether all our children's hymns are spiritually helpful; for someone has said that it would be truer to sing

> There is a happy land
> *Not* far away,

> A. Young

and also that a revised version of another hymn would be helpful:

> There's a Friend for little children
> *Beneath* the bright, blue sky.

> Albert Midlane

Furthermore, when Joshua entered Canaan there were enemies left to fight, and when we enter our spiritual Canaan there are still spiritual foes to face. This alone shows that the reference must be to the present life for, of course, there will be no foes in heaven. To project into the future so many of our joys and so much of potential victorious living often leads to spiritual loss, for we thereby fail to realize and rejoice in our present inheritance of grace in the true Canaan of the soul. One example of this is a commentator who assigned to the future the words, "Ye rejoice with joy unspeakable and full of glory" (I Peter 1:8), when quite obviously the whole context is in the present tense and refers to the joy and exultation of the believer here and now.

In the original this inheritance is described by the apostle as "the parcel of the lot" or "the part of the heritage," thereby suggesting that each believer has some portion of this great spiritual inheritance that is especially his own. We share it with our fellow-believers and all are equally possessed of certain privileges; and yet there is at the same time a distinction through the consciousness that each one has his own particular part in this wonderful "lot" (cf. Acts 8:21).

This heritage is further described as belonging to "the saints in the light" (Gr.). As already noted, the word "saint" invariably describes the Christian's spiritual position, never his actual condition. A saint is one who belongs to Christ, and so this inheritance is seen to be the possession of those who are themselves possessed by Him. Further, the reference to "the light" is particularly significant as expressive of the true character of the Christian position (cf. John 1:4, 5; Eph. 5:8-14) and includes the three elements of truth (e.g., II Cor. 4:4), purity (e.g., I Tim. 6:16), and fellowship (e.g., I Peter 2:9). There is much in the Bible on this subject that calls for meditation. "God is light" (I John 1:5); Christ is "the light of the world" (John 1:6-10; 8:12); and the Word of God is described as "a light" (Ps. 119:105). Christians have been called out of darkness into God's light (see v.13; cf. I Peter 2:9); and on this account they are described as "the children of light" (I Thess. 5:5). It is not surprising, therefore, that the future home of the soul is described by St. John as an abode of light and glory (cf. Rev. 21:23 to 22:5).

Special attention, however, should be paid to the work of the Father in this connection. He is said to have "made us meet," a word which is literally "made competent," being found in only one other passage (II Cor. 3:6). Bishop Moule renders it "qualified" (*Colossian Studies*, p. 50), for it contains the idea of sufficiency, with the meaning that God has endowed us with a spiritual equipment sufficient to possess and enjoy this spiritual heritage. This, of course, is in regard to our judicial position, and one day we shall be "meet" in actual condition as well (II Tim. 2:21). In the words of C. H. V. Bogatsky's quaint prayer: "O to be daily *meetening* for the inheritance of the saints in light! May my eye, my heart, and my hopes be there, because Jesus is there; and it is the sight of Him that will be the cream of all our pleasures" (*A Golden Treasury for the Children of God,* p. 261).

2. The Deliverance (v. 13). The next part of the work of the Father on our behalf is described as our deliverance from the authority (Gr.) of darkness. This reference to darkness is impressive as showing the contrast between it and our spiritual inheritance in the light (v. 12). Darkness is always connected with the three features of error, impurity, and misery; and, of course, all those things that are untrue, unholy, and unhappy are characteristics and results of sin. Men have always "loved darkness rather than light, because their deeds were evil" (John 3:19). Thus, the Christian is to avoid hating his brother because to do so would be to walk in darkness (I John 2:11); and to walk in darkness is to do the very opposite of holding fellowship with God (cf. I John 1:6). To the same effect St. Paul speaks of casting off "the works of darkness" (Rom. 13:12). Our Lord had already spoken with the utmost solemnity of "the power of darkness" (Luke 22:53), and when the apostle speaks of it here he is apparently referring to that same unrestrained and tyrannical influence which is brought to bear upon those who belong to Satan. All who are outside of Christ are under that usurped authority or power, being led captive by the devil at his will (cf. II Tim. 2:26).

This work of the Father, then, is to deliver, or, rather, "rescue" us from that baleful authority. The verb is impressive, meaning "snatched," in the sense of the freeing of a captive. God does this by bestowing on us His own divine life and enabling us thereby to get free of the bondage of spiritual death. The word "rescued," moreover, is in the aorist tense, which indicates actual deliverance, pointing to a time in the past when this "rescue" was completely and finally brought about. It demonstrates the great interest and love of our heavenly Father that He should do this for us in Christ by the gift of His divine grace.

3. The Transference (v. 13). It is not sufficient, however, for God to have delivered us from the kingdom of darkness; there is a positive side to His work on our behalf as well as a negative side. He has at the same time "translated" us into an entirely new kingdom which is called "the kingdom of His dear Son," or, "of the Son of his love" (*A. S. V.*). We have here one of the New Testament passages which reminds us that the kingdom of Christ is already in existence as a spiritual reality. In the next age this kingdom will be visibly manifested, but for the present it is internal, not external. It consists of those who have experienced spiritual life, and into its fellowship the Father admits every true believer who has received His

Son by faith. This is the distinction between the visible church of professed followers and the invisible church, the spiritual kingdom, of those whose actual experience is "righteousness, and peace, and joy in the Holy Ghost" (Rom. 14:17).

The kingdom is described as that of the Son of the Father's love. Thus it is the kingdom of our Lord, and of no one less than divine. As we know, love is the essence of God's character (I John 4:16) and, since the Son is of the same nature as the Father (John 1:1, 14), it follows that His kingdom is one of love. The contrast is evident between tyranny, bondage, cruelty, sorrow, and love, freedom, privilege, and joy.

The word "translated" is of particular interest because it refers to such a complete change. It is found only five times in the New Testament, but always in this sense of a definite removal or turning away (cf. Luke 16:4; Acts 13:22; 19:26; I Cor. 13:2). The corresponding passage in Ephesians (1:6) sheds light on this divine act whereby God freely bestows on us the grace of acceptance in Him who is His own beloved Son.

From all this work of the Father, two great truths emerge:

1. These Are Facts. The verb in each case indicates something already done, something that is absolute and not merely contingent. The value and importance of divine grace are shown in this emphasis on the Father's act. Our inheritance, our deliverance, and our transference are not matters involving our own effort or merit, but blessings that we simply receive because of what has been accomplished by the Father. From first to last, merit is ruled out of everything in connection with true Christianity, and all is of grace. This emphasis on actual facts provides an inspiring foundation for our spiritual life. God has already accomplished these things, and it is for us not only to receive, but also to enjoy them.

2. These Facts Are thus To Be Factors in our Lives. Because of what God has done we are to respond to Him and to live to His glory. The true Christian life is fourfold: (a) we are to trust; (b) we are to be thankful; (c) we are to obey; (d) we are to bear testimony. Thus the facts become forces in our experience which rejoice the heart of God, give blessed assurance to our own souls, and glorify Him before others.

THE EFFICACY OF THE PRAYER, v. 9

We have now seen what the apostle desired for the Christians of Colosse, and in so doing we have learned some of the deepest secrets of Christian living. But also it is impossible thus to dwell upon the substance and purpose of such a petition without discovering some of the characteristics of St. Paul's prayer-life, to the end that our own may be so guided and inspired by the Holy Spirit (cf. Rom. 8:26) that it may become spiritually rich in itself and intensely efficacious for others. Returning to verse 9, we note that—

1. There Was an Urgency in Praying. *"Since* the day we heard—." From the moment the tidings came by Epaphras of the Christian life in Colosse, the apostle's heart had been lifted to God in keenness of interest and in earnestness of entreaty for blessing on all the believers there.

2. There Was a Constancy in Praying. "We . . . do not cease to pray—." Again and again he asked, and kept on asking, since these Christians whom he had never seen were felt to be in special need of graces from God.

3. There Was an Intensity in Praying. "And to desire—." This was no mere lip service. Paul's heart had evidently been stirred to the core by what he had heard of their faith and love, their hope and witness (cf. vv. 4-6); and there arose a deep longing to seek for still fuller blessing on their behalf.

4. There Was a Unity in Praying. "Since the day *we* heard—." Nor was he alone in these petitions; they were offered in union and communion with others. Just as the Epistle associates Timothy with its message (v. 1), so he was connected with St. Paul in prayer, and so, doubtless, were the other friends mentioned in chapter 4. Individual prayer is mighty, but united prayer is mightier still, one of the most potent forces within the Christian Church (cf. Matt. 18:19, 20).

These are the outstanding characteristics of the apostle's prayer-life, and they reveal, perhaps more clearly than anything else, what he was and how he lived.

In this section we have studied one of the fullest, deepest, and most precious of the apostle's prayers. As we consider its union of thought and experience, of profound teaching and equally profound revelation of his own Christian life, we learn four of the most urgent and necessary lessons for the Christian life of today:

1. The Value of Character. The details of the apostle's prayer show what he felt was true Christian witness. It consists, according to him, of being rather than doing, or at least of being with a view to doing, rather than proceeding in the reverse order. It is what we are, not what we say, certainly, that gives the best testimony to others of the reality of our Christianity. This is very prominent here, as elsewhere in the Epistles, so that when it is said, as it often is on purely moral grounds, that "character makes the man," we as Christians naturally add the complementary truth, "Christ makes the character."

2. The Value of Experience. The apostle's prayer is marked by a full, deep, real Christian experience, and it is evident that he feels the necessity and importance of this on behalf of the Christians for whom he prays. Such an experience is always based on a personal acquaintance with God and this, in turn, can come only through the Word of God. As we have seen, every emphasis on "knowledge" shows that St. Paul is concerned with spiritual experience as one of the chief marks of a growing Christian; and St. John seems to have the same conviction (cf. I John 2:12-14). The "little children," though immature, possess the inestimable benefit of forgiveness and are in spiritual touch with their heavenly Father. The "young men," though not yet ripe in Christian experience, are vigorous and strong, having overcome Satan because of the indwelling of God's Word. The "fathers," mature believers, are those who "know," and this seems to be the culmination of everything. And yet knowledge of the Father and of the Word are associated with the "little children" and "young men" as well, thereby showing, surely, the absolute necessity of a personal experience of God if our Christian life, at whatever stage, is to be what it is intended to be.

3. The Value of Balance. Growing out of these aspects of truth is a third one which is twofold:

The first part of this shall be given in words quoted by Bishop Moule: "Beware of an untheological devotion" (*Colossian Studies,* pp. 55f). There is no contradiction between mind and heart, between theology and devotion. Devotional hours do not mean hours when thought is absent; on the contrary, if devotion is to be real it should be characterized by thought. Meditation is not abstraction, nor is devotion dreaminess. "Thou shalt love the Lord thy God with all thy . . . *mind*" is an essential part of "the first and great commandment" (Matt. 22:37, 38). If genuine thought and sound theology (literally, "knowledge of God") do not characterize our times of devotion, we lose some of the most precious opportunities for grace and blessing. A piety that is mere pietism, ɛvangelicalism that does not continually ponder the profound truths of the New Testament, can never be strong or do any true service to the gospel cause. We must indeed beware of "untheological devotion."

But we must also beware of an "undevotional theology." This is the opposite error, and it constitutes an equally grave danger. A hard, dry, intellectual study of theology will yield no spiritual fruit. Accuracy in the knowledge of Greek, careful balancing of various aspects of truth, wide knowledge of the doctrinal verities of the New Testament—all of these are essential and most valuable. Unless, however, they are permeated by a spirit of devotion they will fail at the crucial point. *Pectus facit theologum*—it is the heart that makes the theologian; and a theology that does not spring from spiritual experience is doomed to decay, to deadness, and to disaster.

When, therefore, our devotions are theological, and our theology is devotional, we begin to realize the true meaning, blessing, and power of the Christian life. Thus we may go from strength to strength, from grace to grace, and from glory to glory.

4. The Value of Intercession. It is abundantly clear from this and several other passages that St. Paul made much of prayer on behalf of others. Not only did he seek their prayers for his ministry, but an important part of that ministry was prayer for them. It has been pointed out that, since those to whom he wrote his Epistles were already Christians, it might seem that the apostle should have concentrated his entire interest on prayer for the unconverted; and yet it is evident that he realized the great need of Christians to grow, to become strong, and to reach as far as possible "the measure of the stature of the fulness of Christ ... [that] maketh increase of the body unto the edifying of itself in love" (Eph. 4:13-16). Thus, just as at every stage of the Christian life we need to be taught more and more, so we need to be continually in prayer for each other. Bishop Moule quotes from an old book, *The Christian Ministry,* by Charles Bridges: "There can be little doubt but we shall find that our most successful hours of employment for our people were not those when we were speaking to them from God, but when we were speaking for them to God" (p. 46). To the same effect are some important words of E. M. Bounds in his valuable book *Power Through Prayer:* "The Church is looking for better methods; God is looking for better men.... What the Church needs today is not more machinery or better, not new organizations or more and novel methods, but men whom the Holy Ghost can use—men of prayer, men mighty in prayer. The Holy Ghost does not flow through methods, but through men. He does not come on machinery, but on men. He does not anoint plans, but men—men of prayer.... Talking to men for God is a great thing, but talking to God for men is greater still. He will never talk well and with real success to men for God who has not learned well how to talk to God for men" (pp. 9, 10, 33).

4 THE PERSON AND WORK OF CHRIST

THE DIVINE SON, 1:14-17

At length the central theme of the Epistle is reached. Prayer and thanksgiving for spiritual blessings lead to a strong expression of faith in Christ. It is a logical, inevitable step from the work to the person, from the redemption to the Redeemer, from the salvation to the Savior. Our Lord's work is efficacious because of who and what He is. The entire passage constitutes one of the most important documents in the New Testament for the study of Christology. Indeed, Bishop Nicholson says that "as a Christological statement it has scarcely an equal, certainly no superior" (Nicholson, *Oneness with Christ,* p. 171). With it may be compared other passages expressive of the apostolic doctrine of the person and work of Christ (Col. 2:9-15; Eph. 1:20-23; Phil. 2:5-11; Heb. 1:2-14; Rom. 9:5; Gal. 2:20; I Cor. 1:23, 24, 30, 31). We shall see that in this passage are taught various relationships of Christ.

1. Christ's Relation to Grace (v. 14). From the thought of the Father (vv. 12, 13) comes the natural reference to "the Son of his love" (v. 13, *A.S.V.*), and then follows the significant statement that in Him "we have our redemption, the forgiveness of our sins." Redemption is one of the six words found in the New Testament to express the work of Christ (cf. Eph. 1:7; Heb. 9:12), the other five being as follows: sacrifice (Eph. 5:2; I Cor. 5:7; Heb. 10:22); offering (Heb. 10:10, 14); propitiation (Rom. 3:25; I

John 2:2; 4:10); ransom (Matt. 20:28; I Tim. 2:6); and reconciliation (Rom. 5:11, *A.S.V.*; II Cor. 5:18; Eph. 2:16-18). The word for redemption in the original seems to mean to loose by a price, while the English, following the Latin, means to buy back, to repurchase (cf. I Peter 1:18). The special thought is thus deliverance from slavery by means of payment (cf. Rom. 3:24) and the removal of bondage and thralldom, just as in the previous verse we saw the corresponding metaphor of a victory and a rescue in time of war.

Moreover, this word rendered "redemption" is significant also for its emphasis on the completeness of the work. The related verb "to redeem" occurs four times in the New Testament (Luke 1:68; 24:21; Titus 2:14; I Peter 1:18), and in each case the thought is of deliverance wrought through the death of Christ. But, it may be noted, nowhere are we told to whom the payment was made, thereby avoiding the old and persistent error that it was the devil (although Dimock in his *The Death of Christ* acutely points out that the idea contained the germ of a real truth). Scripture is content with emphasizing the actual payment of something infinitely valuable in the sight of God, that which the apostle Peter may well call "the precious blood of Christ" (I Peter 1:19).

The specific aspect of redemption mentioned here is "the forgiveness of sins," always the first element of the Christian message. Although the word "forgiveness" is one of the most familiar, it may be questioned whether many who use it realize the remarkable force and fulness of its meaning. Forgiveness is never defined in Scripture, but the word itself means "removal," or "sending away." This necessarily includes the remission of the penalty, the removal of the condemnation, and also the actual sending away both of sin (the root) and of sins (the fruit). Never once do we read of the forgiveness of guilt or the forgiveness of condemnation, but only of the forgiveness of sin and of sins. The word must, therefore, mean something equivalent to the fulness of redeeming love and grace, covering past, present, and future, and embracing position and condition, standing and state, character and conduct. Nor can forgiveness mean only and merely the negative aspect of release, but must involve also the positive element of restoration, including saving, cleansing, justifying, purifying, sanctifying, illuminating, welcoming, blessing, and glorifying. A careful study of the usage of the word in the New Testament will prove this, however novel and surprising it may seem. Of course, we are accustomed to distinguish between forgiveness and justification, but there is a sense in which forgiveness may be said to include everything from the beginning of Christian experience to the end, because of the clear reference in Scripture to the "sending away" of sin and of sins. Thus redemption and forgiveness are two of our possessions ("we have"; see also Eph. 1:7). They come from Calvary, and a third, derived from the empty tomb, is "access" (Rom. 4:24 - 5:2). From Pentecost we have a fourth, "unction" (I John 2:20); and from Olivet a fifth, "we have a building of God" (II Cor. 5:1), our resurrection body.

Now, from redemption and forgiveness, the apostle turns to our Lord's relationship to deity (v. 15), to creation (v. 16), and to providence (v. 17); and so we pass on to another relationship of Christ.

2. Christ's Relation to God the Father (v. 15a). This is the basis of redemption. There could be no forgiveness of sins unless Christ were both God and man, for only a divine act could "send away" human evil-doing. He is described as "the image of the invisible God"; and the word "image" seems to include the two ideas of representation and manifestation (cf. II Cor. 4:4; Heb. 1:3). In similar language St. John speaks of Christ as "the Word" (John 1:1), meaning thereby the identical thought and exact expression of God. For this reason John could continue: "No man hath seen God at any time; the only begotten Son, who is in the bosom of the Father, he hath declared him" (John 1:18, *A. S. V.*). To the same effect are some words of His own: "He that hath seen me hath seen the Father" (John 14:9).

It has often been pointed out by writers on this Epistle that in these words about Christ's person the apostle Paul destroys all the erroneous teachings that were already beginning to exert influence in Colosse. Instead of the various emanations from the Godhead that were considered to be links of intercourse between God and the world, the apostle declares, this doctrine of Christ as the sole One in whom God was manifested in human life is not only true but vital. He is the adequate and essential expression of the divine nature. He fully represents God because in Him dwells the fulness of deity. He is the sole revealer of God, actually manifesting the invisible. His character is a true revelation of the divine glory.

Some years ago, at a ministers' meeting a paper was read drawing the conclusion that Jesus Christ was a little more than man and a little less than God, an expression of the old error of the fourth century against which the Nicene Creed was formulated. The minister who was called upon to open the ensuing discussion said immediately that this view would not do for him, because he for one was a sinner needing a Savior and that Savior must be God as well as man. In words that deserve to be quoted again and again, Bishop Moule has declared: "A Saviour not quite God is a bridge broken at the farther end."

> Man fain would build a bridge to God
> Across the fathomless abyss

That lies between his earth-bound soul
　　And heaven's perfect bliss.

He takes his knowledge, small and vague,
　　The great inventions he has wrought,
His mightiest efforts, finest plans,
　　And his profoundest thought.

He binds them with his strands of straw,
　　His strings of tow, his ropes of sand,
With all the power and all the skill
　　Of cunning brain and hand.

Through swirling mists he strains his eyes;
　　Above the unseen torrents' roar
He pushes forth the makeshift thing
　　And hopes to touch the shore.

But when he seeks to cross the chasm
　　With eager heart and step elate
He finds his bridge too short to reach,
　　Too frail to bear his weight.

Oh, baseless dream! Oh, useless toil!
　　Oh, utter and eternal loss!
For God has laid, to span the void,
　　His Son upon the cross.

And when man's broken bridges fall
　　And sink into the gulf at last,
Still wide and long and safe and strong
　　The Bridge of God stands fast.

　　　　　　　　　　　　　—Annie Johnson Flint
　　　　　　　　　　　　　(used by permission)

3. Christ's Relation to Creation (vv. 15b-17). His connection with the world is next mentioned, and He is described as "the first begotten (Gr., cf. Acts 13:33, 34; Rom. 1:4; Heb. 1:6) of all creation" (v. 15b). The whole tendency in the teaching both of Paul and of John entirely forbids the interpretation "first of creatures" (Rev. 3:14). Both writers conceive of our Lord as the principle and cause of creation (from which creation actually originated), and also as preeminent above creation, head as well as source. Thus He has preexistence and He has sovereignty. He must, therefore, be the mediator between creator and creature, and this function is also implied in His sonship. A relationship of love always communicates itself, so it is logical that both primary and plenary self-communication is the eternal generation of the only begotten Son of God. Creation is a further act of self-communication and therefore is carried on through the mediation of the Son.

Moreover, the context makes it perfectly clear that this reference to Him is to One who is separate from creation, and not simply a created being, however exalted. It indicates Christ's unique supremacy over creation, just as in verse 18, as we shall see, the same word is used of His relation to the Church. There are also three prepositions (v. 16) that further show the relation of Christ to creation: "*In* him were all things created" (*A.S.V.*); "all things have been created *through* him" (*A.S.V.*); and the same have been created "*for* him." In other words, all things were made by Him, are sustained in Him, and tend toward Him in a unity of which He is the principle. Thus He is seen to be at once the sphere, the agent, and the beneficiary of creation, which is stated to include all things in heaven and on earth, both visible and invisible, "whether thrones, or dominions, or principalities, or authorities (Gr.)." In Him, therefore, was the *kosmos noetos,* the world as it existed in the divine mind (John 1:3, *A.S.V.* marg.: "That which hath been made was life in him"). There is, therefore, but one link between God and creation, namely, the Son (Rev. 4:11).

Even more than all of this, we are told (v. 17), what we call Providence is associated with our Lord, for this very same being ("he himself," Gr.) is said to be before all things, and all things find in Him their consistency and coherence. Nothing, therefore, could be clearer than this series of pronouncements expressive of the priority, sovereignty, and continuity of Christ in relation to nature. It will be seen, moreover, that in his use of these terms the apostle is not referring at all to the Incarnation, but to the preexistence of Christ, His consequent priority over all else that exists, and His essential relationship to God the Father and to the universe. The undeniably cosmic quality of these verses thus prevents our being limited in our thinking to the sphere of Redemption, great as this is. In fact, a thoughtful writer has said that it is as though the second person of the Trinity took *creature* form for the purposes of creation (cf. "*Elohim* . . . image . . . likeness," Gen. 1:26; cf. Prov. 8:22-31; John 1:1-5), as He afterwards took *human* form for the purposes of redemption (cf. Isa. 49:1; John 1:14; Phil. 2:7; Heb. 10:5).

In this wonderful passage, furthermore, in which the apostle seems to find himself almost incapable of expressing fully the divine thought in human language, we encounter some of the deep things of life. Let us consider a threefold philosophy which these verses set forth:

   a. The Philosophy of Religion. This is seen in Christ's relation to God the Father. The fundamental problem of today, and of all other days, is the essential deity of Jesus Christ. Nothing can be called Christianity that does not start here in the absolute oneness of Christ with the Father as "the image of the invisible God" (v. 15). This is no mere abstract theological principle but a truly vital necessity that touches ordinary life at every point, so that nothing less than this will suffice. It is noteworthy that the words in the Nicene Creed "being of one substance with the Father" commended themselves to the whole Christian Church after the Council of Nicaea had dispersed, because they represented the vital truth of our Lord's oneness with God the Father as the sole basis of human redemption.

   b. The Philosophy of the Universe. This is seen in the fact that Christ has the same relation to the natural world as He has to the spiritual world. Bishop Lightfoot, in a memorable passage, calls attention to the great loss that we suffer by neglecting this wonderful truth of Christ's relation to nature. He very pointedly remarks that "the sympathy of theologians with the revelations of science and the development of history" would be much more hearty "if they habitually connected them with the operations of the same Divine Word who is the Centre of all their religious aspirations." The Bishop also remarks that by the neglect of this connection "our theological conceptions suffer in breadth and fulness." On the other hand, he continues, "the recognition of this idea, with all the consequences which flow from it," would more than in any other way make possible that "harmony of knowledge and faith, of reverence and research" which we all feel to be essential to a complete life and a strong influence (Lightfoot, *Colossians,* pp. 114-15). Bishop Moule similarly points out how this thought of Christ as the "Cause, Head, and Goal of the created Universe" binds both worlds into one, and he adds that "this is a precious gain when our hearts fail us on the border-line between the two." Not only so, but it makes nature so much more real and personal, the Bishop goes on, because "it connects the remotest star . . . with Him. It bids us, when we feel as if lost in the enormity of space and time, fall back upon the Centre of both . . . our Lord Jesus Christ who died for us." This and much more should be pondered by every earnest thinker who rejoices to realize that Christ is not only the Savior of the soul, but also "the ultimate Law" of the universe (Moule, *Colossian Studies,* pp. 80-82).

   c. The Philosophy of Individual Life. This is seen in the fact of redemption (v. 14). It is of special importance to realize that this redemption is in union with Christ and is also a present possession, for notice the dual force of the phrase "in whom we have. . . ." When this unspeakable blessing of redemption is seen to be ours as a precious reality here and now, because of our union with Christ, we have learned one of the secrets of true living and can rejoice with "joy unspeakable and full of glory" (I Peter 1:8).

THE DIVINE REDEEMER, 1:18-20

In developing the great theme of the Epistle, the divine person of Christ, His relation to the natural world (vv. 15b-17) is now to be paralleled by His relation to the spiritual world.

1. Christ's Relation to the Church, the New Creation (v. 18).

The familiar word *church* deserves careful study. The English word comes from an Anglo-Saxon corruption of a Greek term signifying "that which belongs to the Lord." However, the Greek word, *"ecclesia,"* translated "church" in our New Testament, means an assembly of people called together. Its classical equivalent was originally applied to a gathering of Greek citizens who were summoned from their homes and private capacities to some place of public assemblage. In the Greek version of the Old Testament, the Septuagint, the term is the translation of a Hebrew word referring to the gathering together of the people of Israel. It is also used in Acts 19:32, 41 to describe the town meeting of the people of Ephesus. In the Christian sense the word always indicates a society of Christian people in one of three meanings: the local use, the congregation in one place, a house, or a city (cf. 4:15; see p. 139; I Cor. 1:2; Philem. 2; see p. 153); the general use, the aggregate of Christians at one time in different places (cf. I Cor. 10:32; 12:28); and the universal use, the Church of Christ considered as embracing all places and all times (cf. Acts 20:28; Eph. 1:22).

The reference here and in the companion Epistle to the Ephesians is to a spiritual organism, not to an ecclesiastical organization; and the thought of the Church Universal in both Epistles, as consisting of those who are spiritually united to Christ and who form His body is, as Bishop Moule points out, the primary idea of the Church, and all other meanings are to be regarded as strictly secondary to it (*Colossian Studies,* p. 83, fn.). Certainly it will be found that all New Testament uses of the word "church" will fall under one or other of these heads.

Further, it is of the utmost importance that we rigidly confine ourselves to the New Testament for our doctrine of the Church. For all that is essential, as distinct from what is circumstantial and purely local, we must refuse to go one hairsbreadth beyond "the law and . . . the testimony" (Isa. 8:20). For instance, the Church is never to be limited to any officials or leaders, but is the whole body of Christians. Men about to be ordained are sometimes said to be "entering the Church," when the correct indication is that they are entering the ministry, having usually been "in the

Church" for some time previously. This is one instance of how thought and language may degenerate into error. Nor is there in the New Testament any hint of one precise form of ecclesiastical organization or government. Development and outward form came from within as befitted a spiritual body expressing its life in earthly manifestations. As the need arose for this or that office, this or that function, it was met, but there was nothing fixed. Everything was flexible, and growth was according to the requirements of a spiritual community.

It is probable, however, that between the first mention of the word "church" in Matthew 16:18 and the use of the term in Ephesians and Colossians there is no other reference to the Church as a whole, but only to particular parts of it in their earthly manifestations. This widest, fullest, and, of course, truest sense of the term is well defined in some familiar words found in *The Book of Common Prayer*—"the blessed company of all faithful people." It is also particularly interesting to notice the treatment of this doctrine of the Church in Colossians when compared with the teaching of Ephesians. In both cases Christ is called the head (v. 18; Eph. 1:22), but in Colossians the emphasis is placed on His attributes as such, while in Ephesians the stress is laid on the unity of the body, the Church. Moreover, it is singularly suggestive to observe the difference in the appeals made in these Epistles in regard to the same practical duties. Thus, for instance, in Colossians believers are to avoid untruthfulness because of their relation to Christ (3:9-11), while in Ephesians the same duty is inculcated from the standpoint of their relations to other Christians (Eph. 4:25). This is only one of a number of comparisons through which these aspects of "Church truth" are clearly seen.

The thought of Christ as the head of the Church implies three great principles in the spiritual realm as well as in the physical, viz., life, unity, and sovereignty. He is at once the source of our spiritual life, the guarantor of all spiritual unity, and the supreme spiritual authority. He is the One who, because He bestows life, controls all believers, who are therefore expected to render Him love and loyalty. The more completely this fact of our union with Christ as the head is realized, the fuller will be the expression of our spiritual life in fellowship and in obedience as members of His body.

> O what blessings flow from grace,
>   Treasured up in Christ our Head!
> He who perfected life's race
>   Bore sin's burden in our stead.
> Christ our Ransom doth appear
>   In the glorious courts above;

> Righteousness Divine we wear,
> Loved with everlasting love.

Then Christ is described as "the beginning," or author, and actually the original is reminiscent of the Greek term in verse 16, rendered "principalities." This root, according to Lightfoot, involves both priority in time (cf. I Cor. 15:20, 23) and originating power (cf. Acts 3:15) (Lightfoot, *Colossians,* p. 155). It teaches that Christ is the great energizing origin of everything in connection with the Church, His body. Then follows a further statement, "the firstborn from the dead," and again the thought looks back, this time to verse 15 where Christ is spoken of as "the firstborn of all creation" (*A.S.V.*). Thus the same word is used of Him in relation to grace as to nature. The thought here, however, is associated with the resurrection and indicates again priority and origin. He has priority in regard to His own resurrection and, because of it, He is the source of our resurrection.

We find from a study of the subject in St. Paul's Epistles that God had several beneficent purposes in Christ's resurrection. There was, first, our justification (Rom. 4:25); second, there was the validating of our faith and witness (I Cor. 15:14); and, third, there was the providing for our comfort (I Thess. 4:14-18). But, more vital even than these because it includes all of them, by the resurrection He was designated "the Son of God with power" (Rom. 1:4). Although Son of God already by reason of His eternal relationship with the Father (v. 15), Christ became by His resurrection the source of spiritual power to all who receive Him (cf. Rom. 14:9; Eph. 1:19, 20; 2:5, 6).

This spiritual relation and position are intended to fulfil one more purpose—"that in all things He might have the preeminence." Christ was already preeminent in the realm of creation ("is," v. 15), and now He is shown to have become (Gr.) supreme in the realm of grace (Phil. 2:9-11). While this thought, of course, is intended to apply to the whole Church (Eph. 1:10, 22), it is impossible to avoid recalling, as an individual application, the sad and solemn contrast with the only other place in the New Testament where the word *preeminence* is to be found, namely III John 9. Those who, like Diotrephes, love to "have the preeminence" cannot possibly recognize the preeminence of Christ. As has so often been said, "if He be not Lord of all, then He is not Lord at all."

Thus in nature, in providence, and in grace, Christ is preeminent; and it is surely fitting that from this key statement by the apostle should come the title of our original volume. This was the divine purpose for our Lord, this is His rightful place even now, and in the future it will be realized in all its fulness. What a glory it lends to the Christian to know that his

Master is not only spiritually related to the Church, but even physically and eternally related to the entire universe! We can look up into space and realize that Christ made it. We can survey history and know that Christ has been ruling and overruling it. We can contemplate the Church and rejoice to know that Christ is its head, its Lord, and its foundation. Nothing has ever happened, is happening, or will happen, apart from Him.

2. Christ's Relation to Redemption (vv. 19, 20). The basis of what has been said about this wonderful and glorious unity of the entire universe in Christ is now shown to be His deity, for only thus could He hold such a transcendent position in the realms of nature and of grace. Thus we read that "it pleased the Father that in Him should all fulness permanently dwell" (v. 19, Gr. aorist). The Father's pleasure concerning Christ is noteworthy not only here, but elsewhere in Scripture (cf. Isa. 42:1; Matt. 3:17; 17:5; Eph. 1:5). It shows at once the loving interest of the Father in the redemptive work of His Son and the vital necessity of that redemption being accomplished by none other than a divine being. The word "fulness" expresses what has been called by Dr. John Rutherfurd "all the plenitude of Deity," and he states that it includes "whatever is contained in the Divine nature in all its depths of eternal existence, righteousness, wisdom, power, holiness, goodness, truth, love" (*The Epistles to Colossae and Laodicea*, p. 54). The term is found often in the companion Epistle, and it is particularly interesting to notice there the association of the thought with each person of the Trinity (cf. Eph. 3:19; 4:13; 5:18). It is also found later in this Epistle (Col. 2:9) indicating, as here, the entirety or completeness of the Godhead. Indeed, of the eleven occasions on which the word *fulness* is found in St. Paul's writings, no fewer than six are in these two Epistles, Ephesians and Colossians. There is no doubt, therefore, that here, in combination with a word implying permanent abode, Christ's Godhead is regarded as altogether apart from time and all other limitations. "Any limitation, therefore, of the meaning of *Pleroma* (fulness) which would make the indwelling of the fulness of the Godhead in Christ a matter either of the future or of the past only, is inconsistent with what is said of the indwelling of the *Pleroma* in Him in ch. 1:19; 2:9. The reference in both passages is to the timeless and eternal communication of the Godhead from the Father to the Son" (Rutherfurd, *The Epistles to Colossae and Laodicea*, p. 56).

This permanent fulness, betokening deity, is intended for the purpose of reconciliation—"to reconcile all things unto himself" (v. 20)—namely, everything that had become alienated and severed through sin. Elsewhere St. Paul similarly teaches that God is reconciling the universe to Himself through the person and work of Christ (II Cor. 5:19; Eph. 2:14-22). In the latter passage it is interesting to notice the emphasis placed on the unity of the Church by the fact that this reconciliation is connected with the uniting of Jews and Gentiles into one body for the permanent habitation of God. When it is said that Christ reconciles "all things," it seems to mean that in Him there will be no discord of any sort, for both reconciliation and peace come through "the blood of his cross" (v. 20). Peace is the result of reconciliation with God, and this is the twofold peace of Scripture, sometimes described as "peace with God" (Rom. 5:1), or as "the peace of God" (Phil. 4:7); and both have their source in "the God of peace" (Phil. 4:9). The acceptance of Christ's atoning sacrifice through faith brings peace to the soul; and this consciousness of reconciliation with God causes, in turn, a blessed sense of restfulness to spring up in the heart; and thus, and only thus, do we have the very peace of God Himself within us.

Thus the Creator has become the Savior. The Son of God is manifested in redemption; and His mediatorial function in the Church follows from His role in creation. It was the great contention of Athanasius that the author of creation must of necessity be the Redeemer, and so His relation is parallel in both spheres: He is the archetype, the source, the formal cause, and the final goal, both in the universe of created beings and in the assembly of redeemed humanity, the one great link in both spheres between God the Creator and man the creature.

It has often been pointed out that part of a similar expression in Philippians 2:10, "things under the earth," is significantly omitted here in verse 20. This phrase is reminiscent of the powers of darkness (cf. "down," II Peter 2:4; "under darkness," Jude 6). While, of course, there will be total submission to Christ, either willing or unwilling, in order that He may be acknowledged by all as Lord (Phil. 2:11), yet here, where spiritual reconciliation is the subject, there is a limitation to "things in earth" and "things in heaven." This is perhaps a hint of what is found elsewhere, that somehow or other creation has been affected by human sin (cf. Gen. 3:17; Rom. 8:19-22). "As there seems to be a physical unity in the universe, if we may believe the guesses of science, so, says Holy Scripture, there is a moral and spiritual unity also in Jesus Christ" (Bishop Barry in Ellicott's *Commentary*, pp. 25, 26). It is not, however, that universal reconciliation means universal salvation, because we know that, while the work of Christ is sufficient for all, it is efficient only for those who actually accept it. It is indeed God's purpose to save all men, but not all of them will come to Him for life. He impels but never compels.

As we have seen, the method of this reconciliation is "the blood of his cross" by the means of which God has "made peace" in Christ. It is particularly noteworthy that the One who makes the peace is God the Father. This is another reminder that the atoning sacrifice was not due to the love of the Son only, but also to the love of the Father: "God so loved the world, that he gave . . . " (John 3:16); and "Christ . . . loved us, and hath given himself for us" (Eph. 5:2).

As the entire passage clearly teaches what God the Father thinks of Christ, it becomes necessary and important to ask what *we* think of Christ (cf. Matt. 22:42). If He is all this to His Father, it follows that He ought to be everything to us. The whole passage may be summed up by saying that Christ should be to us and should have from us these four realities: (1) *Life.* He is at once the source and the support of it, for His work is our redemption, bringing an end to all self-righteousness. His atonement accepted, our life should belong to Him alone. (2) *Love.* This should be both a proof to others of our profession, and a power for helping them; for His grace is our strength, bringing with it an end to all self-dependence. (3) *Lordship.* This naturally and necessarily follows from all that has preceded. (4) *Loyalty.* This comes from a French word associated with law and faithfulness to it; it has been well defined as "legality with love." Christ's glory is to be our overriding object, which means an end to all forms of self-pleasing.

Thus in individual life and in church life, in witness, work, worship, or warfare, "that in all things he might have the preeminence," there must be acceptance of Him, trust in Him, obedience to Him, and proclamation of Him as supreme and incomparable.

> Then who this day will rejoicing say,
>   With a grateful heart and free,
> "Thou King Divine, my life shall be Thine,
>   I consecrate all to Thee"?
>
> We daily live and we daily give
>   For some object near the heart,
> Some purpose bold, some name that we hold
>   Where the gushing life-springs start.
>
> But oh! 'tis wise when the heart can rise
>   And carry its wealth away
> Where the angels fall; He deserveth all
>   That we at His feet can lay.
>
> A life that serves where a love deserves
>   The life and the love we give
> Is a life sublime, on the fields of time,
>   A life it is grand to live!
>
> Then let each this day rejoicing say,

With a grateful heart and free,
"Thou King Divine, my life shall be Thine,
I consecrate all to Thee!"

THE DIVINE REDEMPTION, 1:21-23

After such an outstanding passage concerning the person of Christ (see also Eph. 1:20-23; Phil. 2:5-11; Heb. 1:1-14), it is not surprising that the definite results of the work of Christ are now to be set forth. Indeed, it is quite natural that this whole great subject of Christology shall be at once applied to the fact of redemption; and so in these verses we see some of the fundamental elements in the redemption process that arise from the consideration of the Redeemer's divine person as discussed earlier. To do this, however, the apostle goes back a little, and speaks of:

1. **Alienation (v. 21a).** It is interesting to notice the way in which this verse commences: "And you," just as in the parallel passage (Eph. 2:1). It would seem as though in both cases St. Paul, having dealt with redemption in general (v. 20; cf. Eph. 1:19, 20), follows this by calling attention to the particular manner in which Christ's work is intended for those to whom the apostle writes. The statement about their past life is impressive in its solemnity. "Having become permanently estranged" is the literal rendering, showing not merely the former state from which they had fallen, but the subsequent fact of their alienation. This does not necessarily mean open and gross sin, but rather that state of heart which comes from a deliberate opposition to God. We notice, first, the guilt of it, incurring condemnation, and then what may rightly be called the folly of it, because sin means leaving light for darkness, purity for defilement, dignity for humiliation, harmony for discord, life for death, and heaven for hell.

This estrangement is further described in the phrase "enemies in your mind by wicked works" (v. 21). Alienation involves actual hostility to God because the assertion of self must of necessity imply rebellion against Him. What a terrible description of the results of sin—mind wrong, conduct wrong, causing not only estrangement from God, but also enmity against Him! This enmity arises first in the mind because the thoughts and feelings are affected; and then it expresses itself in "wicked works," acts of hostility, because the inner life is morally bad. This picture of depravity is both true and sad: true to what we know sin has done for human life; sad, because it means the loss of everything that tends to make human life safe, strong, and satisfying (cf. Rom. 8:7; Eph. 2:12; 4:13).

2. **Reconciliation (vv. 21b, 22a).** Then comes the blessed and glorious contrast between the past and the present. The Colossian Christians had been at one time alienated, "yet now" (v. 21)—a favorite phrase of the

writer (cf. v. 26; 3:8; Rom. 3:21; Eph. 2:13)—there has come reconciliation. Instead of enmity there is friendship and devotion; and He who has accomplished this reconciliation is none other than God Himself, thereby showing His marvelous condescension. In this situation it was actually the offended One who was seeking reconciliation. This is the meaning of another passage (II Cor. 5:18) in which the apostle speaks of God in Christ reconciling the world to Himself. This action is also a proof of God's perfect righteousness for, while it does not affect the divine grace (cf. John 3:16), it of necessity involves the divine government. There could be no reconciliation between God and man unless it were accomplished on the basis of the divine character of righteousness. It is impossible for God to be indifferent to sin, even though He loves the sinner.

Then the apostle goes on to show how this reconciliation has been brought about: "in the body of his flesh through death" (v. 22). In these words is a brief statement of the Incarnation, "the body of his flesh," and of the Atonement, "through death." Christ was born in order to die, and when it is said that He "came into the world to save sinners" (I Tim. 1:15), we are reminded again both of Bethlehem and of Calvary. Christ died for the ungodly (Rom. 5:6), the Just for the unjust (I Peter 3:18), and sinful men are reconciled to God only by the death of His Son (Isa. 53:6).

> Bearing sin and scoffing rude,
> In my place condemned He stood,
> Sealed my pardon with His blood,
> Hallelujah! What a Saviour!

> —P. P. Bliss

3. **Presentation (v. 22b).** The purpose of this redeeming work of Christ is now stated. The verb "to present" is particularly interesting for its three different applications in St. Paul's Epistles, each suggesting a helpful truth. Sometimes an oblation is presented to God (Rom. 12:1); or it may be that a bride is being presented to her husband (II Cor. 11:2; Eph. 5:27); or perhaps a subject is to be presented at court (II Cor. 4:14-18). Whatever be the precise significance here (whether of sacrifice, spouse, or subject), it is a beautiful thought that our Lord, having redeemed us by His death, is to present us "before the presence of his glory with exceeding joy" (Jude, v. 24). The three words indicative of the condition of the believer when thus presented are also noteworthy: "holy and without blemish and unreprovable" (v. 22, *A.S.V.*). There is to be entire consecration ("holy"); the absence of all disfigurement ("without blemish"); and the impossibility of any accusation against him ("unreprovable"). This threefold description

may perhaps be regarded as inward, outward, and upward, or internal, external, and eternal (cf. Rom 8:32-34; Heb. 9:14, 15). There is to be not merely salvation here, but hereafter, not only deliverance from sin's guilt, defilement, and power, but also from its very presence. Christ died that we might one day stand before God "perfect and entire (or mature and complete), lacking in nothing" (James 1:4, *A.S.V.*). Nothing less than this expectation is to be the crown and culmination of our Lord's redemptive work.

4. Continuation (v. 23). But betwixt past and future comes the thought of "the little while between." The believer who has been redeemed and who is to be presented is, meanwhile, to "continue in the faith." The only way in which the work of Christ in the past can be completely carried out, and the purpose of God in the future fully realized, is by the present faithfulness to the gospel of those who are in Christ. It is not so much that there was real doubt of the Colossians' being "in the faith," as might seem indicated by the English word "if," but rather that to assume their present continuance was the best guarantee of it. If something *is,* it is a fair assumption that something related and antecedent to it *was.*

It is possible now to summarize the apostle Paul's development of the truth of reconciliation in relation to the whole subject of redemption. It is first shown in its ideal form ("all things," v. 20), and then in its actual working out (the effect on those "wicked works" of yours of that "death" of His, vv. 21, 22); and yet it is conditional—to paraphrase verse 23a from the Greek: "as ye will continue in the faith, grounded (in Christ) and settled (in your own minds)."

There is nothing magical about this continuing. St. John calls it abiding (cf. John 15:4-11; I John 2:28), and it is the secret of blessedness. The true Christian life means yielding everything to God (Rom. 6:13) and then remaining in that attitude. Thus, and only thus, shall we enter into a spiritual experience of light and liberty, joy and power. Even amid human failure to realize all that is ours in Christ, there comes an ever-deepening conviction that this experience is both the complement of justification by faith and the means by which we are sanctified, still by faith. These fundamental realities constitute the heart and core of that gospel which, for saint as well as for sinner, is "the power of God unto salvation" (Rom. 1:16).

This position is one of (a) permanent foundation ("grounded"), of (b) steadfastness ("settled"), with (c) the absence of any adverse motion ("not moved away") which tends to shake the believer from "the hope originated by the gospel" (Gr.). The elements of this hope are desire, expectation, and patience: not desire only, as so often in human aspiration, for we may want what we do not really expect; not, on the other hand, expectation only, for we may be expecting what we do not desire; but, rather, desire and expectation combined, and exercised with that patience, or endurance, which can await the full realization. Hope as a grace is very different from a mere spirit of hopefulness, or a natural buoyancy of temperament. It is a distinctly Christian virtue, the result, as we have seen, of union with God in Christ. Those who have accepted the redemption discussed in this passage find themselves firmly fixed and grounded in Christ Jesus and rejoicing "in hope of the glory of God" (Rom. 5:2; cf. I Cor. 15:58; Eph. 3:17-19).

5. **Evangelization (v. 23b).** We have seen the need of reconciliation, because of alienation; the means, which was the atonement; the purpose, which was presentation; and the proof, which was continuation. We now come to the preaching of reconciliation, or proclamation. There are three elements of this gospel of reconciliation which here call for attention: (a) it was heard; (b) it was preached in all the world; and (c) it was a gospel of which Paul was a minister. It is interesting to note that in verse 7 we read of a minister of Christ, here of a minister of the gospel, and in verses 24 and 25 of a minister of the Church—the only true and logical order, for it is Christ who, through His gospel proclaimed and accepted, adds "to the church . . . such as should be saved" (Acts 2:47).

Thus we see in this central passage of the Epistle the whole gospel, including atonement for sin, acceptance of the sinner, holiness for the saint—viz., full salvation—and every part of it proclaimed all over the world by those who have received it. As we consider its elements of power and blessedness we see that our sacred duty is (1) to believe it, (2) to receive it, (3) to live it, (4) to enjoy it, and (5) to spread it.

5 THE PRESENTATION OF THE CHRISTIAN MINISTRY

At this point the apostle turns from the Christians of Colosse, whom he is addressing, to speak of himself as a preacher of the gospel that they had heard and received; and from the statement of its universality (v. 23b) he proceeds to relate some of his own personal experiences. Hitherto he has been concerned with our Savior's relation to the universe, to the Church, and to individual Christians; and from the consideration of the divine redemptive work, past, present, and future, comes the presentation of the ministry as a means of redemption's implementation. Specifically, St. Paul refers to himself and his own ministry, which, besides being related, first, to Christ as the source (v. 7) and, second, to the gospel as the message (v. 23), is also related to the Church as the sphere. The fact of a "ministry of reconciliation" (II Cor. 5:18) naturally leads the apostle to think of his own opportunity as a preacher of the gospel, and he is evidently glad of the occasion to glory in his office.

1. The Delight of the Ministry (v. 24a). One characteristic, in particular, of the apostle's ministry is here emphasized, the element of personal satisfaction—"I rejoice" (*A.S.V.*). In so writing he indicates what should be one of the dominant features of the believer's life and work for Christ, as suggested by Bishop Wynne's fine book *The Joy of the Ministry*. Lightfoot calls this "a sudden outburst of thanksgiving" that the apostle, who felt himself personally unworthy, should be allowed thus to serve his Master. There is also an emphasis on the word "now," and Lightfoot suggests that

61

the force of it is "when I see all the glory of bearing a part in this magnificent work" (*Colossians,* p. 162). St. Paul was evidently ready to rejoice even though bound by chains in Rome, and he implies that nothing was to be permitted to affect his deep satisfaction. As we all know, it is easy to be joyful when everything is bright, but very different when, as with the apostle, a sudden check comes to an active career. There may be the need to wait in some prison for the day of trial, meanwhile longing for release not only for freedom, but in order to continue the beloved work.

2. The Discipline of the Ministry (v. 24b). By a remarkable paradox this joy is spoken of in connection with suffering. It was a present and continuous fact in Paul's experience; indeed, it was the sphere in which he may be said to have lived, and yet he was ready to rejoice. This is but one instance of such joy, as in his ministry he endured all things for Christ (cf. Acts 20:23, 24; Rom. 5:3; Phil. 2:17).

This suffering was also for the sake of others, on their behalf, for their advantage ("for you"; cf. II Cor. 1:4-7), but the apostle seems to speak of supplementing a deficiency, as though something had been left over for him to endure, i.e., "that which is lacking of the afflictions of Christ (*A.S.V.*)". What this means will best be understood when we see that his personal sufferings were regarded as distinguishable from and yet identifiable with those of Christ. The phrase "the afflictions of Christ" is unique in the New Testament, and can only mean the afflictions which He Himself endured—His own afflictions. The apostle says that he supplied what was lacking in these, but to what afflictions of Christ can he refer? Certainly not to His expiatory sufferings on the cross, which were, as we know, perfect and complete (cf. v. 20; Heb. 9:25-28; I Peter 3:18). These need no supplement whatsoever; they are not only complete but they are unique, and they are eternal in their significance and their efficacy. But surely the apostle's reference is to those individual, personal afflictions in which Christ lived on our behalf during His earthly ministry (cf. Isa. 53:4; Matt. 8:17).

In this connection it is useful to consult the commentators. Lightfoot points out that the sufferings of Christ must be considered from two standpoints, either as atoning or as exemplary, the one possessing sacrificial efficacy, the other ministerial utility. In the former case, he agrees, the sufferings are perfect and complete, since our Lord's work is both unique in purpose and different in kind from that of His servants. There is no reference here to atonement since, as we have noted, the word "affliction" is not found elsewhere in reference to the sacrifice of Christ on the cross. From the latter standpoint the afflictions of every saint and martyr may rightly be said to supplement the afflictions of Christ, and the Christian Church is built up by acts of self-denial that continue those begun by Him. Indeed, that which is lacking, says Lightfoot, will never be fully supplemented until the struggle with sin and unbelief is brought to a close. Thus the idea of expiation is wholly absent from the passage, and when this is understood we are free to give every word of the apostle's striking statement its full meaning, and yet avoid all suggestion of vicarious satisfaction, which is entirely foreign to the context (Lightfoot, *Colossians*, p. 164).

Other commentators take very much the same line. Bishop Moule says that St. Paul is not thinking of our Lord's passion, but of His sacred life-work as teacher, healer, guide, and endurer. In these tribulations our Lord was preeminent but not unique, for He left toil and suffering for His flock to endure after He quitted the earth (Moule, *Colossian Studies*, p. 99). So also, Maclaren in his felicitous exposition reminds us that "Christ truly participates in the sufferings of His people borne for Him. He suffers with them." It follows, then, that the meaning of this passage is that "every sorrow rightly borne, as it will be when Christ is felt to be bearing it with us, is fruitful of blessing" (*The Expositor's Bible, The Epistles of Paul to the Colossians and Philemon*, p. 120). Thus, while from the standpoint of the atoning sacrifice we of today cannot contribute anything to the sufferings of Christ, yet from the standpoint of personal life and sympathy there is very much in which we can be identified with Him (cf. Matt. 25:41-46; Acts 9:1-5). We can have fellowship with His afflictions and also imitate His patience and courage in suffering. Then the entire aspect of sorrow and trial becomes changed as we realize that

> In every pang that rends the heart
> The Man of Sorrows has a part.

This experience is intended for the whole Church. It is not only for individuals, but for the entire community of Christians; and it is particularly interesting to notice the contrast between Paul's literal "flesh" and Christ's spiritual "body," the Church. It is a beautiful and inspiring thought that each Christian can and should endure afflictions on behalf of the entire body of believers. This is the real meaning of suffering, namely, the education, training, and disciplining of the soul (Heb. 5:8). However, there is no possibility of merit on the part of any Christian, or even on the part of the entire Church, because our Lord's sufferings that wrought salvation were sufficient, yea, more than sufficient, to atone for the sins of the whole world. But after the Atonement had been made there was still suffering to be endured for the establishment of the Church; and wherever the apostles went they suffered as they preached, and as they suffered they preached the more earnestly. In these afflictions we in our turn can share, and this is the inspiring and beautiful truth the apostle emphasizes here. It has been expressed thus: "We cannot create the vital seed, but we can plant it, and tend it, and water it, and we can labour for an abundant harvest. And thus it is that our filling-up of the sufferings of Christ is not done on the hill called Calvary; it is done on the long road which begins at the empty tomb, and which stretches through Jerusalem and Samaria, and reaches the uttermost parts of the earth. In the Christian redemption our sufferings are not fundamental; they are supplemental. Sacrificial disciples are needed to proclaim the sacrificial work of our Lord. Only in this way can we fill up 'that which is lacking of the afflictions of Christ.' " We must not be daunted, therefore, if called upon to suffer, for thereby we shall be permitted to set forward the progress of the Church and the accomplishment of God's purpose.

3. **The Description of the Ministry (vv. 24b, 25).** The apostle calls himself here a minister of the Church, just as he had formerly spoken of himself as a minister of the gospel (v. 23). He also describes himself elsewhere as a minister of Christ (II Cor. 11:23) and as a minister of God (II Cor. 6:4). These varied aspects of his service show how we in our time can work in order to accomplish the divine will.

St. Paul's ministry is also described as "according to the dispensation of God" (v. 25). The word "dispensation" seems to suggest the entrusting of a great responsibility, like the management of an estate, or, as Lightfoot renders it, "stewardship in the house of God," in the capacity of an administrator (Lightfoot, *Colossians,* p. 165), one who dispenses or distributes supplies; and he adds that the words "to you-ward" (*A.S.V.*) indicate that this responsibility was placed on the apostle for the benefit of the Gentiles (Eph. 3:2; Rom. 15:16).

Further, the work is intended "to fulfil the word of God," that is, to bring to completion the message of God's grace (cf. Rom. 15:8-12). The apostle was never content with anything perfunctory; he put his whole soul into everything he did and thus fulfilled, or "filled full," the divine gospel entrusted to him.

4. **The Delineation of the Ministry (v. 26).** The apostle's reference to himself as a minister (v. 25) naturally leads to a fuller explanation of "the word of God" that he proclaimed. Whenever an ambassador arrives for the first time in a foreign capital, he has to present letters of introduction from his chief-of-state to the head of the nation to which he has been appointed. By these he is proved to be the true, authorized representative of his own country, and they are fitly called "credentials," the means whereby he is given credence, or, is proved, believed, accepted. St. Paul here may be said to be presenting his "credentials," and something of the kind was probably in his mind when elsewhere he spoke of himself and

other Christian ministers as "ambassadors for Christ" (II Cor. 5:20), those who are appointed to represent their Master before men. It is fitting that they, too, should possess and show proofs of genuineness, and what these are can be discovered from the many examples of apostolic preaching and teaching in the New Testament. It is as necessary for Christian people today as for the Bereans of old (Acts 17:10-12) to test the Christian ministry as to whether or not it agrees with Scripture and thereby proves itself to be from God. Indeed, the analysis of the Pauline ministry is particularly worthy of careful consideration because of its application to all who proclaim the gospel of Christ.

The apostle calls the divine message "the mystery," a word that is especially significant. It is found some twenty times in the New Testament, more than half of which instances are in St. Paul's Epistles, and invariably it means, as here, something wonderful that was once hidden "but now" (v. 21), though not generally recognized, is revealed to those who will accept it by faith. We may note in passing some of the important uses to which this word "mystery" is put—namely, to designate the following concepts: the union of Jews and Gentiles in the Church (Rom. 11:25; 16:25; Eph. 1:9-14; 3:3-10; 6:19); the wisdom of God (I Cor. 2:7); the resurrection of the body (I Cor. 15:51); the Church as the bride of Christ (Eph. 5:32); the incarnation of God in Christ (Col. 2:2; 4:3; I Tim. 3:9, 16); the problem of lawlessness (II Thess. 2:7, A.S.V.).

5. The Message of the Ministry (vv. 27, 28a). Here, however, the apostle apparently is writing about something that not only had always been hidden, but also had been revealed only a little time before—something, therefore, which, until that revelation was made, had not formed a part of the divine message that St. Paul had to make known. This seems to have been the special feature of the stewardship committed to him (v. 25; Eph. 3:1-12). He goes on to speak of "the riches of the glory of this mystery" (v. 27), and each term needs thorough attention. First, he uses the word "riches," evidently to denote some possession an abundance of which fully satisfies the owner. Certainly these Epistles of the Captivity are particularly noteworthy for their references to the wealth of the gospel (cf. Eph. 1:7, 18; 2:7; 3:8, 16; Col. 2:2; see p. 75f.). The word "glory" is also found frequently, to describe the magnificence and splendor of the Christian message (e.g., Eph. 1:18; 3:16; Phil. 4:19). Then the apostle proceeds to define the "mystery" as "Christ in you, the hope of glory" (v. 27).

What does he mean? At first sight it would seem as though he meant only that those Gentiles who belong to Christ are saved by Him; but their salvation through Christ had assuredly been revealed in older Scripture (cf. Gen. 12:3; Isa. 49:6, 7, etc.). We are told also that He "illuminated" older truths through the gospel (II Tim. 1:10, Gr.). Yet in the parallel passage, Ephesians 3:1-12, the mystery is said to have been hidden from all previous generations and never to have been announced until it was revealed to St. Paul. In fact, this passage clearly indicates that the reference is not to the salvation of Gentiles by Christ, which was not secret at all, but to the great truth that they should be associated with the Jewish nation in one spiritual body on terms of perfect equality in Christ. This, it would seem, is also the meaning of the text here; Christ was to be in the Gentiles "the hope of glory" in the fullest sense of the term, so as to include all the blessings of the gospel. Gentile believers were to enjoy the hope of supreme glory, and Jewish Christians obviously could have nothing more than this. The presence of Christ in the heart is both pledge and foretaste of that glory which will be ours at His Coming. If, therefore, this is the meaning of the passage, as it certainly is of the one in Ephesians, it presupposes Christian fellowship, Gentile believers being equally enriched in the fulness of the blessing of Christ. This would mean not only equality of acceptance in Him, but also equality of association in the Church, which is His body.

Thus we have "the riches of the glory of this mystery," and all three words in the pregnant phrase are also well worthy of notice in the reverse order—viz., "mystery," "glory," "riches." The beloved F. B. Meyer once used the apt illustration of a man returning to his old home, after many years of absence abroad, and sitting down with his mother as though with a stranger. At first she does not recognize him, and this means "mystery"; then he reveals himself to her, and in her delight the result is "the glory of this mystery." Lastly, he tells her of his remarkable prosperity in a far country and of the wealth he has brought home to her; and this is "the riches of the glory of this mystery." So is it in things spiritual: at first we do not realize all that is stored up in Christ, but He reveals Himself to us, and in that revelation will be found "the riches of his grace" (Eph. 1:7). This is also the great and precious thought in the apostle's mind when he exclaims concerning God the Father: "He that spared not his own Son, but delivered him up for us all, how shall he not with him also freely give us all things?" (Rom. 8:32).

The passage also tells us four things that sum up the essential features of the Christian evangel:

a. A person—"Christ . . . whom we preach." The gospel is a personal proclamation. While it is true, of course, that we can also speak of "what" we preach, yet this is only secondary. The theme of Christianity is not a theory, not an institution, not a book, not a set of rules, not simply a code of morals nor a system of philosophy, and not even merely a statement of truth or of principle. It is manifestly impossible for personalities such as we rightly claim for ourselves to love, to worship, or to pray to a principle; nor can we deny to God what we also claim for ourselves, namely, individuality. No, Christianity is a living person, with whom all these things are connected and from whom they proceed. It is the peculiar characteristic of the religion of Christ that we cannot take the message and set aside the speaker of the message. There have been great teachers in the history of the world, like Socrates, Plato, Confucius, Buddha, Mohammed, in whose writings, along with much human error, can be found many truths of beauty and value; but those truths can be appreciated and appropriated without reference to the person who uttered them. These sacred books of the East, including the Koran, may be read and followed without knowing or caring who wrote them. But it is altogether different with the teaching of Christ, for His person is inextricably bound up with what He taught. This is because all that He says centers around Himself; He is the substance of His own revelation and instruction. When He speaks of the Kingdom, He is the King; when He declares the terms of entrance therein, they are faith in and devotion to Him, each concerned with the disposition of the heart toward Him. His constant declaration was "*I* say unto you," and the cause He advocated, the salvation He wrought, the future He promised—all depended on Himself.

b. A provision—"which is Christ." This one great object of preaching is expressed in one word in verse 27, while in the next He is called "Christ Jesus" (v. 28); and these two names contain the entire significance of His person, embracing the facts of His life and work in order to show His transcendent value. We often ask with Shakespeare, "What's in a name?" thereby suggesting our own careless answer, but to the Jews names meant a great deal. While the name *Jesus* refers to our Lord's historic appearance as man, *Christ* is associated with His transcendence beyond anything merely human, for it is the translation of the Greek equivalent of the Hebrew word *Messiah,* and in it are comprised all of God's purposes and preparations for the redemption of mankind. The word means *the Anointed One,* and looks back on God's determination to set apart or consecrate His Son to be the Savior of the world. From Eden onward this divine purpose is seen to make progress, as the race is gradually taught, through type and prophecy, the need of a prophet to reveal God to man, a priest to redeem man from sin, and a king to rule and direct human life. In this threefold provision of prophet, priest, and king, all included in the word *Christ,* man has a solid foundation. It is the combination of the two elements, the divine and the human, that gives the person of Jesus Christ His significance and value. As man He is accessible, and as God He is able; and thus we find everything in Him for yesterday's guilt, today's needs, and tomorrow's possibilities.

c. A possession—"in you." Without these two little words the former truths would be virtually useless. There must be a link between the first century and the twentieth, some relationship that will make Christ real to us today. Certainly the historical manifestation of Jesus of Nazareth is not sufficient, and so the apostle speaks of "Christ in you." The objective person, the historic personage, must be inwardly appropriated so as to be made a subjective, experimental reality in our lives. It is not enough that He came to earth, lived, died, and rose; He must be personally abiding in the heart of each one of His followers (cf. John 14:17-23). Those who recognize intellectually the historical Jesus, or even accept the facts concerning Christ's divine person and work, find that these avail them not until they have been supplemented by the spiritual reception of the living, present Savior and Lord. Credence of mind must be followed by confidence of heart. Christ must be welcomed into the soul by repentance, enthroned in the heart by faith, enjoyed in the mind by surrender, and manifested in the life by obedience.

d. A prospect—"the hope of glory." These words complete the pregnant phrase and refer to the future, just as the foregoing ones relate to past and present. It is impossible to live without looking forward or to avoid inquiring about the future. "Hope springs eternal in the human breast." Whether the mind contemplates the uncertainty of the present life or the certainty of some sort of future existence, man is compelled by his nature to wonder if he may feel secure. The only possible answer for real assurance is found in the words of the apostle, "Christ in you, the hope of glory."

If there is one thing that makes the future uncertain for us in relation to peace of mind and happiness of heart, it is sin. When that is put away through the acceptance of Christ, all fear of the future life goes with it, for He is the Savior of all who believe; and only through Him is this possible. Then, with the actual consciousness that Christ is ours in personal possession, we can face the immediate future just as confidently and cheerfully. Like St. Paul, we know Him now in whom we believed in the past and are therefore persuaded of His power in the future to bless, guide, and protect (II Tim. 1:12). The abiding and indwelling presence of Christ is the pledge as well as the foretaste of future glory; and it is our experience of Him that quickens the assurance that such light for the mind in perplexity, such joy for the heart in sorrow, and such strength for the will in weakness—in a word, so wonderful a spiritual blessedness—will last forever. To have Him is to have pardon and peace, purity and power, heaven begun and life everlasting entered. As someone has said, all things that will make us blessed hereafter we have here, for what makes a Christian happy in life and in death is that the Christ he has now is the Christ he will have then.

He even has his home in heaven for the One he knows and loves best is there already; and whereas once we thought that home was heaven, now we know that heaven is home. Thus we see that Christ, past, present, and future, in the glory of His person and work, is all-sufficient—sufficient in all circumstances, in all places, and at all times.

This, then, is the blessed and glorious theme of the Christian ministry—Christ: the divine person; the anointed Savior; the revealer of God; the atonement for sin; the guide, satisfaction, and completion of life; the refuge of the past; the stay of the present; the hope of the future.

6. The Methods of the Ministry (v. 28b). We shall now see by what means this great message is to be brought into contact with men; and again there are four thoughts to ponder.

a. Admonition. The apostle speaks first of "warning," and this is especially necessary in the case of those who have not received Christ, for it means telling them of their sin and its certain results. Yet even afterwards this method must be prominent, because believers are also, alas, only too apt to have superficial views on this subject. To warn is like applying salt (Matt. 5:13), which prevents surrounding corruption, and it is concerned with the moral aspect of Christianity. The New Testament claims to apply the principles of Christ to all parts of human life and does not shrink from laying bare anything and everything that hinders the soul from coming to God or from maintaining relationship with Him. There is to be something more than the prophesying of smooth things, for the gospel is not "soothing syrup"—it deals with alternatives that must be faced. In these days we hear so much of the love of God in contrast to His righteous hatred of sin, as though the two attributes were irreconcilable in one divine nature, that it is well to remember that some of the most terrible words ever uttered were spoken by our Lord Himself. The Christian preacher and teacher, therefore, needs to sound this note of warning to the indifferent and careless, to the presumptuous and willful, to lay bare the sins that are holding them captive, to show them their grave danger, and to claim their lives for the ownership of Jesus Christ instead of the devil.

b. Instruction. Then will follow "teaching," which is like light (Matt. 5:14), another side of ministerial witness. This seems to have special reference to those who have just begun the Christian life, and it may perhaps be called the intellectual side of the gospel. But teaching is needed at every stage of the journey, for the Christian system is essentially educational and virtually inexhaustible. Those just setting out require the alphabet of the gospel. Those who have gone some distance need instruction proportionate to their capacity. Those who are "fathers" in the Church (I John 1:13) and veterans in the fray must have the strong meat of divine truth and the wisdom of the perfect, or mature. Yes, at every step of life's pathway, from the beginning to the end, we need the finger-post of divine teaching, indicating: "This is the way, walk ye in it" (Isa. 30:21). Sermons and addresses, lessons and lectures are intended not only to provide quiet resting places; rather they are to be fresh starting-points for the future. The true discourse is not something which makes the hearer so fatigued that he is unable to think. Rather should it be such a lifting up of Christ as the one true source of life that it will refresh the jaded spirit, inform the inquiring mind, comfort the anxious heart, and guide the submissive will, thus bracing the whole nature of the believer for the toil and warfare ahead.

c. Application. The words "every man" are found three times in this one verse, and such repetition shows clearly the apostle's idea of the scope of the Christian ministry. The false teachers against whom he was writing had much to say of a wisdom for a peculiar few only (cf. 2:8, 18), but St. Paul's soul spurned such restrictions and rejoiced in a gospel for all. However, he maintains here that Christianity also has a wisdom but it is intended for everybody, and the doors are flung open boldly with an urgent invitation to all who will to enter and to learn. Here is our source of power—the universality of the gospel as a message for all nations, all stations, all capacities. It is a message for rich and poor, old and young, respectable and outcast, peer and peasant. This is because, amid all the differences of sphere and capability, there is the same nature, the same sin, the same need; and therefore there must be the same salvation.

But these words "every man" suggest also the individual application of the gospel as well as its universal extent. It is not only a message for all but a message for each, one by one (John 6: "all . . . him" [v. 37] ; "all . . . it" [v. 39] ; "every one . . . him" [v. 40]). The Christian preacher thus is able to say, "I have a message from God unto *thee*" (Judges 3:20). There is need to emphasize this individual, even solitary, aspect, for our lives are our own. Notwithstanding our surroundings each one of us lives in a little world of his own; for, whatever else we do with others, we think alone, we breathe alone, we die alone, and we shall awake on the other side alone. And so God's truth comes to man alone, dealing with him as an individual, as well as one of a number, "warning every man, and teaching every man."

d. Assimilation. The addition of the phrase "in all wisdom" further emphasizes the difference between the false teachers and St. Paul. He claimed to teach every single man all the wisdom that particular man could grasp, dealing with him according to his particular nature and as far as his particular capacity allowed. Inasmuch as each individual has his own peculiar characteristics, it was the apostle's aim to deal with him wisely, giving him spiritual "food convenient" (Prov. 30:8)—whatever he could accept and assimilate. In this statement Paul displays a marvelous penetration and grasp; he claims all real knowledge as from and for Christ and therefore to be possessed, at least in part, by everyone who belongs to Christ.

These, then, are the Pauline methods whereby Christ was made known to men: warning and teaching, used universally and wisely. "Who is sufficient for these things?" we may ask with him as on another occasion; and the answer he gave was swift and definite: "our sufficiency is from God" (cf. II Cor. 2:14 to 3:5, *A. S. V.*).

7. The Motive of the Ministry (v. 28c). It remains to consider another feature of the Christian ministry stated here very definitely. What is it all for? Why this message and these methods? Why does the apostle do all this work? He has a specific object in his preaching, his warning, and his teaching.

a. Perfection. This purpose is first suggested by the word "perfect," which means here, as often elsewhere, maturity, ripeness, both of character and of experience. Perfection never means sinlessness but almost always the condition of the mature in contrast with the immature believer. From the moment of our conversion we are to make progress, until we all arrive at the full ripeness of our position in Christ (Eph. 4:13).

This, indeed, is the one and only object of the gospel, full salvation and nothing short of it. Nothing short of it will satisfy our heavenly Father, for this is His purpose concerning us. Nothing short of it will satisfy our Savior, for this was the supreme object of His life and work. Nothing short of it will satisfy the Holy Spirit, for holiness means "whole-ness." Therefore, nothing short of sanctification must satisfy us, as it is the crowning object of Christianity itself—not to make men happy, *except* as a consequence of holiness; not to deliver from sin, *except* as a means to holiness. If both pulpit and pew were always maintained in the light of God's holiness, how many dreary platitudes would be left unsaid and how many respectable, easy-going lives shaken to their very foundations! "Perfect"! Yes, this will be an accomplished fact of the future, in our modern sense of the word also. Therefore it should be the object of our present concern. There will be the entire removal hereafter of all defects through sin and the complete possession of all that God has designed for us. It will not be a one-sided growth, but a symmetry of character—the heart purified, the will controlled, the mind instructed, the imagination healthy, the conscience sensitive, the body sound.

This maturity is intended for all and is therefore possible for all; so once again the apostle emphasizes the universality of his message by using the term "every man." No sin must be excused, no weakness palliated, even with differences in capacity, for each such potential must be and can be, up to its limits, ripe and mature, full and perfect. Since capacity grows by use, we need to exercise the grace of God now in order hereafter to realize our fullest possible measure of perfection.

The motive of the ministry is further explained by the term "in Christ Jesus," showing that all this development is to be realized not in ourselves, but in Him. Further, as "in Christ" is the source of our life here, so "in Christ" will be the source of our maturity hereafter. His righteousness is imputed now and will be imparted then. It is especially notable that, according to these verses, we commence here below with "Christ in" us, and we end yonder above with ourselves "in Christ."[1]

b. Presentation. "That we may present every man" is the phrase that shows the completed purpose. Here is the beautiful picture of the minister presenting his converts to Christ, introducing them as such to Him. As we have seen (v. 22), the thought finds a threefold illustration in the New Testament (see Rom. 12:1; II Cor. 11:2 and Eph. 5:27; II Cor. 4:14). Just as at a royal levee or drawing-room some are presented to the sovereign by others, so here we have the picture of "ambassadors for Christ" (II Cor. 5:20) presenting their disciples to the King of kings, and, moreover, presenting them "perfect in Christ Jesus," free from all that is unholy and unworthy. This is surely the ultimate goal of the Christian worker, and for this he lives and labors. Happy the man thus privileged, for it must be the highest possible joy to stand before the throne of God at last and say: "Behold, I and the children whom Thou hast given me!" (Heb. 2:13, *A.S.V.*).

8. The Might of the Ministry (v. 29). St. Paul not only preached but worked, and everything he said and did was in relation to the great end just stated—"whereunto I labor also" (*A.S.V.*). His position as an apostle of Christ involved far more than a mere proclamation of the gospel; it included effort and fatigue. Like an athlete in a contest, of whom both Greek words here are used, as Lightfoot points out (Lightfoot, *Colossians,* p. 169), the apostle strove with all his might. Yet there was also the inspiring realization that, whilst he worked, Christ was working too, and that in proportion as Paul labored Christ strove mightily in him to accomplish this great purpose. It is one of the most encouraging assurances of Christian service that our work may and can be done in exact proportion to God's work in us. "It is God who worketh in you both to will and to work" (Phil. 2:13, *A.S.V.*). In all our service, therefore, let us keep before us the knowledge that we are "striving according to his working,"

---

[1] See also the phrases: "walk in him" (2:6); "rooted and built up in him" (2:7); "complete in him" (2:10).

which is ready to operate in us "mightily," that is, with divine power (cf. Eph. 3:20).

As we look back over this marvelous passage telling of the Christian ministry, we cannot help but notice, with wonder and thankfulness, (1) the magnificence of the theme; (2) the simplicity of the purpose; (3) the thoroughness of the method; and (4) the reality of the life. These constitute the sole, supreme, and satisfying warrant of gospel preaching, and whenever they are found they invariably authenticate themselves to the needy soul and the inquiring mind. Along with these there are practical features implied all through the passage that are as applicable to us today as to the apostle himself. These may be summed up in five words, each of which carries its own meaning and message to those who belong to the Lord.

1. Sonship. This is not only the basis of the gospel message but also the presupposition of all true labor for God.

2. Service. As sons we are called upon to witness, to war, and to work in connection with this gospel.

3. Stewardship. This implies no ordinary service but responsible work. As our experience of Christ deepens and broadens He entrusts to us still more important tasks, for His true ministers are honored by being called "stewards of the mysteries of God" (I Cor. 4:1).

4. Suffering. Our task of witnessing to Christ will often involve opposition, and even hostility, and in all ages God's servants have even had to "suffer hardship" (II Tim. 2:3, *A.S.V.*). This can be a glory to us if only we regard our suffering as the apostle thought of his, as helping forward the cause of Christ and as glorifying God.

5. Satisfaction. In all life and work for the Lord, there wells up in the consecrated heart a spring of joy that He should have deigned, first, to receive us and, then, to use us in His vineyard. There is nothing on earth to compare with the perennial joy that comes through our committal to Christ by faith, resulting in our communion with Him and His control of us in faithfulness of life and effort for the sake of our God and Savior.

Thank God for St. Paul and his view of what the Christian ministry should be! May the Lord enable us who serve Him today to be equally faithful "ministers of his, that do his pleasure" (Ps. 103:21).

6 THE POWER OF CHRIST

The chapter division at this point is in one sense misleading, because it tends to prevent our observing that the subject matter is continuous, dealing still with St. Paul's own ministry; and yet the opening word "For" clearly indicates the close connection of 1:29 and 2:1, 2. The apostle has already referred to his preaching, and to his effort on behalf of the Christians in Colosse; now he will show that he has anxiety for them as well. The whole chapter, indeed, is a remarkable unveiling of a minister's heart, a revelation of the right attitude toward his converts. And yet the very anxiety expressed in the opening verses leads logically to a wider theme, the one that contains the heart of the Epistle and is applicable to all ages; for those things that were a concern then, though not existing now in the same form, point us to essentially the same errors and therefore to the same general principles counteracting them.

CONFLICT (vv. 1-3)[1]

The apostle Paul has not been content to preach only; he now has a ministry of prayerful concern for his readers, even from his Roman prison;

---

[1]Much of this section is taken from the author's small volume entitled *The Prayers of St. Paul* (Edinburgh: T. & T. Clark, and New York: Chas. Scribner's Sons, 1914), long out of print.

and he wishes them to know of this effort on their behalf. He is particularly desirous here, as in many other passages, that believers should lead the finest, strongest, and best lives. There is no doubt that such a life, when fully lived by God's people, is one of the most powerful testimonies to the reality of the gospel. For this reason, the apostle says, he prays for them, as he so often does elsewhere.

1. Paul's Prayer-Life (v. 1).

a. Paul's prayer-life is described as a conflict. If ever the Latin saying, *orare est laborare,* "to pray is to work," were true, it was true of St. Paul, for to him to pray was to labor with all his might. He uses here, as elsewhere, the figure of an athlete (cf. I Tim. 6:12; II Tim. 4:7), and the phrase "great conflict" (v. 1; cf. 1:29:4:12) shows his intense earnestness. Indeed, prayer regarded as a conflict includes the two ideas of toil and strife. The toil of prayer shows us the actual work involved in it. Sometimes, however, we hear the statement, "If you can do nothing else you can pray," as though prayer were the easiest of all types of Christian service. As a simple matter of fact, it is the hardest; and, further, no man knows the real meaning of it unless he experiences what it is to "labor" in prayer. The strife involved in prayer implies opposition—a struggle against unseen foes, the forces of one who wishes above all things to check and thwart our petitions, since "restraining prayer, we cease to fight." We discern something of this opposition in the verb "wrestle" (Eph. 6:12); and the words of the hymn are as true as they are familiar—

> And Satan trembles when he sees
> The weakest saint upon his knees.
>
> William Cowper

The apostle knew by actual spiritual experience that to pray was to arouse against himself a mighty opposition, and it was this malignant force that made his prayer-life such a "great conflict."

No believer should be surprised at his prayers being "hindered" (I Peter 3:7), for it is quite evidently one of Satan's main objects to get him to restrain the spirit of prayer. The Christian man or the Christian church continuing constant in prayer may rest assured of animosity on the part of the hosts of spiritual wickedness in high places. Conversely, we may be certain that Satan scarcely troubles himself about the believer or congregation whose private, family, or public praying is neglected or thought little of. Prayer is not solicitude only, but a struggle; it is not merely anxiety, but activity as well.

The practical question for us, therefore, is whether this is our conception of prayer also, or whether, instead, we are merely playing at prayer and not regarding it with true seriousness. Bishop Moule tells how a caller, kept waiting at the door of one of the Puritans, was told by a servant: "My master is at prayer this morning and has been long in getting access." All such experiences, comments the Bishop, have "a message for all believers. They remind us that prayer, if true, is a transaction worth taking laborious pains about, if we find this needful to 'get access' " (Moule, *Colossian Studies,* p. 124). Yes, if we really know what it is to have "great conflict" in prayer, happy are we. If we do not know, we may well ask God to search our hearts and change our minds about this vital matter.

b. Paul's prayer-life was characterized by unselfishness. It was not at all self-centered, but, on the contrary, it was on behalf of others: "what great conflict I have for you, and for them at Laodicea" (v. 1, *A.S.V.*). Intercession is the very essence of prayer. If our seasons of prayer are taken up largely with requests for our own needs, however urgent and genuine, we are failing at a crucial point; but if our prayer time is spent mostly in offering petitions for others we shall soon find that our own blessings begin to abound. "There is that scattereth, and yet increaseth" (Prov. 11:24).

c. Paul's prayer-life also implied sympathy. In this case, moreover, such intercession is the more outstanding because the Colossian Christians were not personally known to the apostle—"as many as have not seen my face in the flesh" (v. 1). He was actually praying thus urgently for people whom he had never met and probably never would meet. This is not easy—indeed, it is very difficult; but it is a real test of spirituality. "Out of sight, out of mind," it is sometimes said; and we are tempted to limit our prayers to friends whom we value, causes in which we are interested, subjects near and dear to us. Not so the apostle, whose great heart went out to the whole Church of God in every place where he had been told that small groups of Christians were to be found. When sympathy and even anxiety are felt for those who are personally unknown, the reality of such feelings as well as the consciousness of the perils facing them may be the more readily appreciated. Paul's sympathy was at once quick, wide, and deep, and it is one of the supreme tests of true spirituality to have such a sympathy. Ours may be quick and yet narrow, or wide but not deep, or even deep and not wide; but to be at once quick, wide, and deep in sympathy is to be following in the footsteps not only of the apostle Paul, but of Christ Himself.

As we ponder these things—conflict, unselfishness, sympathy—do not our hearts condemn us? Instead of engaging in conflict while praying, how easygoing have been our prayers! Instead of being unselfish, how self-centered—instead of being sympathetic, how contracted, and perhaps even critical! Thus does the great apostle search and test us as we dwell on his wonderful life of prayer.

2. Paul's Petitions (v. 2a). What were the specific objects for which the apostle prayed so earnestly on behalf of these unknown Christians? What were the precise gifts that he sought for them from God? This conflict in prayer had definite purpose and these same gifts have perennial appropriateness for all His people.

a. The apostle asked for spiritual strength—"that their hearts might be comforted." Since St. Paul always went to the very center and core of things, it is not surprising to find him mentioning the "hearts" of these Colossian Christians. The heart in Scripture denotes the center of the moral and spiritual being, including intellect, feeling, and will. Thus, if the heart is right all else will be right, for "out of it are the issues of life" (Prov. 4:23). St. Paul prays that these hearts "might be comforted," and the word has a threefold meaning—to be encouraged, to be exhorted, and to be strengthened. Comfort thus includes the three elements of endurance, courage, and consolation, and the apostle wishes these Christians to be strong, fearless, and full of good cheer as they face the errors and difficulties that surround them. This, of course, is the full significance of the term "Comforter" as applied to the Holy Spirit, for He is the One who gives strength, courage, and consolation. This, too, is the true meaning of that familiar phrase in *The Book of Common Prayer.* "Hear what comfortable words our Saviour Christ saith"—words that minister strength, fortitude, and cheer—"unto all who truly turn to Him." The fact that this thought of hearts comforted was often in the mind and on the lips of the apostle shows the importance he attached to it (Eph. 6:22; II Thess. 2:17). With such hearts Christians can face anything, but with hearts that remain weak, fearful, and sad the Christian life is a prey to all the temptations of the Evil One. It is exactly similar with a church or any assemblage of Christians, for one of the greatest needs in such a community is for the centers of lives to be made strong, courageous, and full of joy. Then it is that such groups live, grow, and witness for Christ in the "demonstration of the Spirit (the Comforter) and of power . . . the power of God" (I Cor. 2:4, 5).

b. The apostle asked for spiritual unity—"being knit together in love," or, quite literally, being compacted, harmoniously fitted together (cf. Eph. 4:16). He prayed that these Christians might be joined together, knit together, and kept together. Solitary Christians are apt to be weak Christians, for in this sphere as in all others "union is strength." If Christian people are not truly knit together, the cause of Christ may suffer, for through the severances caused by division the enemy can keep thrusting his darts which must be parried alone. That is why the apostle elsewhere urges believers earnestly to strive "to keep the unity of the Spirit in the bond of peace" (Eph. 4:3). One of the greatest powers that Satan wields today is due to disunion among the genuine people of God. It is true alike of the Christian home, congregation, and denomination that this wedge of discord can become one of the enemy's most powerful weapons. On the other hand, where the brethren are able to "dwell together in unity," there the Lord commands His blessing (Ps. 133:3).

This unity, however, is only possible "in love." It is the love of God to us that unites us to Him, and it will be the love of God in us that unites us to our brethren. Indeed, there is no power like love to bind Christians together. We may not see eye to eye on all aspects of the truth we hold; we may not all use the same methods of worship and service; but if we love one another God dwells in us and among us, and He can add His own seal of blessing to the work done for Him. Let every evangelical Christian be fully assured that, in so far as he is striving, praying, and laboring for the union of God's people in love, he will be doing one of the most influential and blessed pieces of work for his Master and, at the same time, one of the greatest possible pieces of disservice to the kingdom of Satan. Contrariwise, the Christian man or Christian church practicing separateness and exclusiveness because of non-essential differences of opinion or policy is one of the best allies of Satan and one of his most effective workers.

c. The apostle asked for spiritual certitude—"unto all riches of the full assurance of understanding." There was to be no vagueness or uncertainty in their lives or in their doctrine, but the very opposite, a rich certitude that would enable them to meet every peril, every problem, with courageous confidence. Wealth is a favorite metaphor of St. Paul's, used to denote the fulness and abundance of the Christian life as conceived by him. Mark how he piles phrase upon phrase, speaking not merely of understanding but of fulness of understanding and, finally, of the wealth that is fulness of understanding. To the writer of these words, the mind was one of the essential powers of man in connection with the Christian life. So far from thinking, according to a modern fashion, that the less one uses the mind the better Christian one is, St. Paul, following his Master, ever emphasized the duty and glory of loving God "with all thy mind" (Matt. 22:37; cf. Rom. 7:25, etc.). This wealth of the full assurance of understanding means an abundance of conviction, both intellectual and moral, that Christianity is what it claims to be, and that the Christian life is the perfect satisfaction of all the varied needs of man's nature. As Bishop Moule paraphrases it, the apostle prays that the Colossians may "rise to the whole wealth of the full exercise of their intelligence" (Moule, *Colossian Studies,* p. 126).

Such a firm conviction on the part of an understanding mind, as it has also been expressed, or "full assurance," is one of the purposes of God in connection with Christianity. Thus, when writing to the Thessalonians, St.

Paul spoke of His gospel as having come to them "in much assurance" (I Thess. 1:5). Furthermore, it is interesting to note that the same word occurs in three distinct connections: the "full assurance of faith" (Heb. 10:22), referring especially to the past; the "full assurance of hope" (Heb. 6:11), referring solely to the future; and, in this passage, the "full assurance of understanding," with its definite bearing on the present. In the same spirit St. Luke writes to Theophilus: "That thou mightest know the certainty of those things, wherein thou hast been instructed" (Luke 1:4). The New Testament is thus shown to lay particular emphasis on the necessity for believers to enter fully into the certitude that comes with true Christianity; and yet today the lack of this clearness of thinking and of testimony is one of the most serious failings of the professing Church.

Not only is a firm conviction of the understanding one of the greatest needs, it is also one of the greatest blessings of the Christian life. If a believer cannot say with the apostle, "I know . . . and am persuaded" (II Tim. 1:12), he is lacking in one of the prime essentials of a vigorous experience. But how does it come, this whole wealth of the full exercise of intelligence? It is surely the result of the foregoing "comfort" and "love," for hearts made strong mean minds fully assured, and hearts full of love mean intellects full of knowledge of the loved One and conviction concerning Him. Let no one say that "love is blind"; on the contrary, it is true love that not only sees, but knows. It was the apostle of love who was the first with spiritual insight on that memorable early morning on the lake of Galilee, exclaiming: "It is the Lord" (John 21:7). Similarly today, it is the Christian with a heart strong in courage and full of love who will have this wealth of the fulness of intelligence; and the same is true of a church, for when it is strong and united in love there will come such an influx of conviction and certitude that the world will be impressed by its demonstration of the absolute truth of the Christian gospel.

3. Paul's Purpose (vv. 2b, 3). "To the full knowledge of the mystery of God, even Christ, in whom are all the stored-up treasures of wisdom and knowledge" (Gr.). Here, again, we have a favorite word of the Epistles, "full knowledge," that is, ripe, mature experience; and it means the experience of all that is summed up in the one name *Christ*. In view of the dangerous errors then rife and increasing, implying a special knowledge of spiritual things confined only to a few, to an intellectual aristocracy which later developed into a sect called the Gnostics, literally "those good at knowing," the apostle is here laying stress upon the blessed possibility of every Christian becoming acquainted in personal experience with all the knowledge of God that is stored up in His Son. As in a former passage (1:27), the word "mystery" means a secret once hidden but now revealed; and it is clear that Christ Himself was the specific mystery the Colossians were to know. The use of the present tense "are" indicates that these things were continuing realities and that in possessing Christ the believers possessed all things, and that there was no necessity to go outside Him for the guidance and certitude that they needed.

This is another great Christological passage, following closely upon the one in the previous chapter, and showing both what St. Paul thought of Christ and also how Christians were to be protected through this concept of divine wisdom from the false wisdom around them. The apostle has declared Christ as the image of God (1:15), as the head of the Church (1:18), as the One in whom all fulness dwells (1:19), as the Redeemer from sin (1:20), as the hope of glory (1:27); and now he speaks of Him as the One in whom may be found the only divine revelation. There is no mistiness here, no vagueness, no hesitation, no limitation, but a full, free, open opportunity for all believers to become acquainted with Christ in His divine perfection.

Today, as in every age, there are those who teach that salvation is by human knowledge, that further information and so-called "deeper truth" are our greatest needs. This is essentially the error of Christian Science and all the other false cults of our day. But salvation cannot come from either ideas or ideals, or else the disciples would have been wonderfully "saved" after those unique three years with Jesus. The great need of man, rather, is redemption, and he must be saved through the acceptance of Christ as Redeemer before he can be taught spiritual lessons. Our safeguard against the dangers that abound today is the same as in Paul's time—a personal, divine Savior, received by faith. Then, and then only, will come a strong intellectual foundation, a constant spiritual progress, and the fine upbuilding of an edifice of moral character that will abide to eternity and abound to the glory of God.

This is the crowning-point of the apostle's prayer, for in the full knowledge of Christ everything else is included. In Him are, indeed, "all the stored-up treasures of wisdom and knowledge"; and "the Lord shall open . . . his good treasure" (Deut. 28:12) to the "good man" who "out of the good treasure of the heart bringeth forth good things" (Matt. 12:35; cf. Isa. 33:6). This wisdom and this knowledge, at once intellectual, moral, and spiritual, form the safeguard from all error, the secret of all progress, and the guarantee of all blessing.

As Bishop Moule so eloquently declared in a sermon preached at Durham Cathedral in 1906, each of us "is a spiritual being, made in the image of the eternal Wisdom and Love, redeemed from his fall by the action of the Eternal, borne onward by His grace (as regards the purpose of the divine mercy) to an eternal destiny of bliss, and holiness and loving power; and that every range of existence, every law of thought, bears profound relation to Him, the Son, the Word, the Christ, 'in whom are hid all the treasures of knowledge,' and who is not only the Head of the Church, nor only the Lover of the soul, but also the Keystone of the universe of creation; 'in Him all things consist.' "

Let this prayer, then, be the subject of our constant and careful study. We shall find in it much to rebuke the shallowness, the selfishness, the dullness, and the sluggishness of our own prayers; and we shall also find in it a model of instruction and the inspiration of all true petition and intercession. Indeed, the believer who profits from this outpouring of the apostle's soul, as from each of his other prayers, will apprehend some of the deepest secrets of a devoted Christian life which, when fully lived, is one of the best possible testimonies to the reality of the gospel.

CAUTIONS (vv. 4-23)

At this point the apostle Paul tells the Colossian Christians that he is speaking thus in order that they may not be led astray. He does not assume for one moment that they had already wandered, but only warns them against the possibility. In every connection it can be repeated without hesitation or apology that the only safeguard against error for the Christian is a full knowledge of Christ (cf. v. 3).

1. A Warning Against Persuasive Error (vv. 4-7).

· *a. The peril (v. 4).* This particular danger was that of false reasoning based on specious arguments that might easily lead astray the unwary and unstable. It was on account of this peril that Paul had spoken so strongly about himself (v. 1), about the Colossians themselves (v. 2), and about Christ (v. 3). People are easily influenced by attractive forms of speech, and sometimes a charm of manner and an eloquent utterance will hide the falsity of a speaker's reasoning. Thus the apostle, notwithstanding his satisfaction with the genuineness of these Christians, could not avoid giving them a word of warning. His whole soul pulsed with reality, so that he shrank from anything that might "delude . . . with persuasiveness of speech" (*A.S.V.*). The day of such a peril, of course, is by no means over. There are many today who are easily captured by cults of various kinds, so persuasive as to endanger the spiritual life by their erroneous doctrine and "specious discourse" (Gr.); and thus the need of caution is as great as ever.

b. The praise (v. 5). Although the apostle spoke in this way he was not unmindful of the reality and strength of the Colossian Christians. He was absent in the flesh, but present with them in the spirit, looking upon them with joy and feeling satisfied that all was well with them, even though they were surrounded by danger. This is a fine feature of the true

Christian worker who sees the good points in those whom he wishes to help, for by recognizing their strength rather than their weakness, he encourages them to greater efforts in the right direction. The specific point of Paul's appreciation of the Colossians is what he calls their "order" and the "stedfastness" (*A.S.V.*) of their faith toward Christ. By most writers this phrase in the original is thought to be a military term, meaning an "orderly array" and an "unyielding battle-line." The apostle was certain that if only there came to be a personal and ever-increasing experience of Christ there would be an all-sufficient safeguard against every foe—in fact, the one and only protection against all forms of danger. It is exactly the same today. Whatever errors may be prevalent in our modern era, however numerous and specious may be the perils of life, the panoply of God is union and communion with Christ, in all the fulness of His divine person, His redeeming work, His risen life, and His constant fellowship through the Holy Spirit dwelling in the heart. Given this close relationship, all will be well, since "God was manifest in the flesh" (I Tim. 3:16), the person and work of the Lord Jesus Christ, and He possesses in Himself everything that the soul of man could need for time and for eternity.

c. The protection (vv. 6, 7). After the preceding verses, with their strong emphasis on faith in Christ, it might seem that anything further on this subject were unnecessary; but the apostle evidently feels that this great theme must be mentioned again, so intense is his concern to see these Christians kept steadfast in the true faith. He therefore speaks of the necessity of continuing as they had begun. They had "received Christ Jesus the Lord" (v. 6) by faith (cf. John 1:12), and they were to continue to "walk" in Him.

Thus there is here a simple illustration of the relation between the acceptance of Christ in conversion and the appropriation of Him in sanctification (cf. I Cor. 1:30). The latter may indeed commence at the time of the former, or it may follow after. If after, the spiritual experience of the believer is first instantaneous, then progressive; it is first an act, then an attitude; it is first a crisis, then a process; it is first an obtaining, then a maintaining. There is not growth *into* grace, but growth *in* grace already given, not a "second blessing," but a subsequent work of grace, although it need not be separated by so much as an hour of time from the initial surrender of the will to Christ Jesus as Lord.

Each part of this grand title is noteworthy. First, our Savior is "Christ," the Anointed One, the Messiah, the divinely-commissioned person. Second, He is "Jesus," the human, the historical personage. Third, He is "the Lord," the personification of supreme control over heaven and earth. These people in Colosse had accepted Him in this threefold capacity: He was already their divine Messiah, their Savior Jesus, and their Almighty

Lord. This was the sum and substance of their Christian life, and they were to continue as they had started, expressing this life by consistent conduct in union with Him. The thought of "walking" in connection with the profession of Christianity is a familiar one in the Epistles, the idea expressed being that of a complete and continuous manifestation in both character and conduct of all that is involved in the initial acceptance of our Lord Jesus Christ.

It is told of a traveler, staying with the good Johann Bengel of Germany, that one night, while occupying the next room to that of the saintly scholar, he listened closely in the hope of hearing the last devotional murmurings of the day on the lips of this beloved servant of Christ, for surely Bengel would utter some rapturous prayer. Soon the good man, wearied from his toil, gathered up his books and, kneeling, he prayed, "Lord Jesus, I thank Thee that things are still the same between us." Then he arose, retired, and fell asleep. As he had received Christ Jesus the Lord so he was walking in Him. It was the same fellowship still, moment by moment, hour by hour.

Now follow, in verse 7, three significant participles, all referring to the further progress of the Christian life. The first of these is "having been rooted" (Gr.), implying that the Colossians were like trees that had been permanently planted in the right soil (cf. "no root in themselves," Mark 4:17). To be stately and strong there must have been a firm, strong, living root. Then the metaphor changes, and the tense as well, and the apostle speaks of their being "continually built up" (Gr.). The thought is that of Christ as the foundation of a structure on which the Colossian Christians were presently being built. Then comes the third thought of being "continually made stedfast," for this is another present tense, implying continuous experience. Lightfoot thinks that "faith" here is like the cement of the construction that helps to strengthen and solidify it (Lightfoot, *Colossians*, p. 175). Then the apostle bears witness to the value of the instruction that these Colossians had received from Epaphras, for all this was to be done "even as ye were taught" (*A.S.V.*). It is not enough for evangelists to win men for Christ; they must instruct their converts in those principles of Christian doctrine and living which alone can safeguard the soul and prevent it from backsliding.

With another change of metaphor the apostle speaks of these Christians "abounding in thanksgiving" (*A.S.V.*); and the thought of thankfulness in this connection is singularly suggestive and impressive. Bengel, in one of his characteristic comments, says that "thanksgiving makes lawful and makes glad, and shows the use of things which others load with prohibitions." Similarly, Bishop Moule says that "there is a great and profoundly reasonable power in holy thanksgiving to bring home to the soul the reality of the treasure for which the thanks are given" (Moule, *Colossian Studies*, p. 130). Again he remarks: "No heart is more vulnerable to doubt and to spiritual delusion than the unthankful heart which will not walk in the sunshine of the Lord" (Moule, *Colossian Studies*, p. 131). No fewer than six times in this brief Epistle is this thought of thanksgiving to be found (see also 1:3, 12; 3:15, 17; 4:2).

2. **A Warning Against Vain Knowledge (vv. 8-15).** Everything in the preceding part of the Epistle has been leading up to this, the apostle's first definite reference to the existence of error, against which it was necessary to provide further and fuller safeguards. The caution already given (v. 4) is developed into a warning about a special peril, and the apostle appeals to his readers not to allow themselves to be deceived (v. 8). Much that appeared wise and welcome was really human and worldly, having no relation to Christ. The exact expression of the original shows the danger to be not imaginary or future, but present and pressing; to be deceived would involve their being ensnared and secured as a prey. The word rendered "maketh spoil" (*A.S.V.*) is found only here and is paraphrased by Lightfoot as "carries you off body and soul" (Lightfoot, *Colossians*, p. 176). These converts had been rescued from the power of darkness (1:13), and now they were to watch lest they be taken back into a worse condition. The danger was that of a pretended knowledge, a "philosophy which is a specious make-believe," or, as it may well be rendered, a "vain, deceitful philosophy," the emptiness of purely abstract thought. This word "philosophy" also is found only here, and the accent of scorn associated with it is particularly noteworthy. Christianity is not primarily a philosophy, literally, the love of wisdom, even though Christ is "the wisdom of God" (I Cor. 1:24; cf. entire passage, I Cor. 1:17 - 2:16). He is wisdom because He is life, and the various problems associated with philosophy, such as those of human existence, nature, man's relation to God, all are to be considered in the light of Christ as the life of the soul, "the power of God" as well (I Cor. 1:24).

There is a great deal in current thought that is attractive, even fascinating, but when properly examined it is seen to be "not after Christ" (v. 8). This is the test of movements, of institutions, of books: are they "after Christ"? It is a great mistake to think that every form of philosophy is capable of being harmonized with Christianity. The two rocks on which most philosophies split with it are those of sin and redemption, and yet no system of thought can be regarded as worthy of the name of "wisdom" which does not reckon with human depravity and find a place for divine redemption from it. As Bishop Moule points out, the trouble at Colosse, and in modern communities as well, is that philosophy so frequently contradicts Christ and is not "according to Him." Men often want "a

Christ according to the system of thought, not a system of thought according to the blessed Christ" (Moule, *Colossian Studies,* p. 142). Yet this does not mean any disparagement of the human intellect, for the word of Christ is as clear as ever, "Thou shalt love the Lord thy God with all thy . . . mind" (Matt. 22:37); and the marvelous effects on the thinking powers when a man receives Christ are well known. "Let a man of elevated and penetrating understanding get a true view of the Christ of God, as the Word shows Him, and the Spirit glorifies Him, and he will have a subject-matter for his whole mental power such as he never had before" (Moule, *Colossian Studies,* p. 143).

The hollow pretense of knowledge is further described as according to "the tradition of men" and "the rudiments of the world" (v. 8). It was evidently a matter of empty sham, of idle fancy or silly trifling, or even of abstract thought only. In another passage (Gal. 4:3, 9, *A.S.V.,*), the word rendered "rudiments" (or "elements," marg.) is applied to Jewish ceremonialism, while here the same idea seems to refer to similar practices in paganism. This is still rampant today, disguised under such a designation as "the spirit of the age" and characterized by love of show, of pleasure, of fashion, and of purely physical beauty.

It is natural to make modern applications in regard to the bearing of this warning upon ceremonialism in worship for, as Maclaren points out, "enlisting the senses as the allies of the spirit in worship is risky work" (Maclaren, *Colossians,* p. 192). This is especially because, while they are generally thought to be helpful to the soul in approaching God, actually they are just as likely to prove harmful, and even disastrous. "The gratification of taste and the excitation of aesthetic sensibility, which are the results of such aids to worship, are not worship, however they may be mistaken as such. All ceremonial is in danger of becoming opaque, instead of transparent as it was meant to be" (Maclaren, *Colossians,* p. 193).

It is not surprising, therefore, that a great preacher should dare to say that "of the two extremes, a Quaker meeting is nearer the ideal of Christian worship than High Mass," and that "a Christianity making much of forms and ceremonies is a definite retrogression and descent." It has even been urged, and with good reason, that we must be particularly careful lest we mistake the worship of music for music in worship. Worship is something that goes far deeper than the senses, although quite often, when our senses are stirred, we think our worship is the more acceptable. But no worship is deserving of the name that does not penetrate to the spirit and does not express itself in sincerity of word and genuineness of conduct (cf. John 4:23, 24).

Once again the true safeguard against this specious danger is shown in a due regard for the divine person of Christ (v. 9). "In him," writes the apostle, "dwells permanently the entire fulness of deity in a bodily form." God is no longer afar off, no longer only an idea, but a living, blessed fact through Jesus Christ our Lord, in whom we obtain that contact with the Father which our lives so greatly need. The word "Godhead" is found only here and is indicative of absolute deity, or God's essential nature and being, as distinct from divinity, or the qualities of His person. The use of such a word is a clear indication of what the apostle thought of Christ. Paul believed that He possesses the fulness of God and that in Him believers are permanently filled full (v. 10a). Thus in the incarnation of Christ (cf. John 1:14) is found the complete revelation and possession of God, and there is no need for them to seek for anything else, because in Him they reach their full potential (cf. John 1:16).

Let us dwell on this blessedly permanent fulness in Christ, its influence on our lives, and what it does for their whole circumference—past, present, and future. First, there is the fulness of redemption, or Christ for yesterday; and this includes His glorious person and His wonderful work. Then, there is the fulness of life, or Christ for today; and this provides both character and conduct with strength for service and for suffering, and with devotion for duty and for discipline. Finally, there is the fulness of hope, or Christ for tomorrow; and this includes assurance in the hour of death or of His coming, and confidence for the ages of eternity. Thus, whether we consider the past, the present, or the future, Christ is all; and in Him, and in no one else, is this fulness, this completeness. Like Paul, we should pray to be "filled with all the fulness of God" (Eph. 3:19); but there are too many Christians who avail themselvs of only one phase of God's fulness. Some draw from His forgiveness only and would exhaust it were it not infinite; some draw from His condescension only and find that limitless, and some from His joy only and yet cannot hold it all. But others go to Him for everything, and are filled from the treasures of life and love, wisdom and power, until the whole circumference of their existence vibrates with a new and resistless energy. Shall we not from Christ's fulness receive a deeper holiness, a nobler character, a truer righteousness, a wider charity?

But Christ is also the supreme authority, "the head," or center of vital force, the source of life and sovereignty, over "all principality and power" (v. 10b; cf. vv. 15, 18); and we are spiritually united to Him. Every *fact* in His life is intended to be a *factor* in ours, e.g., Was He circumcised? So are we. Was He dead and buried? So are we. Was He raised? So are we. Thus Paul turns from theological errors to the practical details of what is meant by being "in Christ," and he uses several figures of speech to indicate the true spiritual position of every believer.

a. Circumcision (v. 11). The Jewish ordinance in connection with the flesh meant separation from evil and dedication to God. The apostle implies here, however, that it was entirely unnecessary for Christians to submit to the external rite, which after all was only a symbol of what the followers of Christ had experienced internally, and that not by human hands, but by the Spirit of God. Lightfoot and others point out three contrasts between the physical and spiritual aspects of circumcision: (1) The character of the latter is inward and spiritual, not external and fleshly. (2) It divests of the whole "body of the sins of the flesh," i.e., the fleshly body as the instrument of sinful tendencies and carnal affections; and thus it is not limited in extent to one part alone. (3) Its author is divine, not human—Christ, not Moses or the Patriarchs. Thus it differs in character, extent, and origin; and the Greek word for "putting off" is a very rare and inclusive term implying energy of action and complete range of operation (Lightfoot, *Colossians,* pp. 181f.).

That the spiritual meaning of circumcision was purification of the person and consecration of him to God seems quite clear, for we read of the need for circumcision of the ear (Jer. 6:10), of the lips (Exod. 6:12), and of the heart (Lev. 26:41; Jer. 9:26). Thus it was at once a figure of putting off the old nature and of regarding the new life as entirely devoted to God. This is an essential principle of Christianity and believers, of course, experience the spiritual reality of it so that they may truly say, "I believe . . . I belong."

b. Burial (v. 12a). As in Romans 6:4,[2] the apostle teaches here that when Christ's body was placed in Joseph's tomb we who believe on Him are regarded as having been "buried (Gr., entombed) with Him." Thus, as in the preceding reference to circumcision, the idea of burial or entombment is used spiritually, and not literally, as some insist who would use it to teach a particular mode of baptism. Whatever our precise position on this rite, it is well to realize that in this passage the material element implied by the metaphor is clearly one of those customarily used in connection with a Jewish tomb, i.e., rock or hardened earth, as in the case of the sepulcher of Lazarus (John 11:38) and also in the case of our Lord's own (Matt. 27:60); it is certainly not water. Indeed, it would be difficult in any circumstances to prove that burial should be regarded as literal when every other part of the passage is spiritual and figurative, as we have seen and shall continue to see. Furthermore, to literalize either of the parallel passages (cf. Eph. 2:4-6 as well as Rom. 6:4) comes perilously near the

---

[2]For a treatment of this verse, see the author's volume *The Epistle to the Romans: A Devotional Commentary* (Grand Rapids: Wm. B. Eerdmans Publishing Co., 1945), pp. 166-67, with footnote on latter page.

teaching of what is known today as baptismal regeneration. Yet only to mention this is to show how inconsistent is such a view of St. Paul's position on the Atonement. We ought to read the phrase "Buried with him by reason of the [or, His] baptism unto death"[3] in the sense of experiencing, or being initiated into, His death (cf. Luke 12:50—"I have a baptism to be baptized with"; see also Mark 10:38, 39). Everything in this verse, therefore, is clear in its consistency, and beautiful in its depth of meaning and power of expression if we but recognize the subject of it as our symbolic identification with Christ. This is clearly for the high purpose of a close spiritual union with Him, even to participation by faith in His very death and burial.

 c. Resurrection (v. 12b). The same is true of the phrase "risen with Him," for again the believer is shown to be identified with Christ through being raised with Him in His resurrection "from the dead" (Rom. 6:4), not from baptism (Eph. 2:6). This union is one of those spiritual realities which form the basis of everything else in the Christian life; and solely by "faith in the working of God" (*A.S.V.*) can we benefit by the resurrection of Christ, for only thus are moral effects produced (cf. Rom. 10:9; Phil. 3:10, 11).

 d. Quickening (v. 13). Union in resurrection is shown to be followed by the gift of a new life, eternal life, including, of course, regeneration now and immortality hereafter; for the future is but a continuation of the present, being identical in essence. God not only raised us up in and with Christ, but also imparted the new life in contrast with the spiritual death which came by reason of sin. The words "dead in sins" (see also Eph. 2:5) refer to moral inability to meet God's requirements, and not apparently to moral insensibility to God's appeal, or else there would be no responsibility on the part of the sinner. The gospel in fact appeals to man's consciousness of responsibility. He is responsible for willingness to receive, and it is to this receptivity that grace appeals. When he is willing for grace to enter in and do its work, his instincts which have been affected by sin are restored.

> Down in the human heart,
> Crushed by the tempter,
> Feelings lie buried that grace can restore.

>   —F. J. Van Alstyne

---

[3]This is the author's paraphrase from the Greek; but see also K. S. Wuest: *An Expanded Translation,* Vol. III, p. 36.

The "uncircumcision" of our flesh is a term doubtless used by the apostle, as was its opposite (v. 11), for the sake of its symbolic meaning for the Gentile readers of this Epistle. Arising out of this "quickened" condition comes the blessing of forgiveness—of "all trespasses." Sin is here symbolized as a debt, with the thought implied that though we have nothing with which to pay, God freely and fully remits the obligation (Luke 7:42).

The emphasis on the words "*in* Him" (vv. 9-11) very plainly shows that the source of all spiritual power lies in the union of the soul with Christ. But not only so—we are circumcised, and buried, and raised, and made alive "*with* Him" (vv. 11, 12, 13), suggesting a spiritual fellowship. All this is associated with a definite confidence in God as the object of our trust and as the source of all spiritual blessing. Scripture is very emphatic in regard to the way in which faith links us to God as the means of obtaining grace and power.

Thus at every point Christ and the believer are identified. When our Lord was circumcised, we were circumcised with Him; when our Lord died, we died in Him; when He was buried, we were buried; when He rose, we were raised; and when He was quickened, we were quickened. To these great truths we may add that when He ascended, we ascended; and, as in one of the parallel passages, Ephesians 2:4-6, now that He is at God's right hand we are seated with Him in heavenly places. In this spiritual unity will be found the only guarantee of faithful adherence to what is true and of fearless abhorrence of what is false. This emphasis on the spiritual life as distinct from mere knowledge and even philosophy (v. 8) will be found as potent today as ever. When faced with ideas which under specious guises of one sort or another tend to lead us astray, it is not too much to urge that a careful attention to a passage like this one will do more than anything else to protect against them. Thus, old errors, which continue to appear in new forms, may be met and vanquished just as in St. Paul's day. Yes, union with Christ affects both thought, the full exercise of mental powers, and action, the translation of thought into redeemed, victorious living.

This becomes the more evident as we contemplate what we were apart from Christ and what He has done for us. As we have seen, we were dead and He made us alive; we were unforgiven and He forgave us. Now comes a further statement of what is involved in pardon (v. 14): He has "blotted out the bond written in ordinances that was against us, which was contrary to us" (*A.S.V.*). The word "bond" that is said to have been "against us" and "contrary to us" would seem to refer primarily to a note of hand, or hand-written document, signed by Jews when they promised to obey the law (cf. Deut. 27:26; Gal. 3:10). But the apostle is writing to Gentiles—

those included in the word "us"—and so the phrase covers all forms of positive decrees in which moral principles are embodied or religious duties defined (Rom. 2:14, 15). Thus is indicated an obligation to perform legal obedience to "ordinances," and this is doubly emphasized by the two phrases "against us" and "contrary (or, directly opposed) to us," suggesting not only the validity of the law as over against lawlessness, but also the active hostility of it toward those who cannot keep it. We are debtors to it, and yet we are absolutely incapable of meeting its demands.

Grammatically there is here a double change in the parts of speech utilized: instead of participles a finite verb appears, and it is not in the aorist, but in the perfect tense, expressive of the feeling of relief at completion—"he ... took it (the bond) out of the way," or, literally, "he removed it and put it out of sight." Christ has fulfilled the law for us and has thereby cancelled it, this thought of abrogation being even more emphatic than erasure; it is also a document torn up and cast aside, destroyed by Christ's death (cf. Gal. 6:14). The apostle's phrase gives a vivid, symbolic picture of our Lord nailing the cancelled document to His cross in token of His complete victory; and thus the law is now powerless to insist upon our obedience or to inflict any punishment for its infringement, because the death of Christ has entirely destroyed it, so far as obligation to obey it for salvation is concerned.

> Thou hast our guilt sustainèd
> Upon the cruel tree
> That we might share Thy glory
> For all eternity!
> Thy precious side was wounded,
> From whence the life-blood flowed,
> The debt we had augmented
> Was cancelled by Thy blood.

Not only was the writing against us erased and the bond itself torn up and cast aside, but these actions are seen to be the result of Christ's complete victory over all the hostile powers of evil (v. 15). The term ordinarily translated "spoiled" or "despoiled" is a very rare word, if it is not peculiar to this Epistle (v. 11; 3:9); but the Greek Fathers preferred the alternate rendering that appears in the text of the Revised Version of 1885 (English) and in a footnote in the American Standard Version, literally, "having stripped off and put away" the powers of evil. Then they interpreted the phrase thus: Christ took our nature, and evil immediately gathered around Him in hostile array; each defeat of it led to a new assault, until the end came and victory was complete. Then the "principalities and powers" that had clung to our Lord in a stubborn attempt to impede Him were torn off forever (John 12:31). Our victory is involved in His; we are divested of the very garments of sin and death in Him (cf. Zech. 3:1-5), the difference between us and Him being, of course, that He divested Himself of temptation only, but divested us of actual wrongdoing. This interpretation not only is grammatical, but is consistent both with St. Paul's teaching in general and with his use of the same word in verse 11 and in 3:9, whereas the usual translation, "spoiled," violates this usage and grammar as well.

Then, we are told, Christ "displayed" these evil powers, as a victor would exhibit captives or trophies, not so much to make an example of them as simply to proclaim His victory over them; and this He did "boldly," noticeably, as opposed to something done in silence or stealth (II Cor. 2:14), "in it"—"his cross" (v. 14; cf. Eph. 2:16). The violence of the metaphor justifies the phraseology; for the paradox of the crucifixion consisted of triumph in helplessness and glory in shame, and so Paul is saying that the convict's gibbet has become the victor's chariot.

Thus the main truth of this section seems to be the blessed, spiritual completeness of our Lord's victory on the cross. Through the death of Christ we obtain forgiveness of sins, the abrogation of the law, and victory over the power of sin. We were guilty; He cancelled the bond. We were hindered by the law's requirements; He has taken them away. We were held in bondage by sin's power; He has triumphed over every form of evil. Thus we see emphasized the great realities of the spiritual life: what we were and what we are; what was ours by nature and what is ours in Christ. Indeed, there are few things in the New Testament more impressive than the wonderful variety of the truths connected with the cross of Christ. His death is the ground of our pardon, the basis of our peace, the secret of our purity, and the source of our power. It is of no wonder that the apostle cried, "God forbid that I should glory, save in the cross of our Lord Jesus Christ" (Gal. 6:14).

> See Him ascending up Calvary's hill,
>   Jesus, our Kinsman-Redeemer!
> Payment is made to the very last mite;
> Signed is the contract and finished the fight;
> "Settled" is writ o'er the bill in God's sight;
>   "Finished!" Oh, glorious Redeemer!

The spiritual comfort contained in this passage is inspiring too. We can look backward, and outward, and onward, and know that all is well. The law that was hostile to us is entirely destroyed. The power of sin that held us in bondage is completely broken. The rites and ceremonies of religion, in so far as they may concern themselves with our justification, are done away in Christ, and to return to them would mean that Christ is not sufficient. As one writer has put it, "Dead men have nothing to do with ordinances." They were useless to us when we were dead in sin, and we are useless to them now because we have died with Christ. Thus we rejoice as we contemplate past, present, and future, and thankfully recognize that "Christ is all" (3:11).

Bishop Moule very appropriately introduces at this point these verses of a hymn that should, perhaps, be better known:

> He gave me back the bond;
> It was a heavy debt;
> And as He gave He smiled and said,
> "Thou wilt not Me forget."
>
> He gave me back the bond;
> The seal was torn away;
> And as He gave He smiled and said,
> "Think thou of Me alway."
>
> . . . .
>
> It is a bond no more,
> But it shall ever tell
> All that I owed was fully paid
> By my Emmanuel.

> —Charles Sabine

Here it was felt necessary to descend to more specific matters, and so now there comes the application of verses 8 to 15, first in regard to practical concerns (vv. 16, 17), and then in regard to doctrinal questions (vv. 18, 19). It is significant that the majority of Christians have always been slow to apply principles to conduct or to see the precise bearing of great truths on the details of daily life. But now St. Paul proceeds to specify the actual errors from which he would have his readers keep themselves. Because of what Christ had done for them, they were to beware of every form of error.

3. A Warning Against Legalism (vv. 16, 17). The serious danger is that of the loss of Christian liberty, and this is the point of the word "therefore" in verse 16. Because Christ has cancelled the bond of the law and has forever destroyed it, and since He has gained complete victory over all the powers of evil, Christians are to beware of becoming entangled again in anything that would lead them away from Christ and from the fulness of their privileges in Him. Thus the argument is much the same as that in Galatians 5:1-13. Because believers are free they are not to choose to yield themselves again to the bondage from which they have been so completely delivered. It is generally thought that the dangers against which the apostle warns the Colossians are both Jewish and Oriental in origin, the former referring to legalism, and the latter to the question of angelic mediation.

It is the first of these which St. Paul emphasizes in these two verses, and he specifies five matters (v. 16), warning the Colossian Christians not merely against the observance of these things, but also against those who would call them to account for not observing them, for they ought not to be matters for judgment. Questions of food, drink, and three types of festivals were evidently considered of serious moment by certain people in Colosse; but Christian people were not to be misled by mistaken insistence on things that were no longer essential.

Eating and drinking are, of course, unimportant spiritually for the reason that God's Kingdom is not a matter of food and drink (Rom. 14:17) but of things spiritual. Mosaic distinctions were first regarded as to be abolished (Mark 7:14, 15); then their abolition was graphically illustrated (Acts 10:11-16), and formally declared (Acts 15:28, 29). As Lightfoot points out, the law of Moses referred almost wholly to meats, but the rigorous Colossian prohibitions probably went, as did those of the Essenes, far beyond the Mosaic regulations and forbade animal food altogether and also wine (Lightfoot, *Colossians,* p. 191).

"A feast day" (*A. S. V.*) is a reference to the annual festivals of the Jews, such as the Passover, and "a new moon" is an allusion to the sacrifice on the first day of every month (Num. 28:11-14). The mention of "a sabbath day" clearly indicates the Jewish Sabbath as one of those institutions from which we are set free in Christ. There was exhaustive enumeration of such days (cf. the LXX); and we are reminded of Paul's similar warning in Galatians 4:9-11, where the order is reversed—"days, and months, and seasons, and years" (Gal. 4:10, *A. S. V.*).

No one must for an instant suppose that the observance of the Sabbath Day (lit., "rest day") can in any way procure or help to procure salvation. However, the Sabbath is something infinitely greater than a merely Jewish institution, for it was "made for man" (Mark 2:27) by God Himself and dates from the creation of the world (Gen. 2:1-3). It is very significant that it was just as the ceremonial and legal aspect of the Mosaic dispensation was being brought to an end that Christ called Himself "Lord also of the sabbath" (Mark 2:28). His cancelling of the bond of the law did set aside the necessity for His people to observe the Jewish Sabbath but, at the same time, because we are "under the law to Christ" (I Cor. 9:21), we have the Christian Sabbath, or Rest Day, "the Lord's day" (Rev. 1:10).

This was an indication that Christ's Lordship did not mean abolition of the Sabbath principle, but only a proper interpretation and even a transformation of it. He thus exerted upon it His own authority and, at the same time, applied to it a spirit of liberty that was to be characteristic of the new dispensation. Thus we have a divine institution, dating from the beginning, intended for permanent observance (Exod. 20:11), and perpetuated through the finished work of Christ of which the resurrection on the first day of the week (Matt. 28:1) was the seal.

Christian men and women will, therefore, rejoice in their liberty from everything purely Jewish but will, at the same time, observe with devotion the day of rest that God has now appointed for spirit, soul, and body. While Christ thus resolutely set aside the deplorable bondage that Jewish teaching had associated with the Sabbath, He taught that by the very fact that it has been "made for man" it was meant to prevent a constant absorption in worldly affairs. It was instituted to enable body, mind, and soul to enjoy that cessation from daily work which would enable man to be and to do what God intended. This provision at the very creation of the human race of a weekly day for worship and rest, to the universal benefit of man, is our supreme and sufficient authority for the periodic cessation from toil. We are to seize the opportunity thus given for rest, worship, and Christian service. When this is properly understood it will enable men to realize the will of God; and although there are those who, with what may perhaps be called hyper-spirituality, but certainly not with a due regard to etymology, speak of every day being a sabbath, facts prove beyond question that the observance of the Lord's Day is one of the most essential features of all true spiritual life. Certainly spirituality is not furthered by thinking of every day as exactly alike.

Occupation by the soul with Christ, then, would be the adequate protection against the error of legalism; for the reason why all these things are not to be allowed to encroach upon Christian liberty is that they are a mere shadow of spiritual realities (v. 17), a shadow, according to Lightfoot, thrown before the substance (Lightfoot, *Colossians,* p. 193). Indeed, it is not too much to say that the Greek word usually translated "body" should here have been given an alternate rendering, i.e., "the *substance* belongs to Christ"—even as we often make the two English words interchangeable, speaking of materials which have "body," or substance, to them. Like the law in general, which was a shadow of the good things to come (Heb. 10:1), these things typified what was found and fulfilled in Christ. Thus, to sum up, eating and drinking are symbols of spiritual food (John 6:48-58), the feeding on Christ in our hearts by faith, as the Anglican Communion Service so beautifully expresses it. The feast days are a type of that continuous festival that is ours in Christ (I Cor. 5:8,

Gr.), for all of them were, like the Passover, anticipatory of Christ (I Cor. 5:7) in some significant way. The Jewish Sabbath is a suggestion of both the day that we call the Lord's Day, which is the believer's privilege now, and also of the eternal rest of soul here and hereafter for the people of God (Heb. 4:1-11).

4. A Warning Against False Humility (vv. 18, 19). This next exhortation is even more imperative, dealing as it does with doctrinal errors affecting belief. The apostle uses a very rare word here which seems to refer to the decision of an umpire. The Revised Versions render the phrase "rob you of your prize," and Lightfoot believes the false teachers at Colosse are considered to be persons frustrating those who would otherwise have won the prize (Lightfoot, *Colossians,* p. 193), which is possibly the same as in Philippians 3:14. Other writers, however, translate the words "let no one give judgment against you," and this certainly is the force of the original word, which occurs only here. In either case it means that no believer is to be defrauded of his proper position by being compelled to submit to certain restrictions, because submission would involve the loss of Christian liberty. Anyone who attempted to do this would be taking pleasure in a wrong kind of humility.

But what is the meaning of humility here, and to whom is the reference? Most writers interpret the words as an attitude which led men to worship angels, thinking wrongly that God was unapproachable except through the mediation of celestial beings. If this is the meaning, then of course the humility is indeed false, tending, instead, to a real pride, the word being used ironically, since the Christian knows well that he has not the slightest need to approach God through any such channels, but can enter the divine presence direct (Heb. 4:16; 10:19, 20).

It is sometimes thought difficult to be sure, however, that these Colossians actually needed a warning against angel-worship, unless of course they were strongly indoctrinated in the Oriental concept of the necessity of intermediaries between a holy God and unholy men. Bishop Moule tells us that the Asiatic churches do seem to have been early and widely affected by an angel-worship that was largely developed in the later Judaism; and he quotes Quesnel, a saintly Jansenist (of the Roman Catholic Church) as saying: "Angels will always win the day over Jesus Christ despised and crucified, if the choice of a mediator . . . is left to the vanity of the human mind" (Moule, *Colossian Studies,* p. 177).

Another writer maintains that the reference is to the religious humility exemplified by angels and to the lowly position which they take, veiling their faces before God (Isa. 6:2) as a symbol of reverence, but also because they do not possess the same boldness of access (Rom. 5:2; Eph. 4:12) as do Christians (I Peter 1:12). This would mean that, since believers stand before God in Christ, no one is to rob them of this standing or make them willing to accept a lower position through a false humility. Either of these views makes good sense, although the former is far more universally endorsed, and the latter is perhaps somewhat less easy to follow.

It is a curious and yet perhaps not surprising tendency for human nature to conceive of God as too far off for direct approach, and consequently to seek for intermediaries between ourselves and Him. On the face of it this appears to be a mere confession of weakness, as though we could approach the lower links of some chain between earth and heaven even if unable to reach heaven itself. In reality, however, as Ellicott says, it is not proper Christian humility, "but a false and perverted lowliness, which deemed God was so inaccessible that He could only be approached through the intermediary of inferior beings" (Ellicott, *A Critical and Grammatical Commentary on St. Paul's Epistles to the Philippians, Colossians, and to Philemon*, p. 175). On the contrary, the glory of Christianity is that it is the religion of direct access to God. This is the keynote in particular of the Epistle to the Hebrews, where believers are described by the significant phrase, "those who come right to God" (Heb. 7:25, *Gr.*). The modern tendencies that answer to the error at Colosse are too evident and too prevalent to call for further reference here. Our safety lies continually in direct and immediate entrance "into the holiest in the blood of Jesus" (Heb. 10:19).

Another difficulty in this passage is in regard to the reading of the next phrase. The American Standard Version reads, "dwelling in the things which he hath seen," while the King James Version inserts the word "not"—"intruding into those things which he hath *not* seen." The textual authorities seem to be equally divided, although it is thought that the balance favors the omission of the negative as giving the more difficult reading, which according to the usual principle of criticism is more likely to have been the original. If, therefore, on the one hand, we omit the negative the phrase means that such a person as is here mentioned was concerned only with what his "fleshly mind" could see, viz., the only position he could comprehend. He could neither stand nor walk by faith. On the other hand, the phrase may refer to him as "going into curious and subtle speculation regarding visions granted him" (Joseph Henry Thayer, *Greek-English Lexicon of the New Testament*, p. 206). It is known that these false teachers of Colosse made pretensions of knowing supernatural things by means of visions, and yet these did not rest on faith but were the result of the vanity of the flesh. Sir William Ramsay has shown that the word rendered "intruding" or "dwelling" was a technical term in the mystery-religions of St. Paul's day, and probably means "putting foot on the threshold," or entering on the new life of the initiated (Ramsay, *The*

Teaching of Paul in Terms of the Present Day, p. 287ff). This practically agrees with the marginal reference in the American Standard Version, "taking his stand upon—." Bishop Moule uses the word "invading" and he also favors the retention of the word "not" (Moule, *Colossian Studies*, p. 177), so that the meaning would be that a man who takes a position on the worship of angels is dealing with something about which he knows nothing. In either case the thought is that the Christians in Colosee were not in this way to be defrauded of their true standing in Christ.

An imperative reason is given for this appeal; it is because such an attitude involves the Christian in the error of "not holding fast the Head" (v. 19, *A.S.V.*). Every part of the Church, like the members of a human body in relation to the brain, has its place and function in direct contact with its head, the Lord Jesus Christ. To feel a need for intermediaries would mean disloyalty to Him, because all such false teaching was of the flesh and not derived from Him. They who advocated it were forever found wanting in the apprehension of the revelation of Christ as both God and man, through whom alone we may approach the Father. But those who were right with God in Christ would find that every part of the body was receiving grace direct from God and was growing continually in and through Him who is its head. The erroneous teaching proved, moreover, that the holder of it was not a true member of that body of which Jesus Christ is the head, because it, the true Church, is in vital and direct connection with Him, and is continually benefitting from the inter-communion among all the parts of it.

As Lightfoot points out, the discoveries of modern physiology have made marvelously accurate and appropriate the apostle's choice of words in this verse to describe the parts of the human body. Such distinctions and such force of language, indeed, his contemporaries could not have fully appreciated, for "at every turn we meet with some fresh illustration which kindles it with a flood of light" (Lightfoot, *Colossians*, p. 198). The functions of "joints and bands (ligaments)" are (1) the supply of nutriment ("having nourishment ministered," or, "bountifully furnished"), and (2) the compacting of the frame ("knit together"). In other words, there come through these parts the communication of life and energy and the preservation of unity and order. St. Paul's conception of the relationship of head and body thus includes, says Bishop Lightfoot, "the volition communicated from the brain to the limbs, the sensations of the extremities telegraphed back to the brain, the absolute mutual sympathy between the head and the members, (and) the instantaneous paralysis ensuing on the interruption of continuity" between them. The statement was made by the apostle in the face of the very different opinions entertained by ancient physiologists, and it may possibly reflect favorably upon the competence of the writer's companion at this time, "Luke, the beloved physician" (4:14). But there is here, in any case, a strong argument for the safeguarding of Scripture by divine inspiration in every particular, even in the wide field of secular knowledge.

However, these processes—contact and attachment, nutriment diffused and structural unity attained—are only intermediate to the desired end of growth. Thus the passage goes on to speak in striking fashion of increasing "with the increase of God," as though God Himself grew when His people grew by means of union with His Son. Lightfoot defines this phrase as "that which partakes of God, belongs to God, which has its abode in God. Thus the finite," he goes on, "is truly united with the Infinite; the end which the false teachers strove in vain to compass is attained" (Lightfoot, *Colossians,* p. 198). Bishop Moule interprets the phrase to mean the development of a holiness and a power of which God is source, and secret, and environment—with "nothing between" (Moule, *Colossian Studies,* p. 178). Maclaren says that the "increase" will come from God and "will be pleasing to Him," because it "will be essentially the growth of His own life in the body ... wholesome, solid growth," although there is, indeed, "an increase not of God" and "it is very easy to get an increase of (this) other kind" (Maclaren, *Colossians,* p. 240).

This whole passage has suggested by its reference to Christ the essential privileges of the believer. In verses 9 and 10, Christ is the head, and the believer has his *position* in Him. Here in verse 19, Christ is also shown to be the head, but the thought is of *progress.* We are complete in Him in regard to our place, and we are also nourished by Him and built up in Him. Thus every part of the believer's life is fully met by God's ample provision, and because of this genuine, blessed, and satisfying substance he is urged to avoid anything that would keep him living in the shadows. In short, we must never allow ourselves to be defrauded of any blessing that is rightfully ours in union and communion with our divine Lord and head.

From the doctrinal, the apostle now turns back to the practical, from theology to morality; and it is natural to proceed from the subject of angel-worship to this next aspect of his teaching. He proceeds to show the utter impossibility of any true Christian doing that against which he had been speaking so strongly, and he does this on two grounds: they had "died with Christ" (v. 20, *A.S.V.*); and they had been "raised together with Christ" (3:1, *A.S.V.*). On the proper meaning of these two spiritual facts their entire practical life turned; and this led to:

5. A Warning against Asceticism (vv. 20-23).

a. The safe position (v. 20a). The Christian is here described as having "died with Christ from the rudiments of the world" (*A.S.V.*). The tense of the word "died" is the aorist, implying a definite time in the past, and this, from the standpoint of God, was when Christ Himself died on the cross. So far as the believer's own experience was involved, however, this "dying" took place the moment he received Christ, the One who had died, as his personal Savior. Death always means separation, and this is the reason why it is described as "from the rudiments (or "elements," *A.S.V.* marg.) of the world" (cf. v. 8). It is important that the believer should recognize this death with Christ as a fact, and not as something to which he is now to submit for the purpose of obtaining an experience of it. It is an absolute, an accomplished fact, whether he "experiences" it or not, for there are several statements in the New Testament to prove that when Christ died the believer died also (2:13; 3:3; Rom. 6:1-11; II Tim. 2:11).

The words "with Christ" show that Christ Himself is also regarded as having died "from the rudiments of the world." Lightfoot defines these as "the rudimentary, disciplinary ordinances whose sphere is the mundane and sensuous" (Lightfoot, *Colossians,* p. 200). This seems to mean, first of all, that as Christ was "made under the law" (Gal. 4:4), that is, born under the regime of the law, He was naturally under obligation to fulfil the law during His earthly life, but that when He died this obligation necessarily came to an end. Furthermore, His death was the fulfillment of these requirements in the sense that He was the reality to which they all pointed, so that His death was their abolition. It is for this reason that the apostle so strongly insists upon the believer dying with Christ, for if Christ died "from" these rudiments, or elements, they can no longer be of any authority over the believer. Nothing is to interfere with the perfect liberty of the Christian in his union with Christ, for in Christ he not only died to sin (Rom. 6:2) and to self (II Cor. 5:15), but also to the law (Gal. 2:19).

b. The solemn protest (vv. 20b-22). Based on this fact of the Christian having died with Christ, the question is logically and forcefully put, Why do you submit to the yoke of ordinances? Christ had set them free from these things and they ought not to be capable of desiring to be again in slavery. The three prohibitions (v. 21) are apparently some of the requirements insisted upon by the false teachers. As Maclaren says, "These three prohibitions are not Paul's, but are quoted by him as specimens of the kind of rules and regulations which he is protesting against" (Maclaren, *Colossians,* p. 247). All of them relate to defilements contracted in different ways by contact with so-called impure objects of diet through sense of touch—"handle not, nor yet taste, nor yet even touch." Thus the apostle puts his readers on their guard against these false teachers and goes on to show that in the natural processes of eating and drinking all such things will perish by being used up. This constitutes their unimportance in regard to the spiritual life, and indeed they are definitely characterized by being merely human and temporary, St. Paul quoting to this effect from

Isaiah 29:13—"after the precepts ... of men (v. 22)"—as did our Lord Himself (cf. Matt. 15:7-9; Mark 7:6, 7), when condemning similar practices. It is significant that the teachings of men were actually being observed by God's professing people even while He was being disobeyed. Thus these observances against which Paul was writing were evidently not so much belonging to the Mosaic law, which is now superseded though once authoritative, as they were to the "philosophy" of verse 8, which was wholly vexatious and unwarranted. As a writer well puts it, the special force of this appeal is: "Ye who are in union with Christ, how can ye receive mere human precepts which contradict His will?"

If it should be said, as indeed it has been proposed more than once, that this reference to "ordinances" seems to reflect on the Christian ordinances of baptism and the Lord's Supper, the obvious reply is that these do not come under the same category as those mentioned here by St. Paul. They are in no sense "rudiments of the world," or man-made, or intended for the purpose of providing salvation or guaranteeing merit. They are Christian ordinances instituted by our Lord Himself for use by believers as solemn pledges of grace and reminders of Himself, and they provide just that touch with the material world—through water, bread, wine—which should be a help, not a hindrance, to spiritual life. Indeed, the very simplicity of these ordinances, the only two in the Christian Church, clearly proves the impossibility of associating them with the apostle's warning here, unless of course they are elaborated upon and used in the wrong sense to imply a guarantee of salvation. It may also be pointed out that pure and true Christianity has always been exceedingly simple, free from elaborate ceremonial. This is because it is a universal experience that ritual is apt to lead the soul away from Christ and involve it in a complexity of legalism.

Also, it ought to go without saying that this passage has no reference whatsoever to the avoidance of strong drink, excellent as that practice is, although the phrase has sometimes been lifted out of its context and used in support of such abstention or of any other similar virtue. The whole argument makes this perfectly clear.

c. The spiritual powerlessness (v. 23). Furthermore, in submitting to these false methods of living, the Christian was really doing something absolutely useless for spiritual power and blessing. These ordinances had nothing but a mere appearance of wisdom and were of no real value in remedying the indulgences of the flesh or destroying sin in the life. They constituted a sort of religious service that was purely gratuitous on the part of the worshiper, one not sought or recognized as acceptable to God. They were of the nature of "will-worship," or self-imposed service, and, while they made a pretense of great godliness and humility (cf. v. 18),

101

and even of "neglecting of the body," they were essentially marks of pride that tended to set aside the finished work of Christ in the believer's behalf. It is still important to remember that severity of treatment meted out to the body has no power to remove or destroy the appetites or passions of the soul. Asceticism may try to prevent indulgence in sin, but it is incapable of overcoming the evil that prompts wrongdoing, and thus it is futile as a remedy for what is wrong with mankind. The only way of dealing aright with the body is to regard it as part of the personality of the believer in union with Christ and therefore, by reason of that union, as dead to sin and alive to God.

Looking back over the entire passage from verse 4 of this chapter 2, it is seen that there is a threefold peril. The Colossians are cautioned against being deceived (vv. 4-15), against being judged (vv. 16, 17), and against being defrauded (vv. 18-23). There is the same danger today: the promoters of false religions, philosophies, and systems of thought continue to do their utmost to bring the believer into bondage, and on this account we are to heed the solemn words found here.

But the protection is made as clear as the peril, and this is found all through the section to be simply union with Christ, our head. This union contains wisdom for us, conveys grace and power to us, controls our lives, and enables us to do God's will. This is the force of the prayer in 1:9-11, where wisdom, strength, and the knowledge of the divine will are all included in the apostle's petition. The more we are enabled to realize this assured union with our Lord Jesus Christ, and the more we yield ourselves by faith and surrender to His Lordship as our head, the more effective will be our practical Christian life, both in opposition to what is evil and in furtherance of what is good.

7 THE PRACTICE OF THE CHRISTIAN LIFE

This section is called by A. T. Pierson the turning point in the Epistle. "The first two chapters are doctrinal; the last two are practical, applying the truth"[1] Here is given the second reason for not following the false teachers of Colosse. As the apostle Paul had assumed the union of these Christians in their Lord's death (2:20), so now they are led on to see that they are risen with Him, and that this in particular is a strong reason for repudiating any false way. To be dead with Christ carries with it resurrection with Him, as already stated (2:12), and now the apostle will show that this is the genuine, adequate means of power against any indulgence of the flesh. Holy living is possible, but it must be realized in the right way, not in the wrong way, in God's way, not Satan's. Every part of this passage is important because it gives the essential secrets of Christian holiness; and we shall see also how all true life necessarily springs from true doctrine.

The Source of the Christian Life (vv. 1-4)

1. **The Reminder (v. 1a).** The apostle first calls attention to his readers having been "raised together with Christ" (*A.S.V.*). The English word "if" is employed here in its sense of "since"—"in view of," and the

---

[1] *Newness of Life*, April 1901, p. 52.

verb is in the indicative mood, so that Paul is clearly assuming this resurrection as a fact, admissive of no doubt. That is to say, these Christians were raised spiritually when Christ was raised physically; and this identification was the foundation of their spiritual position. The resurrection is variously presented in the New Testament as at once a proof, a pattern, a power, a promise, and a pledge. It is the proof of our acceptance of Christ's death and of our acceptance with Him (Rom. 4:24, 25); it is to be the pattern of our holy life (Rom. 6:4); it is also the power for Christian character and service (Eph. 1:18-20); it contains the promise of our own physical resurrection (I Thess. 4:14); and it is the pledge of our life hereafter (John 14:19). In the present passage our resurrection is associated with Christ's because we are united with Him in such a way that, whatever He did, we are regarded by God the Father as having done also (2:12; Rom. 6:8).

2. The Realization (vv. 1b, 2). On account of this union with a living Christ, we are called upon to do two things. First, we are to *"seek* those things which are above" (v. 1b), and then we are to *"set"* our "mind on the things that are above" (v. 2, *A.S.V.*). This word "mind" includes the entire personality and refers here to the whole bent of our inner nature, which is to be set in the direction of heaven because Christ is there. We are to see to it that the tendency of our life is toward heavenly not earthly things. The word in the original is very striking, implying concentration of every power on things heavenly (Phil. 2:2, 5; 3:19, 20; see also Matt. 6:33 and Gal. 5:10); and this attitude necessarily follows from our union with Christ. Dr. Pierson expresses it very strongly: "From the moment of faith in Christ, being thus bound to Him and identified with Him, there should be an *absolute cessation of all known sin*—nay, more, the level of earth should be left below and behind for a new level of an essentially heavenly life—lived in Christ."[2] Thus, by realizing our identification with Christ and acting upon it, our condition is made to agree with our position, and holiness is the blessed outcome.

> O Lord, remove whate'er divides
> Our longing souls from Thee;
> 'Tis fit that where the Head resides
> The members' hearts should be.

3. The Reason (v. 3). Since Christ is now in heaven, seated "on the right hand of God" (v. 1, *A.S.V.*), and we are united with Him in His death and resurrection, our life must of necessity be "hid with Christ in God." The word translated "is hid" is very suggestive because it means "has been permanently hidden," and the thought seems to include the two ideas of

---

[2]*Ibid.*

secrecy and safety. Our life is "hid" and therefore unseen by man; it is also "hid" in the sense that it is incapable of being touched or hurt by any evil power (cf. Isa. 32:2). This is one of the glories of the Christian life, and it is not surprising that Christian men of all times have rejoiced in the consciousness of the soul's perfect security in this union with Christ (see Moule, *Colossian Studies*, p. 190). There is a blessed contrast with the purely physical aspect of human life represented by the question asked and answered in James 4:14: "*Your life* . . . is . . . a vapour, that appeareth for a little time, and then vanisheth away." Here the significance is spiritual: "*Your life* is permanently hidden with Christ in God."

4. The Revelation (v. 4). But this is not everything for, although the believer's life is now hidden, one day Christ will be made manifest and then the Christian also will be revealed with Him. Indeed, Christ is actually described as "our life." Here, again, we are in the region of *facts* concerning Him, and these are to become *forces* in our life and experience. We are so identified with Him that not only is our life hidden with Him (v. 3), but He becomes our very life. To understand how this can be is made easier by noting certain New Testament prepositions. St. John tells us Christ promised that the believer should "live *by*" Him (John 6:57); and John himself declares that "this life is *in* his Son (I John 5:11; cf. Acts 17:28; Rom. 5:10, Gr.; 6:2, 3; II Tim. 1:1). St. Paul states that "we live *unto* the Lord" (Rom. 14:8; cf. II Cor. 4:10, 11; 5:15); and he also says that Christ died in order that "we should live together *with* him" (I Thess. 5:10; cf. Eph. 4:18). By Him—the means; in Him—the union; to Him—the incentive; with Him—the fellowship. Nothing could be closer or more definite than this blessed relationship, and out of it comes all spiritual power (Phil. 1:21; I John 5:12). Thus, when the manifestation of Christ occurs, we are to be manifested with Him in glory. Bishop Lightfoot has a helpful comment on this thought of the believer's manifestation: "The veil which now shrouds your higher life from others, and even partly from yourselves, will then be withdrawn. The world, which persecutes, despises, ignores now, will then be blinded with the dazzling glory of the revelation" (Lightfoot, *Colossians,* p. 108). This is to be the crown and culmination of our Christian life, the coming of our Lord and our coming with Him. This is the hope and inspiration of the trusting soul as it looks forward to that blessed day when Christ "shall appear" and all His people shall "also appear with Him in glory" (John 17:22; Rom. 8:19; Rev. 19:11-14).

> Christ died;—but with His latest breath
> He breathed new life in us, once dead in sin;
> He gave His precious life that, by His death,
> He might for sinners Life eternal win.

> "I am the Bread of Life";—the hungering saint
>   On Him, by faith, and in his heart doth feed;
> Strengthened with might, he feels no longer faint,
>   But finds Christ's death, partaken, Life indeed.
>
> "I am the Life";—yes, He doth energize
>   And give fresh power to every palsied limb;
> Death to *our* life—for all the old self dies—
>   But Life from death, since now we live to Him.
>
> But Christ, who is our Life, shall soon appear,
>   And us to higher Life with Him will call;
> Our breath, food, strength within this narrow sphere,
>   In glory still shall be our All in all.

This familiar and yet perennially striking passage is full of blessed teaching concerning Christ and the believer, and from it we cannot fail to realize the emphasis placed on our perfect identification with Him at every stage. Christ is mentioned no fewer than four times in as many verses, in connection with His resurrection, His session above, His union with God, and His coming again. The believer is also mentioned in several ways: first comes our *union* with Christ, then follows our *life* hidden with Him, and lastly the assurance is given of future *manifestation* with Him. We must therefore ponder all these facts and allow them to exert their proper effect on our lives. This is the meaning of St. Paul's great word "reckon" (Rom. 6:11), for we are to account as belonging to us everything that Christ has done and is, and then live in the power of these blessed spiritual realities. When we do so, we shall find both liberty and victory in the face of every thralldom of spirit and of body. Christ's own victory will be ours and so we shall be "more than conquerors" (Rom. 8:37). Yes, occupation with Christ is the secret of everything in the Christian life; and thus the old exhortation "*Sursum corda*"—"Lift up your hearts"—expresses the only right attitude for salvation, for sanctification, and for satisfaction. Be it ours to respond with thankfulness, adoration, and praise, "We lift them up unto the Lord."

THE NEGATIVE EXPRESSION OF THE CHRISTIAN LIFE (vv. 5-11)

Spurgeon is said to have remarked in his characteristically quaint way that this chapter begins in heaven (vv. 1-4) and ends in the kitchen (vv. 22-25); and it is at this point in the chapter that there commences an exhortation to practical Christian living, based on the great truths in the foregoing verses. From the spiritual position of the believer in Christ as risen, ascended, and returning comes the duty of facing a serious problem.

1. The Injunction (v. 5a). This problem was connected with the old sinful nature still a part of those to whom the apostle was writing; and the force of the word "therefore" is very important. Because their life was hidden with Christ, the Colossian Christians were to carry out in it certain spiritual results. The wrong way of living had already been summed up in 2:23, but since these believers had died with Christ (2:20; 3:3), they were to "make dead" or "put to death" their sinful earthly members, also in union with Christ, who is at once the Christian's power and pattern (Rom. 7:4; 8:13). They had died to sin *judicially* (v. 3), and now they were to die to sin *practically* (v. 5). The Greek word rendered "put to death" or "mortify" implies a definite act and is interpreted by Bishop Moule as "give to death" (Moule, *Colossian Studies*, p. 198). Further, it is significant that every reference to our being "dead" or "crucified" is in the past tense, implying not only a definite but a completed action. This means a further step in realizing what is meant by *reckoning* ourselves dead to sin (Rom. 6:11), and is one of the paradoxes of the Christian life. As Godet well expressed it, Christian holiness is fundamentally different from all pagan ethics. Paganism says, "Become what you ought to be"; Christianity says, "Become what you are." Our spiritual condition thus is made to agree with our position in Christ (1:27, 28; 2:6, 10). We are to accept this position as a fact and then live in the power of it. When the soul is conscious that not only did Christ die for its salvation, but that it has been united with Him in His death, there comes a power that enables it to live to God's praise and glory.

In regard to deliverance from the power of sin, which is to be sought, according to this passage, in the death of Christ rather than in any gradual process of sanctification, Dr. Thomas M. Chalmers has a worthy expression of this essential truth:

> The man who—riveting all his confidence in the death of Christ—has become partaker of all its immunities and of all its holy influences, will not only find peace from the guilt of sin, but protection from its tyranny. This faith will not only be to him a barrier from the abyss of its coming vengeance, but it will be to him a panoply of defence against its present ascendency over his soul. The sure way to put Satan to flight is to resist him, steadfast in this faith, which will be to him who exercises it a shield to quench all the fiery darts of the adversary.
>
> We are aware of charges of being strange, and mystical, and imaginary, to which this representation, however Scriptural it may be, exposes us. But we ask, on the one hand, those who have often been defeated by the power of temptation—

whether they ever recollect, in a single instance, that the death of Christ, believed and regarded and made use of in the way now explained, was a weapon put forth in the contest with sin? And we ask, on the other hand, those who have made use of this weapon, whether it ever failed them in their honest and faithful attempts to resist the instigations of evil?

We apprehend that the testimonies of both will stamp an experimental as well as a Scriptural soundness upon the affirmation of my text that he who by faith in the death of Christ is freed from the condemnation of sin, has also an instrument in his possession which has only to be plied and kept in habitual exercise, that he may habitually be free from its power (Chalmers, *Romans,* vol. ii., p. 90f.).

There is, of course, constant danger of disproportion in the statement of this truth; but so there is in everything else. Notwithstanding all such perils, the old saying is just as true as ever, that "abuse does not take away use." Evan H. Hopkins, one of the founders of the Keswick Movement, once wrote: "Does anyone ask, 'What have you lately received which you did not possess before?' I answer, as to my standing in Christ nothing; as to doctrine nothing. But I have been made to see that Christ can as fully meet my need as to walk as He has as to standing; that He is as truly my Sanctification as He is my Righteousness."

2. The Description (v. 5b). The word "members," of course, is used here not physically, but morally. Since our actual limbs may be made instruments either for the world or for Christ, they are thus symbolic of the potentials of the human personality that controls them (Matt. 5:29). The grammatical construction of this verse, however, places these instruments and activities in direct apposition, perhaps for heightened dramatic effect. The sins listed here include both actions and desires in the moral realm, and all of them are often characteristic of our "members which are upon the earth." They are described with singular impressiveness, starting with impurity and ending with a solemn association of covetousness with the heinous sin of idolatry. Note that the word for covetousness in the original means, quite literally, "the having of more." Thus it is not necessarily yearning for what someone possesses, but merely wishing for more than has been given us. The root of all covetousness is simply dissatisfaction, and this soon may become greed. But do we realize that every unworthy desire, whatever form it may take, even a mere grasping after money or position, is really equivalent to idol-worship—putting self in the place of God in our life as the object of our devotion? As we are told by our Lord Himself, "Ye cannot serve God and mammon" (Matt. 6:24).

3. The Condemnation (vv. 6, 7). God's judgment inevitably falls on those who practice these things in which the Colossian Christians had formerly lived, and it is certain to come not only now, but hereafter. The phrase "wrath of God" (v. 6) should be carefully noted here and elsewhere (Rom. 1:18; Eph. 5:6), for it means the divine judicial attitude toward everything sinful.

The Colossians are now reminded that these evil ways did form part and parcel of their life in the old days. The word "walked" (v. 7) always means the outward expression of life, the conduct that comes from the very possession of life. It is frequently found in Scripture to indicate the true outward behavior of the believer (e.g., Gen. 17:1; Eph. 2:2; 4:17; 5:2); in fact, the connection between life and walk is the same as that between cause and effect. It was because these people had "lived" in the sphere of evil that they had "walked" in it, that is, had manifested in their conduct that spirit which was in agreement with it.

4. The Transformation (vv. 8-10). Introduced by a favorite Pauline phrase denoting strong contrast (1:21, 26), there follows an earnest entreaty to put aside not only all the things just mentioned (v. 5), but also those that are now to be included (v. 8). We may characterize the first list as sins of unchastity; and this second one concerns those of uncharity and untruth. The words "put off" (v. 8) are in the imperative mood and are expressive of disrobing. It is as much as to say that, as Christians had "put off the old man" (v. 9; cf. 2:11), they are now to put off his disreputable clothes, his undesirable characteristics.

What is the "old man"? The phrase is used in two other passages: In Romans 6:6, "our old man is crucified," and in Ephesians 4:22, "the old man . . . is corrupt." It is a description of what we were like in Adam as a result of his fall, having the natural characteristics of all unsaved persons. It represents sin in its definite, concrete form, but with different aspects, including the flesh, which is subjective in nature. It is, as Bishop Moule points out, "an abiding element (Gal. 5:16, 17) in even the regenerate and spiritual, though it need no longer—even for an hour—be the ruling element; it may be continuously overcome in a practical and profound manner, in the strength of the new man." The Bishop goes on to remark that the word "corrupt" is literally "corrupting, growing corrupt, morally decaying, on the way to final ruin. Such, from the Divine point of view, is the condition of ideal Man unregenerate, man as represented by and summed up in Adam fallen."[3] "The flesh" is the evil principle within,

---

[3]Moule in *The Cambridge Bible for Schools and Colleges, Ephesians*, pp. 118f.

never in this life eradicated, but by the indwelling power of Christ effectually and continually counteracted.

Sin had no part of the original creation (Gen. 1:26, 27) of a threefold human personality (I Thess. 5:23), so that we must always distinguish clearly between the person, "Ye," and the nature, "old man," and remember that the former is responsible for sin—not for its existence, but for its activities—and the latter is incurable (Rom. 8:7, 8; Eph. 4:22). When given over to sins like hatred and lying, a person is thought of as wearing the clothing of the "old man" but does not become the "old man" again. If the "old man" stands for the unregenerate self, we cannot be at once regenerate and unregenerate (although we may *de*generate). That which a person once was, unregenerate, the moment he becomes regenerate he ceases to be.

Evil habits are not the equivalent of "the flesh." We are not born with evil habits but with an evil nature. Habit is formed by successive acts and may acquire power that becomes "second nature," something additional to our fallen nature. But when the person is united to Christ, the old nature with its evil habits can be "put off" as a stained garment is discarded—not repressed, not covered over, but laid aside.

The Speaker's Commentary[4] defines the phrase "the old man" as "the old self which belonged to the Colossians in their heathen days, and which they put off once for all when admitted into covenant with God and sealed with the Spirit ... The putting off the old man and putting on the new man are ... represented as things past, and the renewing as a thing still going on."[5]

As we have already noted, the two general categories mentioned here (v. 8) are sins of uncharitableness and insincerity, which are expressed both in feeling and in speech: "anger" is an habitual attitude of hatred; "wrath" is a sudden outburst of fury; "malice" means sheer malignity, the vicious nature bent on harming others; "railing" (*A. S. V.*) is slander, false accusation. "Shameful speaking" seems to refer to abusive and therefore impure language. Thus the tongue is sure to show the true character of its owner; and just as its physical appearance is a gauge of bodily health, so the proper use of it in speech is a good sign of the reality of Christian profession (Jas. 3).

One sin in particular was rife in those days and is not unknown now, even among Christians, that of lying (v. 9), and the ground on which this is to be avoided is especially interesting. It was evidently a prominently characteristic feature of the old life of these particular people. A similar

---

[4]Also known as *Holy Bible with Commentary*, edited by F. C. Cook.
[5]Vol. 12, p. 567.

appeal is made in Ephesians 4:25, where the readers are to tell the truth because of their relation to fellow-Christians, while here it is to be because of the believer's relation to Christ. Once again, as in Ephesians 4:22, Paul states that something had actually happened to them and he exhorts them, therefore, to do something definite. They had put off the unregenerate self (v. 9) and put on the regenerate self (v. 10); this was settled at their conversion. We shall see also that besides putting off the doings of the old life (v. 8) there was to be a putting on of the finest elements of the new (v. 12; cf. Rom. 13:14).

This reference to the former unconverted state in contrast with their new position is very impressive and demands thorough study. It was a contrast between sin and Christ, between old and new, and every day this regenerate self, all that the believer was in Christ, was continually being renewed "unto knowledge" (*A. S. V.*), which means, of course, spiritual perception or experience, after the likeness of the Creator Himself. The reference seems clearly to be to the original creation (Gen. 1:26, 27), so that we may express the analogy in this verse as the spiritual man, in the believer's heart, approximating, as time goes on, the primal man, Adam, created in God's own image and according to His standard. As the new birth is a re-creation in God's image, so the subsequent life is a deepening of the image thus engraved; and Christ Himself, as we have already seen, is called "the image of the invisible God" (1:15).

5. The Identification (v. 11). St. Paul now proceeds to show that under these new conditions certain distinctions had been done away. In fact, the word "cannot" (*A. S. V.*) shows the absolute impossibility of any such differences being maintained in the Christian life. The first two are national—"Greek and Jew"; the second two are religious—"circumcision and uncircumcision"; the third two are racial, "barbarian, Scythian"; and the fourth two are social, "bondman, freeman." To the Jew the human race was divided into two classes, Jews and Greeks, circumcision and uncircumcision, each of which scorned the other; while to the Greek (or Roman) the whole world was similarly divided into Greeks (or Romans) and "barbarians." We are told that of these barbarians the Scythians were regarded as one of the lowest types; and it is notable that Cicero classes Scythians with Britons. The reference "bond or free" is especially important in view of the question of slavery in the days of St. Paul, and more particularly because of the fact that one of the messengers who carried this Epistle to Colosse was a runaway slave who was being sent back to his master (4:7-9; Philem. 1-25; see Part II, pp. 149ff). The distinction of bond and free being destroyed in Christ, Philemon was to receive back Onesimus as a beloved brother. The very fact that no word is spoken in the New Testament about the general emancipation of slaves is a striking testimony to the essential truth of oneness in Christ; but of course the abolition of slavery has grown out of this fundamental truth of Christianity, viz., that all are one in Christ. The one and only uniting element was this One who was "all, and in all."

These are simple yet searching principles for today. Are they applicable to us? Are we true to one another? Do we realize what is involved in having "put off the old man" and "put on the new"? Is Christ supreme in our lives and does He mean everything to us? Can we declare that

> To all my vileness, Christ is Glory Bright;
> To all my miseries, Infinite Delight;
> To all my ignorance, Wise without compare;
> To my deformity, the Eternal Fair;
> Sight to my blindness; to my meanness, Wealth;
> Life to my death; and to my sickness, Health;
> To darkness, Light; my Liberty in thrall.
> What shall I say? My Christ is All in All!

In this vitally important and very practical passage addressed to the Colossian Christians, we notice: (1) The threefold call. They were to put to death their members (v. 5); they were to put off all that was wrong in word and deed (v. 8); and they were to realize that they had put on Christ (v. 10). This is followed by (2) The threefold reason. They must remember the certainty of divine judgment on sin (v. 6); they had put away their old habits (v. 9); and they should be enjoying their new position of oneness in Christ and fellowship with Him and with each other (v. 11). Thus they had a new life, a new principle, and a new creed.

> A Way He is to lost ones who have strayed;
> A Robe He is to such as naked be;
> Is any hungry? To all such He's Bread;
> Is any weak? To Him new Strength is He;
> To him that's dead He's Life; to sick man Health;
> Eyes to the blind, and to the poor man Wealth.

THE POSITIVE EXPRESSION OF THE CHRISTIAN LIFE (vv. 12-14)

As in so many departments of life, after the negative comes the positive in Christian living. Not only is the believer to put off the evils of the old life, he is also to put on the graces of the new life. Having "put on the new man" (v. 10), it is necessary to think of the clothes he is to wear, the virtues in which he is to show his new life. In these verses and the ones immediately following, a number of aspects of Christian character and conduct are graphically presented for practical realization.

1. The Spiritual Attire (vv. 12, 13). Believers are described as "God's elect, holy and beloved" (v. 12, *A.S.V.*), or, the chosen, consecrated objects of divine affection, and they are exhorted to clothe themselves with various appropriate elements of the spiritual life (cf. Isa. 61:3, 10). The figure of clothing is found in several other New Testament passages (e.g., Rom. 13:14), and here in Colossians some very beautiful garments are mentioned. The first necessity is "a heart of compassion" (*A.S.V.*), because if the affections are right everything else should follow. Then will come "kindness," the opposite of harshness and severity (cf. v. 8); and the next feature will be "humbleness of mind," or "lowliness" (*A.S.V.*)—the real thing as distinct from the unreal (cf. 2:18, 23). This will express itself in "meekness" and "longsuffering," the very opposite of conduct that is rude and overbearing (cf. v. 8). Sir William Ramsay has called attention to the frequency with which St. Paul brings together the two ideas of meekness and lowliness (e.g., Eph. 4:2), as though this were an echo of our Lord's well-known words (Matt. 11:28-30). Those who are humble in mind will naturally be slow to resent wrongs and will never for an instant contemplate revenge (I Peter 5:5, 6). Dr. C. H. Mackintosh tells us that "the way to be truly humble is to walk with God in the intelligence and power of the relationship in which He has set us. He has made us His children; and if only we walk as such we shall be humble."

> Oh! learn that it is only by the lowly
>   The paths of peace are trod;
> If thou would'st keep thy garments white and holy
>   Walk humbly with thy God.

Keeping up the figure of attire, it is noteworthy that so great a prominence is given to the spirit of forbearance and forgiveness, as though it were a double robe or lined outer garment (v. 13a). The Greek word translated forbearance literally means "holding oneself back from another," that is, in self-control under provocation; and both here and elsewhere (e.g., Eph. 4:32; Luke 6:32-37), the opposite or out-going Christian grace of forgiveness is made very prominent. It is plainly stated that in all matters for complaint or blame a true readiness to forgive should be demonstrated, especially since it is the logical outcome of our Lord's forgiveness of His own (v. 13b; cf. Matt. 6:12, 14, 15), which is to be our example. As the poet William Cowper quaintly wrote of marriage:

> The kindest and the happiest pair
> Will find occasion to forbear;
> And something, every day they live,
> To pity, and perhaps forgive.

113

Thus we may distinguish seven separate yet connected portions of this "clothing," constituting a fine manifestation of worthy Christian living. To be found "wearing" this, we might say, is to be "well dressed," and "in the fashion" of Christ (Phil. 3:21), or, to adopt the apostle's opposite metaphor, to provide a constant recommendation of the gospel by "adorning" it (Titus 2:10).

2. The Uniting Band (v. 14). Again the figure of clothing is used, and reference is made to the "bond" or girdle by which the robes of an Eastern man were gathered about his waist. Over all these spiritual "garments" the Colossian Christians were to "put on love" (*A.S.V.*), as that which binds all the rest together and makes them one. It is interesting that a girdle is spoken of in three Pauline passages: the girdle of truth (Eph. 6:14); the girdle of peace (Eph. 4:3); and, here, the girdle of love, which is called "the bond of perfectness." Love is regarded as the means of uniting and holding together all the elements of the true believer's life, the various Christian graces already mentioned; and it will lead to the ripeness or maturity which is the invariable meaning of the New Testament word for perfection. Love is thus recognized as supreme, related as it is to everything else in the Christian life: to knowledge (Phil. 1:9; I John 4:7, 8); to faith (Gal. 5:6); to obedience (John 14:15); to intercession (II Cor. 9:14; Phil. 1:3-7; II Tim. 1:1-3); and to service (II Cor. 5:14; Gal. 5:13, 14; Heb. 6:10). This is indeed "the love of God" Himself which, St. Paul elsewhere tells us, has been "shed abroad in our hearts through the Holy Spirit which was given unto us" (Rom. 5:5, *A.S.V.*).

> I want that adorning Divine
>   Thou only, my God, canst bestow;
> I want in those beautiful garments to shine
>   Which distinguish Thy household below.
>
> I want every moment to feel
>   That Thy Spirit resides in my heart,
> That His power is present to cleanse and to heal
>   And newness of life to impart.
>
> I want, oh, I want to attain
>   Some likeness, my Saviour, to Thee,
> That longed-for resemblance once more to regain
>   And Thy comeliness put upon me.
>
> I want Thine own hand to unbind
>   Each tie to terrestrial things
> Too tenderly cherished, too closely entwined,
>   Where my heart too tenaciously clings.

> I want—and this sums up my prayer—
> To glorify Thee till I die;
> Then calmly to yield up my soul to Thy care
> And breathe out, in faith, my last sigh!
>
> —Charlotte Elliott

THE SAFEGUARD OF THE CHRISTIAN LIFE (vv. 15-17)

Now come three exhortations that prove still further the reality of the change in living already described (vv. 9-11). The future for the Christian may be thought of here, as elsewhere, as a pilgrim experience. He has already been, so to speak, in a dressing room where he has first undressed (vv. 8, 9), and then dressed himself suitably (vv. 10, 12, 14), and now he is ready for his journey, except for a threefold need: a compass—"the peace of Christ" (v. 15, *A.S.V.*); a staff—"the word of Christ" (v. 16); and a passport—"the name of the Lord Jesus" (v. 17).

1. The Peace of Christ (v. 15, *A.S.V.*). Of all the titles of God, the one used most frequently by St. Paul is "the God of peace," and it may be said without much fear of contradiction that peace is the deepest need of man. This may be noted throughout Scripture (e.g., Lev. 3:1-11; Num. 6:26; Ps. 29:11; Prov. 3:19; Luke 1:70; 2:14; John 14:27; Acts 10:36; and all through the Epistles). What, then, is "the peace of Christ"? The Greek word signifies a pact, an agreement, a bond, while the Hebrew one speaks of rest, security. Both these senses of the English translation suggest a conscious possession of (1) divine pardon, including sins forgiven, burdens lifted, and condemnation removed; (2) divine justification, reinstatement, imputation of righteousness; and (3) the divine presence, with the fellowship and indwelling of the living Christ.

What does the peace of Christ do? Primarily it gives assurance of acceptance with God (cf. Rom. 5:1), and the protection of God (cf. Phil. 4:7, Gr., "shall garrison," a paradoxical use of a warlike term). But here Christ's peace is to be received into the heart as the arbiter deciding the course and ruling the life (Gr., "umpire"). A similar idea and practically the same Greek word is found in 2:18, as we have seen, where the apostle is warning his readers not to let anyone judicially deprive them of their reward as though they were unworthy. This word, translated here "rule," suggests that which settles differences, especially where there is any conflict of thoughts and feelings. Under such circumstances "the peace of Christ" is to decide; and if it be asked how peace is able to do this perhaps the explanation is that just as peace with God is the result of our acceptance of Christ as Savior (Rom. 5:1), so the experience of peace in the soul, in union with Christ and through the presence of the Holy Spirit, will at once settle every difficulty, resolve every conflict, and show us what is the will of God. In this case there is a special reason for such divine peace–the essential unity of the body of Christ, the Church, and to this peace, we are told, every believer has been called. When we are one with Christ, in whom God "called us with an holy calling" (II Tim. 1:9), and also one with Christians, "called in one body," as Paul says here, there is no question as to the great power of divine peace in our lives. We read of "government and peace" (Isa. 9:7), of "righteousness and peace" (Ps. 85:10; cf. Isa. 32:17), and of "grace . . . and peace" (Titus 1:4). Until these prevail universally, however, "the God of peace himself" (I Thess. 5:23, *A.S.V.*) will be with us, keeping us meanwhile "in perfect peace" (Isa. 26:3).

When the apostle adds, "and be ye thankful," he means, in Lightfoot's suggestive phrase, "and to crown all, forget yourselves in thanksgiving towards God" (Lightfoot, *Colossians,* p. 22). True thankfulness, being part of the very essence of the Christian life, will be the natural and inevitable outcome of Christ's peace in the heart. In proportion as we appreciate that which God has done for us and is now to us in Christ we shall realize the divine power for true Christian living (I Thess. 5:18).

2. The Word of Christ (v. 16). The next exhortation refers to "the word of Christ," which we are to allow to dwell in us, accepted by a trustful heart, welcomed by a surrendered will, and obeyed by a loyal life (cf. Ps. 119:165). It is not enough to be taught the truth (cf. John 8:37); we must possess it as a present, personal experience. It is to be "in" us as abiding in our hearts, dwelling in us as in a home where we are consciously to make room for it (cf. Ps. 119:11). As someone has written, "It should not be treated as a stranger or slave, at a distance, but received as an intimate guest." It is to abide in us "richly," or plentifully, in all the variety of its wealth and power (1:27; 2:2; I Tim. 6:17; Titus 3:6, *A.S.V.*). If we follow the King James Version's punctuation, we may say that Christ's word is also to dwell in us "in all wisdom," so that we may know thereby how to live and how to help others live. Certainly, it is in proportion as we meditate on God's Word and fill our minds with its truth that we shall have the consciousness of power and the means of blessing; for everything in the Christian life is in one way or another associated with the Word of God.

But if, in agreement with several great authorities, we make two slight but natural changes in sentence construction, we may connect the words "in all wisdom" with what follows instead of with what goes before. This is how the verse will read according to this suggestion: "Let the word of Christ dwell in you richly; in all wisdom teaching and admonishing one another; with psalms and hymns and spiritual songs singing with grace in your hearts unto God" (*A. S. V.*). The twofold task of teaching and of warning others is very important, and it naturally follows from the possession of Christ's word in our hearts (cf. 1:27, 28). Only as that word is dwelling in all of us abundantly can we be wise enough safely and truly to be the means of blessing to our fellow-believers, and they to us.

The teaching of the Word, moreover, will lead to praise, for even though we may have nothing within us that the world calls musical, we shall be able to sing in our hearts because of the divine grace coming from the Word abiding there. Whatever we can or cannot do with the lips, our whole being will in one way or another manifest itself to God's praise and glory.

This music will take various forms so as to be used in the "teaching and admonishing" of ourselves and of others. The apostle's reference to "psalms and hymns and spiritual songs" seems to indicate something of the corporate life of the early Church, although it is not easy to distinguish these three forms of praise one from another. Perhaps the word "psalms" refers to the Hebrew Psalter, and the word "hymns" to Christian compositions, while the third phrase would naturally include the other two and yet go further in describing all forms of song, so long as they were "spiritual" in nature. No statement is made that the singing of these songs is to be referred, still less limited, to public services of worship, and so perhaps there is included the idea of joyous fellowship at family and other social gatherings, suggesting that praise to God was to be characteristic of the daily life of the believer. There can be no doubt, certainly, that this singing flows from the soul's personal fellowship with Christ and expresses its emotions when alone with Him. It means that the consciousness of God's saving and keeping grace fills the heart with such joy and peace that it cannot but rejoice before Him. Surely it is a fine test of our spiritual condition if our lips are mouthpieces of grace, whether by singing, as here, or by speaking (cf. 4:6).

3. The Name of Christ (v. 17). From the heart the apostolic thought reaches out as widely as possible, to the entire life, and everything is included in an all-embracing twofold principle of doing all "in the Name of the Lord Jesus" and "giving thanks to God the Father through Him." Christianity is a religion, and the Bible a book, not of rules but of principles. It is easy to prefer rules, but life is too intricate for them to be universally set up and applied. Further, principles develop the personality by requiring thought and application, so that, while rules are primarily for children, men and women are better served by principles, and specifically Christian men and women by Christian principles. The Christian minister, likewise, is to be not a director, but an adviser and exemplar, in spite of the very human longing for a definite chart on the one hand, or an escape from responsibility on the other. Here the principle laid down is that everything is to be done "in the name of the Lord Jesus."

"Whatsoever ye do" is a searching phrase found three times in the New Testament (see also v. 23; I Cor. 10:31). Here it has to do with the "name," or revealed character, according to Scripture usage, of the Lord Jesus Christ, and means that the life is to be lived in relation to His authority and in reliance upon His ability in every situation. As we shall see further on, we are told in verse 23 to do everything "heartily," or "from the soul itself" (Gr.), as though directly to the Lord and not, therefore, with an eye to human approval. Writing to the Corinthians, St. Paul says that all is to be done "to the glory of God" (I Cor. 10:31)—that is, with a view to His splendor and majesty. Putting all three references together, we see unmistakably the mark of the true follower of Christ, one who performs all his duties in union with his Savior and in the consciousness that his very soul belongs to the One who died that he might live, and to whom is to be ascribed all the glory for so great a salvation. This will surely take care of life's details, embracing all things, for it is a dominating principle that can be universally applied. It means a participation in the joy of conscious salvation and fellowship and an adequate inspiration for all acceptable service.

We are also to give thanks through our Lord to the Father for all things. Thus we again see the importance and the power of thanksgiving (cf. v. 15). One theologian has summed up this verse as giving us (1) the sphere of Christian duty—"whatsoever ye do"; (2) the principle of Christian living—"do all in the name of the Lord Jesus"; and (3) the tone of Christian service—"giving thanks unto God and the Father by him." Thus no part of our life must be lived apart from our Master or without regard for its relationship to our heavenly Father through Him.

In all of this we have a wonderful picture of Christian living. It is most significant that, while some of the verbs are in the Greek aorist tense, which invariably refers to a definite act, others are in the present tense, which always indicates a continuous action. Thus the former speaks of the Christian position and principle, and the latter of the Christian process and progress; and the one speaks of being "in Christ," and the other of being "for Christ."

1. The Christian Position. This is indicated by the words "God's elect, holy and beloved" (v. 12, *A.S.V.*), namely, what the Christian is in the divine sight. He is chosen of God, consecrated for God, and loved by God; and all this comes through his union with Christ.

2. The Christian Process. The thought of clothing in this section (cf. vs. 12-14) emphasizes the need of a proper outward appearance and the duty of maintaining a seemly conduct. As clothes are an indication of personality, so the expression of inward graces and the impression they convey will show unmistakably "whose we are and whom we serve." Thus there will be not only an experience of justification—Christ for us; of sanctification—Christ in us; but also of manifestation—Christ through us.

3. *The Christian Principle.* To bring about these elements of Christian experience there is a solemn requirement, viz., a deeper knowledge of "the peace" (v. 15), "the word" (v. 16), and "the name" (v. 17) through which we are to be and do "whatsoever" shall bring glory to God. Two great means to this end are the study of the Word—"whatsoever he saith" (John 2:5)—and prayer—"whatsoever ye shall ask" (John 16:23). These are high ideals, and the higher the ideal, of course, the greater the need of power for realization. When we enter fully into the real meaning of Christ's peace, Christ's Word, and Christ's name, we shall have learned the secret of true life in Him.

This marvelous passage may be usefully summed up by noting its concern with the person of our Lord Jesus Christ: (1) We are risen with the ascended Christ; (2) we are hid with Christ (v. 3); (3) we are to appear with Christ (v. 4); (4) Christ is our all, and He is in all (v. 11); (5) we have the forgiveness of Christ (v. 13); (6) we are to have the peace of Christ (v. 16); and (7) we are to do all in the name of Christ (v. 17).

Thus our union with Christ is not only the basis of our spiritual position, but it is also the source, the secret, the satisfaction, and the strength of our spiritual state in its every detail. There will be identification with Christ, occupation with Christ, appropriation of Christ, and manifestation of Christ. Therefore we see once again that, indeed, "Christ is all."

8 THE PROOF OF THE CHRISTIAN LIFE

Like all of St. Paul's Epistles, this one addressed to the believers at Colosse is characterized by a close association between the two aspects of doctrine and duty, character and conduct, principle and practice. Indeed, we may say that in those very Epistles that are most closely concerned with great doctrines regarding the Lord Jesus Christ (as are Romans, Colossians and its companion Epistle to the Ephesians), the apostle is more than ordinarily careful to press home the practical duties arising out of these great truths.

The Christian life is social as well as personal, communal as well as individual, and the same principles are intended for both spheres. In fact, social relations are among the very best opportunities we have of revealing our true Christianity and of showing how genuine is our holiness. Does our experience of Christ have power to enable? "By their fruits ye shall know them," declared our Lord (Matt. 7:20). Or, in this age of pragmatism, it may simply be asked of our profession, Does it work? These social applications of the gospel are now emphasized for our most serious consideration.

HOME LIFE (3:18 – 4:1)

As urged by the apostle elsewhere, the Christians of those early days were to "shew piety at home" (I Tim. 5:4; cf. Titus 2:5), and thereby to prove to all who knew them the reality and power of their spiritual life.

121

Once when a question was asked as to whether a certain man was a Christian, the reply given was, "I do not know; I have never lived with him." Three ordinary but striking instances are used here, expressive of the three main social relationships of life.

1. Wives and Husbands (vv. 18, 19).

a. Wives are exhorted to submission (v. 18). Bishop Moule renders this word as "loyalty" because he feels that it suggests better the ideal of a wife's attitude, which recognizes "a God-appointed leadership" and yet is not, in the strict sense of the term, service (Moule, *Colossian Studies,* pp. 234, 235, footnotes). The service rendered by a slave, or even by a faithful servant or employee, is quite different from the loving devotion and loyal co-operation of a wife to a husband (cf. Rom. 6:14-23 with 7:1-6). In any case, however, this appeal is in no sense contradictory to the essential oneness of male and female in Christ (Gal. 3:28), because grace never contravenes nature. Nor is there anything incongruous with or inappropriate to Christian womanhood, because "order is heaven's first law" in every sphere of life (see I Cor. 11:3). Besides, this exhortation is pointed by the significant words, "as is fitting in the Lord" (v. 18, *A.S.V.*), and enforced by the wife's personal relationship to Christ. This is at once the warrant and the safeguard of submission; because she is "in the Lord" she is to love loyally as befits that union, for those who are one with Him will readily and gladly fulfill His word to "be one flesh" (Gen. 2:24).

b. Husbands are exhorted to "love" their wives (v. 19). It has often been pointed out that the apostle uses no word here expressive of the opposite of submission, like "ordering" or "commanding." Submission is contrasted, instead, with love, which includes all that a husband should be to a wife, and in this will be found the true secret of married life. This is because here, as elsewhere in the New Testament, love is not a mere feeling but also a fact, not only emotion but devotion, not just an attitude but action, not only sentiment but sacrifice. An added injunction is given— Christian husbands are not to be "bitter" against their wives, thus expressing the absence of all selfishness, ill temper, and inconsiderateness from their lives together, and proving that a truly Christ-like spirit actuates them. Comparison should be made between this and the corresponding but much longer passage in the companion Epistle (Eph. 5:22-33), where the husband's attitude to the wife is especially emphasized as illustrating the relation of Christ to the Church, a very searching parallel indeed.

2. Children and Parents (vv. 20, 21).

a. Children are exhorted to be obedient to their parents in everything, (v. 20). The reason given is again the highest possible one, expressive of their own relation to Christ: "this is well-pleasing unto the Lord." The thought of giving pleasure to our Lord Jesus is a fine and inspiring incentive for boys and girls to obey, one that should make its appeal to the experience of the young.

b. Fathers are not to "provoke" their children (v. 21, A.S.V.). Here is an exhortation that probably proscribes all undue harshness while, of course, maintaining proper authority and discipline. They are to be considerate, for children may easily lose heart through overmuch severity and lack of sympathy; and this condition of mind quickly leads to wrongdoing. All who are associated with young people know how powerful in their training and development is the element of encouragement on the part of an understanding adult.

3. Servants and Masters (3:22 – 4:1). It is striking that this subject is dealt with far more fully than are the other two. Lightfoot (*op. cit.,* p. 226) and Rutherfurd (*St. Paul's Epistles to Colosse and Laodicea,* p. 189) think this is due to the special circumstances connecting this Epistle with Onesimus, the escaped slave being sent back to his master in Colosse (cf. 4:9 with Philem. 10; and see the section of this volume on the Epistle to Philemon, pp. 149). Some writers suggest that, as the relationship of master and slave was not so natural nor so elemental as the others mentioned, it needed a fuller and more urgent treatment. Perhaps both these considerations may have influenced the apostle's writing.

a. Slaves, or servants in general, were called upon for a sevenfold obedience. (1) This was to be a complete obedience—"in all things" (v. 22a)—not exercising any right of judgment. (2) It was to be a genuine obedience, springing from an undivided heart and free from all improper obsequiousness (v. 22b; cf. Matt. 6:24). (3) It was also be a thorough obedience (v. 23a), proceeding from the soul (Gr.) and expressive of all the power of the inner being (cf. I Tim. 6:1, 2). (4) It was also to be a spiritual obedience (v. 23b), the slave being conscious of the Lord Jesus as the One to whom his service was primarily being rendered. (5) Thus it was even an encouraging obedience (v. 24a), since the slave was told that he would be rewarded by Christ, who knew what he was doing and why he was doing it. (6) It was thus an obedience that was really a privileged one (v. 24b), for in serving his earthly master he was actually serving Christ, and this would give special dignity to the humblest service day by day. (7) And yet it must be a righteous obedience, because if the slave did wrong there would be judgment, since God is no respecter of persons (v. 25).

b. The masters were almost certainly included in this last reminder to the slaves. It was all too possible in those days for one of them to do his servant an injustice, and if this should happen in a Christian household the master, too, would be dealt with impartially by an absolutely just God (cf. I Tim. 6:1, 2). This gives special point to the following exhortation to the masters to render to their slaves what was "just and equal" (4:1), inasmuch as they were themselves the servants of a Master in heaven. It is interesting to notice that while the apostle does not say one word about the emancipation of slaves, it was certain to come, as it actually did come, by Christian masters doing that which was "just and equal." Through the application of such fundamental principles and human values, all types of slavery with their attendant evils would be thoroughly and permanently undermined and destroyed, and this is still true today.

Thus, on the one hand, in rendering obedience to those in authority, there is to be sincerity, thoroughness, and honor; and on the other hand, in receiving it, there is to be integrity, impartiality, and intelligence.

The *reality* of home life is here especially emphasized, so that it is impossible to exaggerate the value of a truly Christian family; indeed, "there's no place like home"—the Christian home. It is Christianity more than any other influence that has made possible pure, loving, and unselfish home life, but the requirements for it are few and simple, as may be seen from this passage. No home needs an elaborate set of rules to realize even its highest function. If parents, children, and those who serve them in any capacity carry out what is so clearly set forth here, there will be no question as to the peace and joy, blessing and influence of Christian homes everywhere.

But the most striking feature of all is the *relationship* of home life to our Lord. Seven times over this thought of everything being done in His sight is presented in this passage. Wives are to submit "in the Lord" (v. 18); children are to obey as "unto the Lord" (v. 20); servants are to be "fearing the Lord" (v. 22, *A.S.V.*) while they work "as to the Lord" (v. 23); they will receive their reward "from the Lord" (v. 24, *A.S.V.*); and they "serve the Lord Christ" (v. 24), just as their masters are to be impartial because they, too, have "a Master in heaven" (4:1). This is the great principle underlying all the domestic duties implied here.

The *result* of all this in home life is a significant contrast between pleasing men and fearing God, and it has many additional applications today. For example, if only our service to those above us in business, and their attitude to us, were actuated solely by this principle of our relationship to God, it would make a vast difference in much that is done. We would all be working "from the soul" (v. 23, *A.S.V.*, marg.), remembering that our supreme Master is not an earthly one but a heavenly. While there is no merit attached to our work for Christ, there is to be from His hand a blessed and adequate reward of faithfulness.

> O Master dear, the tiniest work for Thee
> Finds recompense beyond our highest thought,
> And feeble hands that work but tremblingly
> The richest colors in Thy fabric wrought.

> We are content to take what Thou shalt give,
> To do, to suffer, as Thy choice shall be;
> Forsaking all, Thy wisdom bids us live
> Glad in the thought that we are pleasing Thee.

Thus in these three great realms of home life the apostle emphasizes truths that will produce righteousness and truth, faithfulness and devotion in our most intimate relationships. Faith makes all things possible; love makes all things easy; hope makes all things bright; and grace makes all things sure. And so not only salvation and sanctification, but sympathy, submission, and service are all associated with "the life that is Christ."

PERSONAL LIFE (4:2-6)

The apostolic appeal now takes a more general turn and, after the doctrinal teaching and the social counsels, St. Paul deals with the personal life of all believers.

1. An Appeal for Earnest Prayer (vv. 2-4). There are several elements in this exhortation.

a. Continuance (v. 2). The apostle urges constancy in prayer, the value of which surely finds its best proof in the Christian's determination to continue its exercise; for thereby he shows both his need of those things which God alone can give and his faith that God will hear. The Greek word employed is singularly interesting and illuminating when its New Testament usage is studied. For instance, the earliest believers "continued" regularly in the temple (Acts 2:46); Simon "continued" with Philip (Acts 8:13); the little boat of the disciples was to wait on our Lord "continually" (Mark 3:9, *Gr.*). These passages all suggest persistence and perseverance, that which Maclaren helpfully describes as "the idea of close adherence as well as of uninterrupted companionship," implying "both earnestness and continuity" (Maclaren, *Expositor's Bible, St. Paul's Epistles to the Colossians and Philemon,* p. 355). This is no doubt the meaning of what is often described as "the Spirit of prayer," or "the practice of the presence of God." It of necessity cannot mean a continuous raising of petitions to the exclusion of other duties and the care of physical needs, but, as someone has remarked, whatever may be the attitude of the body, the soul should be always on its knees. Just as uninterrupted breathing is the natural expression and necessary function of our bodies, so is constant prayer to our souls; and this attitude should nurture in the believer such spiritual elements as submission, desire, trust, fellowship, steadfastness. But in the midst of the bustle of modern life and the stress and strain of our work, there is a tendency to crowd out prayer when, beyond all else, we need it to apply God's power to that work and to fill our lives with His peace and joy. Prayer also has a wonderful way of cleansing our insight and illuminating His Word, and so making light our labor for Him "whose service is perfect freedom." Thus by means of a strong prayer-life we shall find God's presence real, His power felt, His will clear, His service easy.

b. Watchfulness (v. 2). The association of this with prayer is significant. The verb is the one employed by Christ in Gethsemane in reproving the disciples (Matt. 26:38, 40, 41), and it implies an emphasis on alertness and the avoidance of drowsiness or sluggishness. It is to be noted that nowhere are we told *what* or *whom* to watch, since the verb, though in the active voice, is invariably found without the customary definite object. We are not to watch self, for that is too *delusive;* we are not to watch Satan, for he is too *elusive;* we are not to watch circumstances, for they are too *illusive.* Perhaps the absence of any object for this word "watch" means that we are to keep our gaze fixed on Christ, "looking off unto Jesus" (Heb. 12:2, *Gr.*) as we work and as we wait for His return. Being occupied with Him, we shall be enabled to see all that is necessary for us to see, and this will be *conclusive;* and we shall be neither depressed by ourselves and our sins, distracted by our foes, nor disheartened by our surroundings. Then we can say with the psalmist, "In thy light shall we see light" (Ps. 36:9).

c. Thankfulness (v. 2). Praying and watching are to be connected with thanksgiving. This is the fifth time this duty of grateful expression has been emphasized in this short Epistle (cf. 1:12; 2:7; 3:15; 3:17), and it is impossible to exaggerate its importance either here or elsewhere in the New Testament (e.g., Eph. 5:4, 20; I Thess. 5:18). This feature of the apostle's own spiritual life, indeed, is most impressive; and there is no doubt that its absence from ours is invariably a result of weak faith and a cause of faint hope. His words are a reminder that our hearts should be fairly overflowing with praise, for thanksgiving will inevitably lead to what has been called "thanksliving."

d. Intercession (vv. 3, 4). The appeal for watchful, thankful prayer was intended to include remembrance of the apostle's needs as well (cf. Eph. 6:18, 20), and this would prevent his readers' petitions from becoming self-centered. He was an ambassador of the gospel "in bonds" (v. 3; cf. Eph. 6:20; Phil. 1:13), and he desired that nevertheless God would give him unhindered opportunity, "a door for the word" (*A.S.V.*), that he might proclaim "the mystery of Christ" to all who came near him. St. Paul was so conscious of the supreme necessity for manifesting this gospel (v. 4; cf. I Cor. 9:16) that he sought prayer in order that he might be enabled to do it as he was bound to do. As H. W. Hinde has said, "St. Paul was evangelizing, and he called on the Colossians to make prayer their business, and his work the subject of their prayer. No one would say that St. Paul was not a man of prayer himself, but as they could not do that part of the work of the Church which he was doing he would have them help by giving constant attention to prayer. His business was evangelization, theirs prayer." In the same way, today's minister of the gospel, while stirring up his people to greater efforts in service, ought not to neglect the setting before them of prayer as a vital part of the work of the Church. Intercessory prayer should be an important element of our personal life, especially that God's ministers may be blessed in their work. Indeed, there are few means of usefulness more valuable and powerful than that of intercession for our fellow-workers, for it will bring down divine grace on their hearts and lives as well as on our own. On one occasion the late Charles Haddon Spurgeon, when asked the secret of his successful ministry, replied simply, "My people pray for me." In no mere poetic or theoretical sense, but in blessed, practical reality, the words of Lord Tennyson are still true: "More things are wrought by prayer than this world dreams of." But do we realize that souls may be kept back from Christ through our lack of prayer? Do we know that omission or too early cessation of intercessory prayer is actually a sin (cf. I Sam. 12:23)?

2. **An Appeal for Consistent Conduct (v. 5).** Now the apostolic counsels turn to the outward life of the Colossian Christians, with special reference to those persons who are not yet believers, and St. Paul urges his readers to "walk in wisdom," "redeeming the time." The description of the unconverted as "them that are without" (cf. Mark 4:11; I Cor. 5:12), in evident contrast with those who are safely within, is at once significant and very sad, because the unbeliever is not only outside the Church, but he is without God, without Christ, without hope (cf. Eph. 2:12), and therefore without true joy or real power. To be outside one's home is sometimes to be in darkness, in danger, in storm and stress, in loneliness; and when men and women are outside the family of God they are also without fellowship, in constant peril, and in the unutterable darkness of sin. This impressive phrase, therefore, should often strike home to us who are within, and make its solemn and searching appeal for prayer and for effort. Here the apostle suggests two characteristics of Christian conduct.

a. Wisdom. The Christian walk is an important feature of the Epistles, and to "walk in wisdom" means consciously to live the Christian life so as to impress and win those who are "without," that is, outside the unspeakable privileges of grace that motivate and empower the believer. Someone has said that "the Christian is the worldlings' Bible, and sometimes they will read no other." Certainly there can be no doubt that we are continually being watched by those who are not yet followers of Christ, in order to see whether there is any reality in our profession. Bishop Moule makes an impressive point on this passage. He tells of a man who was "totally sceptical" and who, while not unwilling to listen to Christian witness, was made to stumble by the listless air of a certain congregation. He later told of asking himself as he left the church, "Can these Christians possess any secret better than my reason gives me?" (Moule, *Colossian Studies,* p. 261.).

b. Earnestness. The English phrase "redeeming the time" means in the original "buying up the opportunity," which suggests letting no fleeting chance to witness be lost, but instead using every occasion wisely to impress and, if possible, lead to Christ "them that are without." As Lightfoot, referring to the corresponding passage in Ephesians 5:16, says, "The prevailing evil of the times makes the opportunities for good more precious" (Lightfoot, *Colossians,* p. 230).

3. An Appeal for Wholesome Speech (v. 6). Again the tongue is emphasized (cf. 3:8) as an essential instrument of the Christian life, to show that words as well as works need to be true to Christ. Speech was not merely to be pleasant, but to be marked by divine grace; and being "seasoned with salt" meant having such a spiritual flavor that it would never be flat or unprofitable, but forceful and telling, free from all evil, and capable of inspiring others with moral and spiritual blessings (cf. Matt. 5:13). When a Christian bears gracious witness, brightly and yet not lightly, his words will be a blessing to those around him and a testimony to "the God of all grace" (I Peter 5:10), and to the gospel of the grace of God (cf. Acts 20:24).

So today, our speech should be useful, never trivial, helpful, never flippant, forceful, never feeble. Since many of those around us desire to know what Christianity really means, our careful and capable discussion of its serious issues will enable them to understand it better (cf. I Peter 3:15).

We have seen here something of the completeness of the Christian life. This life has its relation to God, of course (v. 2), but also its relation to man—in prayer, in deed, and in word (vv. 3-6). This is the meaning of the word "consistent," which implies something that stands firmly and well all around. Our witness must have no weakness or failure in it such as the unconverted might use as a reason for continuing to neglect or to reject the gospel. It can only be when we pray with perseverance, walk in wisdom, and talk with grace that we shall be of any use to them or show whose we are and whom we serve (cf. Acts 27:23).

This is only possible by the grace of God in response to trust and obedience. It was this same apostle who said elsewhere: "By the grace of God I am what I am: and his grace which was bestowed upon me was not in vain" (I Cor. 15:10); and the same grace is available for us if only we are ready to yield ourselves to God in wholehearted surrender (cf. II Cor. 9:8). Then He must and will be glorified through the notable consistency of our personal lives.

CHURCH LIFE (vv. 7-18)

Now, having considered St. Paul's exhortations to the Colossians as to their personal and social life, it is interesting to catch a glimpse of their church life through his individual greetings. Although we shall study these more fully in the following chapter under the last main heading of our outline, it is possible here, through a general view of them, to see something of the beauty of first-century Christian intercourse. These twelve verses refer (1) to the bearers of the Epistle (vv. 7-9); (2) to the brethren who were remaining in Rome with Paul (vv. 10-14); (3) to some special friends at Laodicea and one at Colosse (vv. 15-17); and (4) to himself as he penned his own personal valediction (v. 18).

In all these verses we should carefully note the great variety of description, for something specific is said or implied about each person mentioned. When the various points are pondered, separately and together, they give us an exquisite picture of the Christian life as it must have been lived in such early Church circles. Among its finest elements were confidence and comfort (vv. 7-11); intercession and assurance (v. 12); zeal and large-heartedness (vv. 13, 14); reciprocity and fellowship (vv. 15, 16); and exhortation and mutual remembrance (vv. 17, 18).

To sum up, all ideals, whether personal, social, or ecclesiastical, need some type of power for realization; and it is obvious that the higher the ideal the greater is the need of power. The secret of realizing our Christian ideals rests, of course, in the person and work of our Lord Jesus Christ, mediated to us by the Holy Spirit. The specific form of this divine power needed in the present instance is to be found in the two verses immediately preceding all these practical exhortations (cf. 3:16, 17): (1) The Word of Christ is to dwell richly in us; and (2) the name of the Lord Jesus is that in which we are to do everything. Thus, when we enter fully into the real meaning of Christ's Word and Christ's name, we have learned the secret of the practical realization of the highest possible ideals.

9 THE PERSONAL CONCLUSION

St. Paul's personal relations with those with whom he labored and with those to whom he wrote are always interesting and instructive. Indeed, the word-pictures of his friends are among the most helpful parts of his Epistles. Those who have read that delightful book *The Companions of St. Paul*, by Dean Howson, will know what profit can be derived from a study of the various references to those who were associated with the apostle. Only brief descriptions are given, as a rule, but these are sufficient to indicate the characters of his companions, and what St. Paul thought of them. Here in Colossians we have a galaxy of workers whom we shall do well to consider one by one, dividing this closing passage of the Epistle under four headings:

MESSAGES THROUGH THE BEARERS OF THE EPISTLE (vv. 7-9)

St. Paul was sending Tychicus (vv. 7, 8) and Onesimus (v. 9) to tell the Colossian Christians about himself; but his beautiful descriptive phrases regarding these two messengers also indicate what should be the relations between fellow workers when truly "in the Lord," the blessed sphere in whom all believers live and labor.

1. Tychicus (vv. 7, 8). He is mentioned five times in the New Testament, first in Acts 20:4, 5, as a companion on Paul's third missionary journey, then here and in Ephesians 6:21, and last of all in Titus 3:12 and

131

in II Timothy 4:12. In all these references we see his close association with the apostle; and it is no wonder that he is here spoken of in a threefold expression of (a) affection—"beloved brother"; (b) approbation—"faithful minister"; and (c) association—"fellowservant" (v. 7). Nor is it surprising that Tychicus should have been sent by St. Paul for the twofold purpose of supplying information about his circumstances to the Colossian Christians, and of encouraging them in their spiritual life (v. 8, *A.S.V.*; cf. Eph. 6:21). The one thought regarding Tychicus which seems to stand out more than anything else is that of faithfulness. Probably he was not brilliant or outstanding, but he was eminently dependable, and this above all was what the apostle needed in such circumstances. The same is true of all our Christian service; God does not seek for certain success or even, necessarily, for unusual ability, but for quiet, humble, genuine faithfulness of heart and life. "Good and faithful servant," Christ says; "Be thou faithful unto death" (Matt. 25:21, 23; Rev. 2:10).

2. **Onesimus (v. 9).** We know from another letter of St. Paul that this was a runaway slave of Philemon's who was being sent back to his master in Colosse, although there is no hint of that here.[1] It seems as though before his flight Onesimus had not been a Christian, but that in coming to Rome he was led to Christ by the apostle. Now, as he was being sent back to his old home, it was necessary for someone to be ready to give evidence of the change that had taken place. This St. Paul does, both here and in his Epistle to Philemon himself. Nothing could be finer than the testimony afforded, nor more delicate than the precise way in which Onesimus is presented to the Christians in Colosse, his former place of residence. He is called the "faithful and beloved brother," words that are almost identical with those used of both Tychicus, his companion on the journey (v. 7), and of Epaphras, the well-known evangelist at Colosse (cf. 1:7). Yes, the former slave in becoming a Christian had also earned the title of brother. He was now to be not only "one of you," the group of believers, but also one with Tychicus, the apostolic companion—"together"—in the ministry of fellowship and sympathy. Furthermore, St. Paul was so anxious that the hearts of the Colossians should be cheered by news of himself that he says: "They shall make known unto you all things which are done here." Thus, at the center of their moral and spiritual lives his readers were to have strength, courage, and consolation through knowledge of God's working elsewhere.

---

[1] For a fuller treatment of this subject, see Part II, The Epistle to Philemon, pp. 149ff.

GREETINGS FROM THE BRETHREN IN ROME (vv. 10-14)

The allusions to the other associates of St. Paul are equally noteworthy. These Christians, together with the two foregoing, have been called "The Comfort Men," for the apostle writes of three of them as men that "have been a comfort unto me" (v. 11); and it is obvious that the fourth, Epaphras, with his fine spiritual gifts, and the fifth, Luke, as St. Paul's "beloved physician" (v. 14), must also have greatly encouraged their leader during his imprisonment.

1. **The Friends of Paul Described (vv. 10-12a, 13, 14).**

a. Aristarchus (v. 10). He was a Hebrew Christian (v. 11) of Thessalonica in Macedonia (Acts 19:29; 20:4), and one of the companions of the second and third missionary journeys. He then accompanied St. Paul on his voyage to Rome as a prisoner (Acts 27:2), and is here called his "fellowprisoner." This must mean either that Aristarchus voluntarily shared the captivity, or else he had been apprehended separately for some reason unknown to us. In any case, he is a sufferer with the apostle and reminds us of how God's will may be done: activity is only one way of serving God for, as John Milton wrote, "they also serve who only stand and wait." It must have been hard for Aristarchus, as we know it was for St. Paul, to be a prisoner, prevented from doing active work for Christ with normal freedom of movement. Those who live in the will of God, however, will find their circumstances, of whatever sort, made subservient to His purposes and even instrumental in their accomplishment.

b. Mark (v. 10). This is a reference, one of eight such in the Acts and the Epistles, to the well-known author of our second Gospel, for which he was early called the "interpreter" of St. Peter's conception of Christ. He was the cousin of Barnabas, and it is thought that his mother's position as the owner of the house where later the Church at Jerusalem evidently met (Acts 1:13; 12:12) may have brought him into contact with actual scenes in the life of our Lord (Mark 14:13-51). Mark was chosen as the personal assistant of Barnabas and Paul on their first missionary journey (Acts 12:25; 13:5), but for some reason he left them on their arrival in Asia Minor. Some think it must have been fear of the hardships in new territory, while others suggest personal feeling because he may have seen his cousin Barnabas being gradually relegated to a subordinate position. Or Mark may simply have had the narrow outlook of the Jerusalem Christians of that period who did not agree with the broad policy of admitting the Gentiles to their fellowship on equal terms (Acts 15:1-6). But, whatever it was, it was evidently a serious flaw in the eyes of St. Paul, for he refused to take Mark on the second journey (Acts 15:36-38).

It is particularly interesting to note this kind allusion to Mark, and even a commendation of him, in the letter to Colosse, where he may well have been going, because it implies that, about eleven years later, the estrangement was at an end (cf. also Philem. 24). Mark had evidently recovered his position and regained the apostle's confidence. Opinions differ as to which leader was right in the matter, Barnabas in his evident partiality, or Paul in his understandable severity (cf. II Tim. 2:3). Perhaps we may say that both were right, for it may well have been that Paul's strictness caused the youthful Mark finally to realize what were the qualities necessary to Christian service, while the natural love of Barnabas gave him encouragement and an opportunity of overcoming his former weakness. It is clear, however, that Mark as a "fellowworker" became a real "comfort" (v. 11) to the apostle, both at this time and subsequently (cf. II Tim. 4:11); and it is thought also that the tone of St. Paul's references to Barnabas, some time after their separation, indicates genuine affection (cf. I Cor. 9:6; Gal. 2:1, 9). It is probable that the reference to Mark by St. Peter (I Peter 5:13) dates from a time after St. Paul's death.

c. Justus (v. 11). Nothing more is known of this man than is told us here, although it is interesting to reflect that one of his names is the hallowed human one of our Lord Himself. He and the two mentioned with him, Aristarchus and Mark, were Jewish Christians—"of the circumcision"—and as such must have been a special gratification to the apostle. It would seem from their being singled out in this way that all the other Jewish Christian leaders in Rome at that time had separated themselves from him and were anything but a comfort. Probably this is what he meant when he referred to the "affliction" that some had added to his bonds (Phil. 1:15, 16). Such a sad state of affairs must have made St. Paul feel still more grateful for this particular encouragement from the three Jewish brethren in Christ whose faithful fellowship had been a real solace in his imprisonment.

d. Epaphras (vv. 12a, 13). The references to Epaphras in this Epistle are particularly striking. During the three years of St. Paul's stay at Ephesus (cf. Acts 20:31), he seems to have been led to Christ and to have carried the gospel to Colosse (cf. 1:7, 8; Acts 19:10), where the apostle himself had never been (2:1). Then Epaphras came to St. Paul in Rome with news of the young church of which he was the evangelist. This news was not altogether favorable, and so Epaphras spent much time in prayer for his converts. As Lightfoot says, he did not return to Colosse as a bearer of this letter, but remained behind with St. Paul as a "fellowprisoner" (Philem. 23); and "it may be inferred that his zeal and affection had involved him in the Apostle's captivity, and that his continuance in Rome was enforced" (Lightfoot, *Colossians,* pp. 34, 35).

The prayer-life of this man will call for more detailed attention under section 2 of this chapter; but we may note here the apostle's fine testimony to his faithfulness. Epaphras was thinking continually of the Asian Christians and working in their behalf (v. 12a), even though he was far away from them. The word rendered "labor" (v. 13, *A.S.V.*) really means keen desire as well as great effort. Furthermore, he was thus burdened not only for Colosse, but for the cities of Laodicea and Hierapolis, so that probably he had been the evangelist to all of these three places in Asia Minor.

e. Luke (v. 14). This, of course, is the author of our third Gospel and of The Acts of the Apostles. He first appears in St. Paul's company at Troas (Acts 16:10); and he went with the apostle to Jerusalem (Acts 20:5, 6; 21:1-18), and also to Rome (Acts 27:1 to 28:16). Now Luke was with his friend while this Epistle was being written; and it is touching later on to observe the words of the great warrior for Christ just before he was beheaded: "Only Luke is with me" (II Tim. 4:11).

It is usually thought that the way in which Luke is here distinguished from the Jewish Christians (cf. v. 11) implies that he was a Gentile; and, if so, he is the only New Testament writer who was not a Jew. Thus two of the four evangelists, Mark and Luke, are among the friends of St. Paul and appear in this passage. Luke is called "the beloved physician," and "my fellowlabourer" (Philem. 24); and very possibly he is the "true yokefellow" of Philippians 4:3. He is often thought to have joined the apostle on account of the latter's malady (cf. II Cor. 12:7), which may have necessitated the frequent attention of a physician. As a medical man, Luke would be a careful, accurate, and accomplished type of person, and something of the sort of scholar and writer he was can be seen from the preface to his Gospel. This shows what he set out to do and the methodical way in which he did it, and it further implies a claim to first-hand, contemporary knowledge of his subject, namely, our Lord as ideal man and Savior of the world. We owe to Luke, under God, the existence of two of the most valuable books in the New Testament, clearly linked together (Acts 1:1). After telling in the first of these that which Jesus "began" to do, until His ascension into heaven, Luke records in his second volume what the risen Lord continued to do afterward by the power of the Holy Spirit through His chosen apostles. We can well appreciate the comfort of his presence, knowledge, and skill to the apostle Paul, especially at this critical time of the first Roman imprisonment.

f. Demas (v. 14). It is impressive and perhaps significant that nothing descriptive is said here about Demas as in the case of the other fellow-workers of St. Paul (Philem. 24). It is possible that already there was a danger of what afterward took place: "Demas hath forsaken me, having loved this present world" (II Tim. 4:10). The contrast between Mark and

Demas is striking; Mark returned but Demas seems not to have done so. Also, the contrast between Luke and Demas, mentioned together here, is equally impressive, the one suggesting faithfulness and strength, the other being associated in our minds with unfaithfulness and weakness.

2. The Prayer of Epaphras Detailed (v. 12b). As a servant of Christ, Epaphras was continually and earnestly engaged in prayer for those whom he had led to his Lord; and this reference to his intercession is important in revealing what was evidently the outstanding feature of his Christian life.

a. The process of the prayer. The greatest service Epaphras could possibly render to these others was to pray for them. Forbes Robertson of Cambridge used to say that, instead of talking with a man, he often found it more profitable to spend half an hour in prayer for him. The exact process by which such intercession brings blessing is, of course, a divine mystery, but it is abundantly clear from Scripture that believers may indeed help each other by prayer, and that even Christian love lacks its deepest significance and greatest force without such mutual remembrance before God. Abraham's prayer for Lot, Christ's prayer for Peter, Paul's prayers for the churches—these all show the value of intercession; and in like manner Epaphras had the welfare of the Colossian Christians ever in mind as he went to the Lord in prayer.

b. The premise of the prayer. The reason why Epaphras was able to pray was that he was "a servant of Jesus Christ." Christians alone can really pray because effectual prayers are only possible when based on the acceptance of the promises of God. Prayer is one of the proofs of the new life: "Behold, he prayeth" (Acts 9:11). Hence this is a service that all believers can render. Epaphras quite evidently could not write the wonderful Epistles of St. Paul, but he could pray, and this we are told he did. Let us therefore be encouraged in this special and blessed work. There are many things outside the experiences of ordinary Christian people, and great position, wide influence, outstanding ability may be lacking for almost all of us; but the humblest and least significant Christian can engage in prayer.

c. The power of the prayer. Further, since "prayer moves the Hand that moves the world," it is obvious that the greatest influence any believer can exert is that which comes through intercession, and so three characteristics are mentioned in connection with the prayer of Epaphras.

It was *earnest* "striving" (*A.S.V.*) for the Colossians. This is the word found in connection with the apostle's own prayers (1:29; 2:1) and is akin to the word translated "agony" and associated with Gethsemane (Luke 22:44). There is in this not so much of our modern idea of pain or anguish, but there is in it assuredly the thought of an athlete, wrestling by putting forth all his strength. This suggests at once the cost of prayer and also the fact that Satanic forces are continually hindering God's people from praying. Be it ours likewise to put all our effort into our prayers and thereby to manifest true spiritual earnestness.

Epaphras was also *persistent* in his prayers, "always striving." He was not content with asking once, but bore these Colossian Christians continually before God. Our Lord had said that "men ought always to pray and never to lose heart" (Luke 18:1, Gr.), and His servant was habitually engaged in this ministry for those who were in great need of spiritual blessing.

The *definiteness* of this prayer should also be noted—"always striving for you" (*A.S.V.*). Epaphras knew those for whom he was praying, and he knew what he wanted for them; and so he made known his requests to God with clearness and force.

This is the kind of prayer—earnest, persistent, definite—that always prevails.

d. The purpose of the prayer. Three words sum up the desire of Epaphras for his friends in Colosse, and they also represent some of the essential elements in Christian character.

(1) Steadfastness of character. He prayed for the Colossians "that ye may stand." There is no doubt that they needed the strength of resistance against error and of persistence in labor for the truth. Many believers are tempted and fall because they are unable to "withstand in the evil day," and many others fail to continue in the Christian life because they lack that perseverance which enables them, "having done all, to stand" (Eph. 6:13).

(2) Maturity of experience. Epaphras also desired his converts to be ripe and mature in the Christian life—"that ye may stand perfect." The word here translated "perfect" is rendered "full-grown" in another of St. Paul's Epistles (I Cor. 2:6), referring to those who are approximating the goal of their spiritual life; and later in the same passage the contrasting thought is of unripeness and immaturity—"babes" (I Cor. 3:1). There is also the solemn thought of the second childhood of those who had gone back from their Christian position (Heb. 5:12, 13) and into what may almost be called overripeness. It is very important here to bear in mind that in the New Testament the word "perfect" never stands for sinlessness, so that there is no allusion whatever in this context to the entire absence of sin. Not only does St. Paul use the word to denote a fully developed or ripening Christian as distinct from a beginner, but our Lord Himself chose it to describe our heavenly Father (Matt. 5:48). In the context of that verse, God is spoken of as sending down His rain on the just and the unjust, being kind indiscriminately to the evil and to the good; and Christ

applies this to His disciples by saying in effect: "Do likewise, not limiting your attentions to the good and beneficent; be mature, rather, as your heavenly Father is." Thus the true Christian will be "perfect" in this sense, realizing the "end" (I Peter 1:9, Gr.), or object, for which he is a follower of Christ. This will mean clearness of spiritual perception, tenderness of spiritual sympathy, charm of spiritual attractiveness, and fruitfulness of spiritual influence.

(3) Realization of assurance. Another element of the Christian life for which Epaphras prayed was a strong conviction—"fully assured in all the will of God" *(A.S. V.)*. He wished his Colossian friends to realize to the full the divine will for their lives and thus to stand firm, as mature, convinced Christians, with complete spiritual confidence in everything connected with God's purpose, whatever it might be. Indeed, the only way in which His purpose may be traced is by doing His will as it is revealed to the soul day by day (cf. John 7:17). The thought of assurance seems to be identical with, or at least akin to, certainty, and the word is found in three other connections in the New Testament: the fulness or full assurance of faith (Heb. 10:22); the fulness or full assurance of hope (Heb. 6:11); and the fulness or full assurance of understanding (Col. 2:2). These mean that the Christian is intended to be quite sure of God's will in regard to his acceptance, his fellowship, and his equipment. He knows and is certain of his position in Christ; he knows and rejoices in his communion with Christ; and he knows and is confident of his provision from Christ. There is nothing higher than this in all of the Christian life, because the will of God is the source, the standard, the strength, and the satisfaction of the believer's whole experience, including salvation and sanctification. When he is fully assured concerning that will for him—its clearness, its blessedness, and its authority, then indeed is he making spiritual progress. Among those things that we know from the New Testament to be according to the will of God for us are the following: salvation (I Tim 2:4); sanctification (I Thess. 4:3); separation (Gal. 1:4); singleness of aim (Eph. 6:6); suffering for well-doing (I Peter 3:17).

Toward these ends prayer is, for us as for Epaphras, the appointed means. Prayer develops spiritual faculties and leads to spiritual maturity. Prayer makes real the presence of God, and in that presence His will naturally becomes clearer and asserts its complete yet blessed authority. The more we pray the riper we become and the more completely assured of the will of God in Christ Jesus concerning us. Further, as we consider what Epaphras was doing through prayer, we see that often intercession is the most necessary and also the most blessed work we can do. Whether our prayers are for individuals or for whole communities of Christians, we ought, as priests "unto our God" (Rev. 5:10), to make the fullest possible use of this ministry of intercession. If anyone should think that this is difficult, the apostle, as we have seen, testifies that the prayer-life of Epaphras did indeed involve "much labor" (v. 13, *A.S.V.*) for his converts. Of him the old Latin motto was true—"to pray is to labor"—with its corollary, "to labor is to pray."

But we also have the blessed secret of it all. For us the Word of God is the supreme expression of His will; and through daily meditation, daily application, daily trust, and daily obedience we shall become mighty in prayer because we are, like Apollos, "mighty in the scriptures" (Acts 18:24). The Word is the fuel of prayer and will prompt, inspire, and encourage us to make petition for ourselves and intercession for others. In particular, it will reveal to us the wonderful intercession of Christ above (cf. Rom. 8:34; Heb. 7:25), and the equally wonderful intercession of the Holy Spirit within (cf. Rom. 8:26; Jude 20); and, because thus linked with the throne through them, we shall, in Lord Tennyson's beautiful phrase, be "bound by gold chains about the feet of God."

Thus surrounded by friends and fellowworkers whom he loved and prized, and who were devoted to him, St. Paul could write cheerfully and appreciatively to Colosse and thereby testify afresh to his Christian experience and confidence.

GREETINGS TO SPECIAL FRIENDS (vv. 15-17)

The letter to Colosse draws to a close with two messages, one general, the other individual.

1. Salutations to Laodicean Christians (vv. 15, 16). There are two readings of verse 15, one referring to a man's name, Nymphas, with a masculine plural pronoun, "their house," and the other to a woman's, Nympha, with a feminine singular pronoun, "her house." Whichever is correct, the reference is to a Christian home in Laodicea, the brethren there being greeted with the person mentioned. The private house as the ordinary place of gathering for the early Christians is an interesting illustration of the simplicity of the primitive Church fellowship. Lightfoot points out that there is no clear example of a separate building set apart for Christian worship within the limits of the Roman Empire before the third century (*Colossians,* p. 241). In Colosse, the Church met in the house of Philemon (Philem. 2), and in Ephesus in the house of Aquila and Priscilla (I Cor. 16:19). When these two removed to Rome, they did exactly the same there as they had done in Ephesus (Rom. 16:5), that is, they opened their home to the assembly of believers. All this is at once a testimony to the value of Christian homes and to the blessedness of Christian fellowship, as well as to the close connection that there should be between home and church; and the more we of today can have all of these blessings the better it will be for the reality and progress of Christian living.

At this point it is interesting to notice that the present Epistle was intended to be read in the Church of Laodicea, while the Epistle sent to that Church was to be read in Colosse (v. 16). Furthermore, it is usually thought that the latter refers to our Epistle to the Ephesians, which was almost certainly a circular letter intended for several Churches. This reciprocal use of the Epistles in various churches forms the germ of that acceptance of writings from apostolic sources which reached its culmination in the canon of our New Testament.

2. Exhortation to Archippus (v. 17). Then comes a tender yet solemn word to one who was probably in need of just such a message from the apostle. No one knows anything more definite of Archippus than is found here, except that in mentioning him elsewhere St. Paul calls him his "fellowsoldier," and the probability is that he was a son of Philemon (cf. Philem. 2),[2] whom the apostle may have known first as a small boy and whom he is now calling to a renewal of childish vows. In any case, it is evident that Archippus had received the important responsibility of ministry, and Lightfoot suggests that this may well have been conducted in Laodicea, a short distance from his home in Colosse (*Colossians,* pp. 42, 307-308). Most writers think that the admonition given here implies some laxity of duty or that, lest he should prove slack, Archippus is urged to take heed and fill up that ministry of his to the full in faithfulness (Acts 20:24; II Tim. 4:5). Bishop Moule quotes Richard Cecil in this connection: "A minister of Christ is often in highest honor with men for the performance of one half of his work, while God is regarding him with displeasure for the neglect of the other half" (*Colossian Studies,* p. 271). Whether this was true of Archippus or not, the apostolic injunction is an appeal to watchfulness and thoroughness in any ministry received from the Lord, that characterizing it there may be such vital elements as simplicity of life, singleness of heart, scripturalness of preaching, strength of sympathy, spirituality of methods, sincerity of motives, and strenuousness of service. Well may we pray in the words of *The Book of Common Prayer* concerning clergy and people, "That they may truly please Thee, pour upon them the continual dew of Thy blessing."

THE AUTOGRAPHIC CLOSE (v. 18)

The apostolic signature and a touching personal appeal bring both the salutations and the Epistle to an end. Paul's handwriting may have changed

---

2 See Part II, p. 149.

through weakness or been hampered by his "bonds," the handcuffs of his prison cell (cf. Acts 28:20; see also Acts 12:6); but his benediction is one of the characteristic Pauline references to divine "grace." This was then, as ever, the spring of all his splendid life and sacrificial service (cf. I Cor. 15:10).

It is manifestly impossible to close this consideration of the apostle's friends without thinking most of all of St. Paul himself, for his references to others are a genuine reflection of his own personality and of those things which he felt to be the most essential features of the Christian life. All through the Epistle, in fact, we have found references to others which reveal much of his own life in relation to God (e.g., 1:3, 24, 25; 2:1, 5; 4:3, 4).[3] Whether, therefore, in preaching, or in praying, or in practice, the apostle Paul is a wonderful example for us. We can do no better than to follow him, even as he followed Christ. His testimony has been well expressed in sonnet form, as follows:

> Now I am one of His; and this my fame.
> Pride, power, wealth, all else is loss.
> I live in time to herald forth His Name
> And light in souls the wonder of a Cross.
> You see me, Paul, an all-consuming flame
> Kindled by Him—I, driftwood, dross.
> You see these hands outstretched to blind and lame
> In healing love. It was not always thus;
> There was a once I strode, cursing the light,
> Eyeing with discontent the spirit free.
> One blood-bent day, a sky-bolt struck my sight,
> And filled my eyes with God-lit truth. I see,
> And now I seek the stars beyond earth's cynic night.
> I live, yet now not I, but Christ my Lord in me!

> —Leslie Rose

----

[3] See also Appendix 1, p. 177.

10 SUMMARY

After going through an Epistle like this one and pondering every phrase—almost every word—in its order, it is spiritually helpful to review it as a whole, and to think of the great themes that occupied the apostle's thought while writing it. Although the circumstances in Colosse were very different from those of today, the Epistle contains so much of permanent truth that even its direct and specific appeals to the Colossian Church may be profitably applied to the Christians of our time.

As we have seen, the main theme of this Epistle from beginning to end is the person and work of our Lord. Arising out of this, it is possible to see clearly what St. Paul thinks (a) of the Christian life, whether of the individual or of the community, (b) of the Christian service that ought to be rendered by God's people, and (c) of the kind of dangers that beset them. Thus it would be helpful to go through this brief Epistle asking ourselves these questions: What does it say of Christ? What does it say of the Christian life? What does it say of Christian work? What does it say of Christian perils? Under these main topics, practically all the teaching of the Epistle can be included. But let us see, by way of summing up, what in particular it means for us at the present time.

1. The Epistle Teaches that Christianity Means Holiness. This theme is presented throughout and in various ways. The apostle's thanksgiving and prayer (1:3-13) are concerned with it, while the practical part of the Epistle (3:5 to 4:6) re-emphasizes both the need and the duty of living a holy life, whether individually, or in the home, or in society. Nothing is more prominent in these pages, as, indeed, all through St. Paul's writings, than the emphasis placed on Christian holiness.

2. The Epistle Teaches that Holiness Is Based on Redemption. It is obviously impossible to be holy without having had our sins forgiven, and this means that only as we are redeemed by grace can we be what God intends us to be. This is another theme of the Epistle which, while emphasized in certain sections (e.g., 1:20 to 2:3), is stated or implied from beginning to end. Redemption alone is the fount of holiness.

3. The Epistle Teaches that Redemption Is Founded on the Deity of Christ. The work of Christ for us must of necessity spring from His person, and only a divine person (1:15-19) can do a redemptive work. The possibility of Jesus Christ being anything less than God would make redemption absolutely unthinkable, since the death of a mere man may not and cannot purchase even his own salvation. It is here that all modern systems fail which do not accept and emphasize the deity of Christ, for without His membership in the Godhead there can be no salvation, no forgiveness, for men.

4. The Epistle Teaches that This Divine Christ Is Available for All. The Colossian Christians, like so many people today, were in serious danger of interposing between themselves and God mediators who could not possibly meet the requirements, and who would in reality tend to shut out God from human life. The apostle flings the door of access wide open and says that "every man" (1:28) without exception can approach God without human or angelic mediation (2:18, 19). This is the chief glory of true Christianity, that it is a means of direct access to God, for through God the Son we have our introduction "by one Spirit unto the Father" (Eph. 2:18).

5. The Epistle Teaches that the Universal Characteristic of the Christian Life Is Union with Christ. The way in which the apostle emphasizes the headship of Christ shows what this means (2:10, 19). The thought of believers being "in Christ" or "in the Lord" runs from beginning to end of this Epistle; and it is noteworthy because of its clear implication of our spiritual union in Him. The saints and faithful brethren are "in Christ" (1:2); our faith is "in Christ Jesus," (1:4); redemption is ours in Christ (1:14); all things hold together in him (1:17); "in him" all fulness dwells (1:19); and every Christian man is to be presented mature "in Christ Jesus" (1:28). All Christians are made full "in him" (2:10); wives, husbands, children, servants, and masters are all, in one way or another, appealed to because of their relationship to Christ, because they are "in the Lord" (3:18 to 4:1); and St. Paul's own friends have the same blessed spiritual position (4:7, 12, 17). Thus we see how the believer is united with Christ in His death (2:20) and resurrection (3:1), and is now living above a life "hid with Christ in God" (3:3).

6. The Epistle Teaches that Union with Christ Is the Only Adequate Protection Against All Error. The Colossian Church was faced with two great dangers (2:4-23), one doctrinal and the other practical; and the apostle points out that both perils can be met, and more than met, by the reality and the power of union with Christ. So is it today; for, whatever may be the danger, either of the Christian man or of the Christian Church, union and communion with Christ, who is at once divine and human, redemptive and sanctifying, is the complete safeguard in the face of every conceivable peril.

Thus everything in Colossians culminates in the grace of God. The closing prayer, "Grace be with you" (4:18), is but an echo of what is found all through the Epistle. The Colossian believers had heard and had known "the grace of God in truth" (1:6) from the very beginning of their Christian life; and this grace had continued with them every step of the way, reminding them of what God was able to be and to do in their lives as they realized to the full their union with Him. It is our privilege, similarly, to realize the efficacy, abundance, and power of the grace of God in all things in our lives, until that day comes when grace will be manifested in glory. Then shall we live forever "to the praise of the glory of his grace, wherein he hath made us accepted in the beloved" (Eph. 1:6).

BIBLIOGRAPHY

Those who wish to give the closest possible attention to this truly vital and precious part of God's Word will be glad to have the following references to the more important books which were available to the author in conducting the study of Colossians and to which he owes much.

1. For grammatical commentaries, involving a knowledge of Greek: Lightfoot, Ellicott, and A. Lukyn Williams in *The Cambridge Greek Testament*. There is also a scholarly and suggestive treatment entitled *A Letter to Asia*, by Archdeacon F. B. Westcott.

2. For English commentaries not involving a knowledge of Greek: Bishop Barry in Ellicott's *Commentary for English Readers;* John Rutherfurd's *St. Paul's Epistles to Colosse and Laodicea*, which is one of the most useful of books, and far too little known; and *The Cambridge Bible for Schools*, by Bishop Handley C. G. Moule.

3. Devotional and homiletical: Alexander Maclaren in *The Expositor's Bible* (a model exposition); Bishop Moule's *Colossian Studies;* Bishop W. R. Nicholson's *Oneness with Christ* (ed. James M. Gray); and Dean Howson's *The Companions of St. Paul.*

PART TWO

THE EPISTLE OF
ST. PAUL, THE APOSTLE,
TO
PHILEMON

11 INTRODUCTION

This short letter is unique among the Epistles of the New Testament. It is the only private communication preserved and included in the canon of Holy Scripture. The Pastoral Epistles, indeed, are addressed to individuals, Timothy and Titus, but their chief purpose is to discuss questions of Church government with fellowworkers and could well have been read in public or otherwise shared. This letter, on the contrary, is written by St. Paul not as one exerting apostolic authority over either an adherent or a colleague, but as friend to friend. The one addressed was Philemon, a layman in the Colossian Church who, we believe from textual evidence, was a convert of Paul's own (cf. v. 19), probably in Ephesus. The letter has to do with the domestic life of Christians and with the ordinary circumstances of that day. It was probably one of many such personal messages not only inspired by the Spirit of God, but prompted also by the apostle's warm heart and friendly nature. It has been said to exemplify Love in Christ, emphasizing the vital importance of His Lordship in the believer's everyday experience as well as in all other realms.

The letter to Philemon belongs, as we have already noted, in the same group as the Epistles sent to Ephesus, Colosse, and Philippi. It is a short letter with no doctrinal teaching, but in it we can trace the working out of some of the great truths set forth in the longer letters written from St. Paul's Roman prison. It has been suggested that the four of them give us a great spiritual square: at the top, Colossians—the ideal head, Christ; at the base, Ephesians—the ideal body, the Church; at one side, Philippians—the ideal Christian in relation to the head; and at the other side, Philemon—the ideal Church member in relation to his fellowmembers.

The Epistle to Philemon is important and interesting for a number of specific reasons: first, it is a *perfect example of Christian character;* second, it is a *perfect model of Christian friendship;* third, it is a *perfect picture of Christian domestic life* in earliest days; and, fourth, it is a *perfect indication of Christianity's attitude toward the world's social organization.*

1. A Perfect Example of Christian Character. There is a wonderful revelation of St. Paul's personality throughout this brief letter. We may trace in it his earnest spirit, his warm love, his delicate tact, his remarkable ingenuity, his complete courtesy, his inexorable justice, even his delightful playfulness combined with easy self-effacement and modesty. It is especially striking to compare the great intellectuality of Colossians as we have just experienced it, and of the other two profound Epistles written at about the same time, namely, Ephesians and Philippians, with the graceful simplicity and sweet kindliness of what Renan called "a true little *chef-d'oeuvre* of the art of letterwriting," and Luther "a masterly, lovely example" of Christian love.

2. A Perfect Model of Christian Friendship. The characters of both Paul and Philemon were refined by the love of God, and their friendship therefore was adorned by courtesy and consideration. However, Paul neither falters nor flatters, nor does he fail to give counsel to his friend; and yet he fully recognizes the justice of Philemon's position in the light of contemporary conditions.

3. A Perfect Picture of Early Christian Domestic Life. As we shall see, here are husband, wife, son, servant, and friends; and the use of such terms as "fellowlabourer" (v. 1; cf. v. 24) and "fellowsoldier" (v. 2) shows co-operation in Christian work among young recruits and veteran fighters alike, with the home the focal point and the base.

4. A Perfect Indication of Christianity's Attitude to the World's Social Organization. It goes without saying that the Epistle recognizes the existence of slavery, which in that day was widespread. Had the system been met by prohibition on the part of the early Church, as it was to be met much later on by the State, society in general might have been disrupted and virtually torn to shreds. If St. Paul, for instance, had denounced slavery, he might, humanly speaking, have created so gigantic a social revolution that his influence and even his doctrinal teaching might have been hindered. By way of illustration, it is well to note that Abraham Lincoln's initial attitude to the question of slavery took into account a similar danger. He would have preferred a more gradual approach rather than an immediate and total abolition, because he knew how alarmingly the economic situation in the southern states would react if all the slaves were summarily liberated. In point of fact, Mr. Lincoln actually proposed as an alternative plan that the slaveholders be recompensed for emancipation by the Federal government to help them over a difficult transition. But the measure was repudiated by his own cabinet, the members of which, it was said, seemed in this case to prefer the expenditure of human life to that of money. Thus we cannot but compare Paul's way of treating the subject of slavery with the manner in which it was finally met by the United States government during the Civil War. The apostle preached principles of oneness, brotherhood, and equality in Christ that would slowly and surely undermine the very foundations of slavery, and in time actually did so. But human brotherhood in Christ is much more than emancipation from servitude, and so Christianity not only succeeded in freeing the slaves of the world, but also taught them, and their former owners as well, that "there is neither bond nor free," . . . but all are "one in Christ Jesus" (Gal. 3:28). Preaching the acceptance of Christ as Savior and Lord is the one sure way of destroying not only slavery, but all other un-Christian systems of life and law.

As we shall see, this letter to Philemon exemplifies the higher law of love revealed in Christ. Onesimus could not get away from Christ though he fled the home of a Christian. After contact with Paul and conversion, he ministered in the name of Christ. Then all barriers were broken down in Christ, and adversity was found to have been a time of greatest victory for Christ. Today Christ can still triumph over adverse social conditions and over the oftentimes serious differences between men that both cause and are perpetuated by a given social order.

The Epistle to Philemon may be divided into three sections. First, the writer commences with a salutation and an expression of thanksgiving for the good tidings received of Philemon and his family (vv. 1-7); then, emboldened by the sense of their close friendship, he proceeds to reveal his object in writing (vv. 8-14); and, finally, he enlarges upon the providential aspects of the incident under discussion, concluding in a very personal and friendly manner (vv. 15-25).

12 THE SALUTATION

As in all the opening sentences of St. Paul's personally addressed
Epistles, this salutation and its accompanying expression of thanksgiving
cast a revealing light upon the writer's Christian character. They are also
rich in suggestion and example for us today.

FELLOWSHIP GREETING (vv. 1-3)

1. The Address (vv. 1, 2). Paul designates himself "a prisoner of Jesus
Christ" (v. 1; cf. Rom. 1:1[1]), and does not refer, as in the majority of his
Epistles, including Colossians as we have seen, to his authority as an
apostle. Instead, he writes as friend to friend, relying on his personal
influence to touch the heart rather than on his apostolic authority to move
the will. This is the first of five such references to his chains (cf. vv. 9, 10,
13, 23). But the words "of Jesus Christ" lose sight of second causes; Jesus
Christ is the author of Paul's imprisonment, just as He is the reason for
men having made Paul a captive.

The apostle includes Timothy in his address as "our brother" (v. 1).
The younger man was not an apostle, and therefore Paul uses this natural,
simple title—another instance of his humility and desire to associate his
fellowworkers with himself in the cause of Christ (cf. Col. 1:1, etc.). Since
Timothy was with Paul during the greater part of the three years at

[1] See the author's *St. Paul's Epistle to the Romans,* pp. 38f.

Ephesus (Acts 19:22), Philemon doubtless knew him personally; and thus weight would be added to the ensuing request.

We may safely assume that the persons addressed in this letter lived at Colosse (cf. Col. 4:9, 12, 17), in the province of Phrygia and situated near the center of what was afterward called Asia Minor: Philemon, the head of a family probably converted through the apostle's ministry, his wife, their son or Christian associate, and the fellow-believers who met for worship in their home. Philemon's Christian zeal and warm fellowship are emphasized (v. 1), and his social standing as leader or sponsor of an assembly of believers is suggested (v. 2). We are told by Chrysostom that Apphia was the wife of Philemon and this seems more than probable. Here she is given the description "beloved," and thus is pictured as a valued associate of Paul's, possibly from the days in Ephesus, and not as a mere chattel or slave in the home, as so often a woman was counted in those early times. It would follow that Archippus might well be the son of Philemon and Apphia. At the very least he was a Christian worker resident in their home at the time, for he is described here as Paul's "fellowsoldier" (v. 2). Elsewhere he is indicated as one who had received a certain "ministry in the Lord," or commission, to which he was to "take heed" in order that he might "fulfil it" (Col. 4:17; see p. 142).

The word "church" (v. 2) as descriptive of any local "called-out" body of believers, of whatever size, is most significant. Moreover, the entire phrase "the church in thy house" is very interesting. A similar expression is found in Colossians 4:15 (see p. 139), referring to a group in the home of Nymphas of Laodicea, not far away. Early Christian life was thus both domestic and ecclesiastic, in the literal sense of the two words. It was a united life, as evidenced by the phrases "fellowlabourer" and "fellow-soldier"; and it was also an uplifting life, for it included children and slaves of the household, thus promoting young recruits and humble workers alike to Paul's own sphere of labor, save that these were in this typical Christian home "at Colosse" and he "in all the world" (Col. 1:2, 6). Thus was there a division of labor and yet a unity of service.

2. **The Salutation (v. 3).** Here are blended a wish and an exhortation. As elsewhere, "grace" and "peace" are closely associated. *Grace* may be thought of as threefold: it is divine love and favor in exercise toward the inferior and the undeserving; it includes the gifts which that love bestows; and it describes the effects of those loving gifts in the lives of the recipients. This great New Testament word has a particularly touching application here: Philemon had had grace shown him and therefore should show grace. *Peace* is one of the greatest results of divine grace; and it includes peace with God and the very peace of God, and also peace with self and peace with others. The origin of grace and peace was twofold: the

source was "God our Father," for so God has been revealed to us; and the channel was "the Lord Jesus Christ," for He once spoke to Paul of "my grace" (II Cor. 12:9) and to the Twelve of "my peace" (John 14:27).

APPRECIATION COMMENDING (vv. 4-7)

The two clauses of verse 4, introduce two distinct yet connected statements, each of which is continued, the first by verse 5 and the second by verse 6. One has to do with praise and the other with prayer and, while distinct in function, the connection both in the Greek construction and in the Christian life is obvious and yet too often neglected.

1. The Praise (vv. 4, 5). "I thank my God," writes St. Paul to his friend, ". . . hearing of thy love and faith." Here the Greek verb is in the first person singular, no longer including Timothy as he so often does (cf. I Thess. 1:2). The thankfulness Paul felt in this case was very personal, even though thanksgiving is usually a prominent note in commencing his more general Epistles, unless there is some special reason to omit it, as in Galatians. Here he is not speaking what the prophet called "smooth things" (Isa. 30:10), not paying compliments nor using flattery, but he is expressing his esteem for a fine character by praising not Philemon primarily, but God, the One who has inspired and enabled. Here is a hint for us: It is the part of wisdom to deal out praise whenever and wherever possible, for it is a nourishing food for virtues and a strong antidote against vices. Love always delights to see the white patches on even the blackest garment of a man's character. To recognize good is to make good better, and it is a safe rule to express confidence unless and until it is shown to be misplaced. The bitter medicine of blame or criticism is more easily taken if it can be administered in the capsule of honest praise.

In this commendation of Philemon's character, Paul mentions first his friend's love and then his faith, not in the reverse and more usual order as he did when writing to the larger group at Colosse (cf. Col. 1:4; see p. 25). In the latter case, of course, the discussion was dogmatic and so that prominence given to faith was appropriate. In the case of Philemon, however, the letter is an appeal to humanity, not to doctrine, and so love was emphasized. On receipt of this appeal, Philemon would see the importance of love in the Christian life. Perhaps this order was also an echo of his personal relationship with the apostle, indicating the good things that Paul had heard of Philemon, probably from Epaphras (cf. Col. 1:7, 8; 4:12; see pp. 29, 134). Love as the manifestation of faith, and Christ as the object of faith—here is the natural order of analysis, showing effect pointing back to cause. It was also the writer's desire to secure another expression of love in relation to the subject of the letter, and to add to its range and comprehensiveness. The phrase "love . . . toward all saints" (v. 5) represents in those early days the scaling of high walls of prejudice, as indeed it still does; but it is preceded by another phrase, "love . . . toward the Lord Jesus"—and that harmonizes everything. In the original, however, there are two different prepositions in this verse, though both are translated "toward." The nearest we may come to it in English is to suggest that our love goes *forward* to Christ and *inward* to our fellow-Christians, or a blending of direction and contact. It is like the spoke of a wheel that points in and out at the same time, united to its fellows by hub and rim alike, so that together they are welded into a single useful instrument.

But, while love toward others arises out of love toward Christ, and both these phases of love derive from faith, there are also two kinds of faith suggested here. Belief *on* Christ is the foundation and belief *in* Christians is the house built thereon. Faith is one basis of a loving character, as in the case of Barnabas, who is described as "a good man" because "full of the Holy Ghost and of faith" (Acts 11:24).

2. The Prayer (vv. 4, 6). ". . . making mention of thee always in my prayers, . . . that the communication of thy faith may become effectual by the acknowledging of every good thing which is in you in Christ Jesus." This was Paul's petition for Philemon and in it he was asking God that the fellowship (as the *A. S. V.* has it; cf. Rom. 15:26; Phil. 1:5; Heb. 13:16), or liberality toward others, the friendly offices of love and sympathy, that had sprung from his friend's faith, might continue to increase. Thus would Philemon be led into an ever-deepening knowledge of the spiritual treasures that were already his.

It is evident that this mature knowledge, the Greek word for which is characteristic of all four Epistles of this period, is in his view a distinguishing mark of a ripening Christian life. It stands for the complete appropriation of all known truth and an unreserved identification with God's will as the goal of the believer's course. Note that Paul does not speak here of possession or of performance. This is because, in this higher sense, to know is to possess and also to perform.

In short, the knowledge here envisioned is the result and reward of faith manifested in love (cf. Eph. 4:13; Titus 1:1, *A. S. V.*), for it was Philemon's own knowledge that Paul had in mind, and not the knowledge that others had of Philemon. And the final goal of "the effectiveness of the fellowship that comes by faith" is actually Christ Himself—"effectual . . . unto Christ" (v. 6, *A. S. V.* and Gr.).

In this expression of desire on behalf of Philemon, the apostle states a great spiritual principle. Beneficence is a means of growth. The heart grows rich, not poor, in giving, "being fruitful in every good work, and increasing in the knowledge of God" (Col. 1:10; see pp. 34ff.). Conduct has a strong influence on character (even though it is more usual to urge the reverse of this statement). It has always been true that when mankind fails to live up to its religion, that religion descends to the current level of human life. The ownership of unoccupied territory, spiritual as well as material, has a way of lapsing with the years, or else the very ground itself deteriorates. If we are to retain gifts we must use them; and the practice of our convictions is the best way of deepening them. In the life of faith each consecrated thought, word, or deed increases our capacity for holding, understanding, and enjoying "every good thing" (v. 6) that has already come into our lives as Christians.

3. **The Joy (v. 7).** "We have great joy and consolation in thy love," wrote St. Paul, wanting his friend to know that he rejoiced and found comfort in the consciousness of their fellowship, even though distance separated them. It had done the apostle good to hear in that far-off prison that Philemon had been so lovingly helpful and hospitable to others. Paul was never afraid of showing tenderness; in fact, he frequently poured out his heart as he wrote, in a way that was at once sincere and manly.

There is often unexpected good in good deeds—results far beyond the immediate, intended benefits—such as a bright light kindled, as here, in the darkness of a prison cell hundreds of miles distant. Philemon had "refreshed" not only the hearts of "the saints" in Colosse, but also the soul of his "brother" in Rome. We may draw a parallel between Paul's rejoicing and comfort in the faith and love of Philemon with the record of our Lord's rejoicing in Luke 10:21. We are told there that He was gladdened by His Father's revelation of "these things," spiritual truths, to those who were but "babes" spiritually; and here His apostle is given "great joy" because "every good thing" (v. 6), each of the elements of the faith, in Philemon has found expression in his spontaneous benefactions to fellow-Christians.

But analyze these opening sentences of the Epistle as we may, we sense in them a feeling of urgency, as though all rules of arrangement in letterwriting were being defied, so great is Paul's anxiety to express the desire uppermost in his mind. Thus we find ourselves nearing the definite reason for the dispatch of this very personal and practical communication.

13 THE HEART OF THE MATTER

As we consider from the apostle's own standpoint the situation of which he wrote, we shall find in this central section of the Epistle to Philemon a fourfold revelation of his character.

LOVE IN DEALING (vv. 8, 9)

St. Paul might well have pronounced a command, an injunction, here, such as popes and bishops, even parish priests and pastors, have not hesitated to issue throughout the Church's history. But he would not do this, choosing instead to utilize the grace of love rather than to exercise his apostolic authority.

1. **The Connection (v. 8).** The word "wherefore" is a link with the previous verse, referring to the love shown by Philemon as refreshing to "the hearts of the saints" (v. 7, *A.S.V.*). Paul is thus introducing a new situation in which he urges his friend to be equally kind. It is not lack of boldness that causes the apostle to write thus, but rather the opposite—it is his confidence "in Christ" as their common Lord that inspires him to waive his apostolic authority. There were, indeed, limits to this authority: one, it was to be exercised only "in Christ"; and, two, it was to "enjoin ... that which is befitting" (*A.S.V.;* cf. Eph. 5:4; Col. 3:18). This word has to do with propriety, or right behavior, in an atmosphere external to the Church, and it is found only in the Epistles of the Captivity.

It is true that many people in authority, even Christian leaders, too often feel a necessity to use force in their dealings with others. Yet there is need for it in fewer cases than some might think likely, and it is wiser to try gentleness, first at least, and to attempt to lead rather than to drive.

2. The Claim (v. 9a). It is "for love's sake" that Paul did "rather beseech" instead of issuing an order. An order applies only to a man's will, but love appeals to his heart, furnishing the strong motive that the will needs to direct the desired action most acceptably and completely. Authority is often the weapon of a weak man afraid of not obtaining obedience. The love mentioned here is evidently not Philemon's own, nor Paul's own, but love absolute, "regarded as a principle which demands a deferential respect" (Lightfoot, *Colossians and Philemon*, p. 335). It is the finest instrument of the strong man who, casting aside any trappings of superiority, is paradoxically never loftier in stature than when he "stoops to conquer." Our Lord Himself was the greatest example of one who might well have commanded but did not (cf. Phil. 2:5-8); and His apostle was giving a glimpse into Christ's heart of love even as he was laying bare his own before his friend.

HUMILITY IN APPEALING (v. 9b)

Paul now brings forward some personal considerations to strengthen the case he is about to present and to enlist sympathy for it.

1. His Age. "Being such an one as Paul the aged," or "the elder," he goes on. However, as Lightfoot points out, the Greek word here can be translated "ambassador" (cf. Eph. 6:20), or one of high rank and of leadership, rather than necessarily of great age (Lightfoot, *Colossians and Philemon*, pp. 335, 336). As man measures his life span Paul was not "aged" so much as prematurely old, through hard work, anxiety, ill health, persecution, and the very burning zeal of his own spirit that had characterized his life. At this time he was only about sixty years of age, as compared with the much more advanced years of the apostle John when he wrote the Book of Revelation. Furthermore, if Archippus, old enough to be a "minister" (Col. 4:17), was indeed Philemon's son, Philemon himself was at this time a man not much younger than the apostle. But both age and leadership, implying long service and varied experience, as they indisputably do here, carry weight and command deference. Paul was one who delighted to be surrounded by young life, such as was represented by Timothy, and his latter Epistles attest his continuing interest in all that went on around him. His life was still characterized by joy and hope (e.g., Col. 2:5), even as when he had joined in midnight song at Philippi (Acts 16:25). He could well have testified that

> When stern affliction clouds the cheek
> And want stands at the door,
> Hope cheers us with her sunniest note,
> " 'Tis better on before!"

2. His Status. Not only was Paul venerable, but he was also a prisoner, and so he may have been drawing a contrast, somewhat playfully, between the words ambassador and slave, usually so completely different in connotation. It was as though he held up his shackled wrist as he wrote and pleaded with his distant friend, "You won't refuse me, a captive representing the cause of Christ!" It was a cumulative plea with great force behind it—Paul the elder, the representative of the Master, but now also a prisoner of His. It was another instance, also, of the relation between sight and faith: to sight Paul was the prisoner of Nero, to faith the prisoner of Jesus Christ, so that the cheerless cell was transformed and its occupant at peace. A. J. Gordon once asked an aged man why he seemed so happy. "Because I belong to the Lord," was the reply. "Are there no others happy at your time of life?" "No," said the aged saint, "the devil has no happy old men!" Such personal considerations and attachments should ever be strong incentives to Christian duty, as when our Lord urged not only righteousness for its own sake, but also for His sake (Matt. 5:10, 11), and because of His disciples' relationship to Him: "If ye love me, keep my commandments" (John 14:15).

TACT IN REVEALING (vv. 10, 11)

In approaching now the main purpose of his letter, the apostle still does not blurt it out at once.

1. The Method. "I beseech thee for my child" (v. 10, *A. S. V.*), he writes simply, as though anticipating Philemon's annoyance at the introduction of the subject. Perhaps he has even now hesitated before plunging into it, for, according to the order both of the Greek and of the English Revision, he is diplomatic and does not mention the name of Onesimus until he has described him, and then hurriedly passes on to place deserved blame, as if in anticipation of Philemon's objection. Paul freely admits that Onesimus, a slave in the service of Philemon (cf. v. 16), had been "unprofitable" (v. 11), good for nothing (cf. Matt. 25:30; Luke 17:10). This is, of course, a playful allusion to the meaning of the slave's name which is "profitable"; and so the apostle hastens to add that now there will be a difference, for Onesimus will be profitable to both friends and thus live up to his name. We know that this would be significant in Biblical times (cf., e.g., Gen. 30:24; 32:28; Ruth 1:20). "In time past ... unprofitable, but now profitable" (v. 11)—these words express Paul's belief in the power of the gospel to change a man's entire nature and make him "meet for the master's use" (II Tim. 2:21, Gr.) and "profitable . . . for the ministry" (II Tim. 4:11).

Paul's tact has been aptly described by Bishop Moule as "an exquisite combination of sympathy and judgment" (cf. Acts 17:22, 23, 28). It was doubtless inborn, and yet it must also have been a product of the good feeling toward other people developed during his long years of Christian experience. Never were ruffled feelings more skillfully or delicately soothed. What a model we have here for all efforts to lead others in right paths! Manner counts for much, as well as matter, and there is a real danger of repelling people by the way we do an entirely correct thing or make a perfectly justifiable statement. Much persuasion is often needed to induce even a good man to do his plain duty. How much more do we need sanctified ingenuity in attracting a sinner to the gospel and wooing him away from sin!

2. The Miracle. "My child, . . . whom I have begotten in my bonds" (v. 10), is the way Paul describes Onesimus the slave (cf. I Cor. 4:15; Gal. 4:19). Of all his converts Onesimus must have been the one doubly dear as a child of the apostle's sorrows and, as in the case of Joseph and Jacob, of his old age (cf. Gen. 37:3). But slaves were an underprivileged and often vicious class of men, and evidently this one had been no outstanding exception. Yet the apostle was quite certain that a miracle of grace, a new birth, had been performed in his heart. He uses the metaphor of a father who is perfectly sure of the identity of his son. It has even been suggested that there are here two allusions to Roman law: one, the right of a slave to request a friend of his master's to intercede for him; and the other, the legal enfranchisement that could be effected by the adoption of a slave as the son of a Roman citizen.

Thus the apostle hopes that the past was to be blotted out and a new start made. Christianity has always wrought such moral and spiritual miracles. It admits no knowledge of hopeless cases where it is given a fair opportunity. We do not blame a medicine for failure to act upon a patient who refuses to take the dose that the physician has prescribed. In each instance, it is the yielding of the will that is the all-important prerequisite to a successful outcome.

INTEGRITY IN FEELING (vv. 12-14)

In these verses Paul's sense of justice is shown to have been weighing, as it were, right and wrong, law and expediency, gain and loss, advantage and disadvantage, and even brotherly love and self-interest.

1. The Principle (v. 12a). The apostle has decided in favor of the law of restitution. This was something deeply ingrained in the Jewish mind, for it had occupied an important place in the Mosaic Law (cf. Exod. 22:1-15; Lev. 6:1-7; 25:27; Deut. 22:1-3). Furthermore, Paul is sending Onesimus back to Colosse as a slave because, according to Roman law, such a course was the only correct one in justice to a master who had been wronged. This does not mean, however, that Christianity sanctioned slavery, which it considered, then as now, a sin against God and an act of treason against fellowmen (cf. Gal. 3:28; Eph. 6:9); but it was bringing the principle of love, not force, to bear upon the system. Christianity hates violence and cruelty and opposes them, not by legislation—that is not its function—but by an appeal to the hearts and minds of individual believers with their God-given powers of promoting truth and right and of exercising loving-kindness.

Dealing with the reasons why Paul encouraged the fugitive slave to enter into servitude again, Dr. J. H. Jowett suggests the following:

> Because, although personal liberty was an exceedingly precious thing—a pearl of great price—there was something more precious still—a pearl of greater price—the welfare of all the · other slaves. A runaway slave, instigated in his flight by the Christian faith, might not only have jeopardized the interests of the struggling infant Church, but would have plunged into even greater hardships all the slaves throughout the Empire. So Onesimus voluntarily went back into bondage, sacrificing his personal liberty for the common good, the good pearl for the sake of the better, and in so doing proved himself a worthy member of the Kingdom of God (*The Folly of Unbelief and Other Meditations for Quiet Moments*, p. 65).

It is scarcely necessary to remind ourselves that certain forms of slavery survive today, and that therefore this lesson from long ago must be learned afresh. A form of servitude that should concern the Christian Church is the enslavement of many by intemperance and addiction to drink. God is often longsuffering with even the willing victims of this iniquitous traffic, but He is not passive concerning ·it, and so His Church must ever be in the vanguard of the devoted social action that undertakes to combat its widespread evils. The individual Christian also must play an active, not a passive role in the abolition of this and all other degrading forms of human slavery and equally in the safeguarding of human rights.

2. The Plea (v. 12b). Onesimus, however, had become dear to Paul, so that the apostle actually refers to this runaway slave as his "very heart" (*A.S.V.*), as though to part with Onesimus was to the writer like losing one of his own vital organs. Such an identification of self with an object of love, especially an unworthy one, leaps all barriers and overcomes even the curse of slavery. It is only in the same spirit of interceding love that

163

Christianity, while warring relentlessly on social evils, will succeed in influencing social outcasts. They must be convinced by the Church of the error of their ways, but also must be shown that they are the objects of love and concern to individual Christians.

3. The Preference (v. 13). An idea of how Paul regarded Onesimus, the converted heathen slave, may be gained from a half-formed purpose that had evidently agreed with his own desire. The verb he used shows both by its meaning and by its tense that he had been "of a mind," as we might say, to retain Onesimus to serve him in a new capacity, in "the bonds of the gospel," a link riveted not by man, but by God. With the words "in thy stead he might have ministered unto me," it is tactfully assumed that Philemon would have wished to do this in person and, since that was impossible, would gladly have lent his slave to serve the apostle in that far-away prison.

4. The Persuasion (v. 14). Yet Paul put aside his personal needs and desires, and for two reasons. First, he would not violate the law by keeping another man's property without consulting him. Second, if Paul had kept Onesimus in Rome, Philemon, being at a distance, might have felt forced to overlook the offense; whereas if he was to have his slave back in his own home he would be able to decide freely in what spirit to receive him. Paul had such confidence, however, in the quality of good will in his friend's character that he took this means of evoking true Christian love and forgiveness for the culprit. As not only the apostle's beloved friend, but also his spiritual son (cf. v. 10), Onesimus could surely count on a cordial reception upon his return home.

Here is the difference between Paul's wish and his will. The outcome was to be a triumph not only for righteousness, but also for the apostle's powers of persuasion against his own self-interest. Yet he desired that his friend's response "not be as of necessity, but of free will" (*A.S.V.*). He wanted it made clear that Philemon was not being pressed into compliance or self-sacrifice. On the contrary, he was to choose freely whether or not he would show himself a beneficent master who spontaneously welcomes his repentant, newly profitable servant.

In all of this we may trace a picture of one of Christ's strongest appeals to us, His friends and followers, for two of His parables show strongly contrasting attitudes. There was the one about the unjust steward who turned a fellow-servant into an enemy and whose punishment led to the solemn pronouncement: "So likewise shall my heavenly Father do also unto you, if ye from your hearts forgive not every one his brother their trespasses" (Matt. 18:35). Then there was the story of the Good Samaritan who turned an enemy into a neighbor, leading up to the divine directive, "Go, and do thou likewise" (Luke 10:37).

14 ELEMENTS HUMAN AND DIVINE

In this, the closing section of his letter to Philemon, St. Paul develops more fully his purpose in writing it. Giving definite expression now to his heartfelt desire in the matter under discussion, he enforces his plea with several tender yet powerful considerations. These reveal more of the great Christian character of the Apostle.

HUMAN DEEDS AND DIVINE PURPOSES, vv. 15-17

That this whole section of the apostle's letter follows closely upon the foregoing one is shown by the introductory and connective word "For," used in order to explain an additional motive guiding the writer.

1. The Wise Suggestion (v. 15). "For perhaps he [Onesimus] therefore departed for a season, that thou [Philemon] shouldest receive him for ever." "It might well be," writes Paul in effect, "that I should have been defeating God's purpose in allowing your slave to leave you, had I retained him in Rome." The use of the mild verb "departed," or better, "was parted" (*A.S.V.*), rather than the emphatic word "fled" that might so appropriately have been employed in this situation, shows both delicacy of feeling and caution of statement.

> Hard words to make a callous conscience wince,
> But words of balm to men ashamed of sins.

165

Paul is suggesting that the incident might have been permitted for the eventual higher good of all concerned (cf. Gen. 45:5-8; 50:20); but to say so categorically was impossible, both because of incomplete human knowledge, and also because others might presume to justify similar deeds by the example of Onesimus. God's judgments are hidden and, while we may often assume that His directive will is working behind the scenes as we see dimly a great divine purpose in human affairs, we know that man still is held responsible for his own actions (cf. Luke 22:22; Acts 2:23).

"Perhaps" is admittedly a difficult word for some of us to accept, but with this connotation it is a wise motto to adopt. Impatience with uncertainty can become a moral flaw that may mar many a measured process of consideration and investigation. Let us be truly scientific in the highest sense, for a humble, cautious "perhaps" often develops into a strongly convinced "verily," while conversely a hasty "verily" as to some key to the divine purpose can all too easily dwindle ignominiously into a hesitating "perhaps" or even into a definite denial of faith.

Yet, in striking contrast, St. Paul was quite certain as to the general principle of God's eternal purpose, even when he was most modest in the application of it. In the wide sweep of eternity, God utilizes evil and works it into the accomplishment of His purposes in a way that is beyond human ken. How little did Onesimus guess the result of his departure from Colosse when he started out! And yet, with no high motives at all, but quite the reverse, he ran straight into the arms not only of a kind friend, but also of a loving Savior. So Paul's confidence seems to grow with each succeeding word, as he sees that the web of circumstance is indeed being woven by a skillful hand. He is watching it take shape with all the interlacing threads in place according to the pattern of the divine purpose, a pattern that will be vindicated only by the emergence of the finished fabric.

Another striking contrast lies in the apostle's words "for a season, . . . for ever." It had been a short absence compared with the magnitude of the work done in it, the spiritual birth and growth that had taken place in the life of the slave (vv. 10-13). But it is also the difference between a brief space of time and a limitless eternity, between temporary loss and everlasting gain, between an old inferior relationship and a new bond of eternal friendship that death itself would not break. Philemon and Onesimus were now primarily two fellow-believers, instead of one a master and the other a slave.

2. **The Kindly Intercession, (v. 16).** " . . . Have him . . . no longer as a servant, but more than a servant, a brother beloved, specially to me, but how much rather to thee, both in the flesh and in the Lord" (A.S.V.). Philemon was being offered not only a gain in time of service, but also an

improvement in its quality. Because he and Onesimus were now one in Christ, it was unimportant whether the latter was a slave or not. Yet he was going back in that capacity; so it was, rather, that his master was urged to receive him as one who was not a slave. As Goldwin Smith wrote: "Such a feeling as Paul supposes to exist in the hearts of Christians as to their relations with each other, though it would not prevent a Christian slave from remaining in the service of his master, would certainly prevent a Christian master from continuing to hold his fellow-Christian as a slave" (*Does the Bible Sanction American Slavery?*).

This relationship is a paradox that can be illustrated today wherever an ideal situation obtains between employer and domestic servant, notably in a Christian home. The employee rightly considers himself or herself a servant even though the master or mistress thinks of the employee as a real friend because of the high value placed on the faithful service rendered. "By love serve one another" (Gal. 5:13) is the way St. Paul expressed this relationship in another of his letters. Here, as has been pointed out, two spheres are included: "in the flesh" Philemon is to have a brother for a servant, and "in the Lord" he is to have a servant for a brother (cf. I Tim. 6:1, 2). This is an instance of true Christian "brotherhood of man," never more needed than now, in Church as well as in State, with its indispensable foundation the Fatherhood of "God the Father of our Lord Jesus Christ" (Col. 1:3, *A.S.V.*), in whom "we might receive the adoption of sons" (Gal. 4:5).

3. **The Gracious Identification, (v. 17).** The apostle's tact and courtesy continue to be very striking as he expresses himself by a phrase in the hypothetical subjunctive mood: "If thou count me therefore a partner, receive him as myself." Looking back to the preceding verse, we see that Paul, having described Onesimus as a beloved brother, adds "*most of all* (Gr.) to me, but how *much more* unto thee," which is another interesting paradox. Then he continues with a tentative connecting clause to the effect that if, therefore, he and Philemon really are partners, or associates, intimate friends and comrades having common interests (Gr.), Onesimus, as one more link between them, should surely be received as each would receive the other.

HUMAN DEBTS AND DIVINE PAYMENT, vv. 18-20

This leads to a second phrase in the hypothetical subjunctive mood:

1. **The Generous Offer (vv. 18, 19a).** "If he (Onesimus) hath wronged thee, or oweth thee aught, put that on mine account" (v. 18). The owing defines the wronging, and both doubtless were sad facts; the slave had probably fled to escape punishment. But Paul speaks tentatively again,

refraining from the use of the word "stole," perhaps to spare the feelings of both master and servant with a semi-playful phrase such as a lawyer uses in court to disarm the guarded attitude of a witness. Yet beneath it all is the implied exhortation to Philemon to forgive this wrong also, as Paul goes on to use the ever memorable words, "Put that on mine account," or "Set it down and reckon it in with what I myself may owe you." Does not this reckoning, or imputing, remind us of the apostle's doctrinal discussion in the fourth and fifth chapters of his Epistle to the Romans?[1] As Dr. C. I. Scofield has so aptly pointed out, verses 17 and 18 are an illustration of the two aspects of imputation: "Receive him as myself," or "reckon to him my merit"; ... "Put that on mine account," or "reckon to me his demerit." These verses also illustrate the two aspects of substitution—exact and equivalent. Exact substitution is the literal idea of the term "vicarious," and it may be illustrated by the well-known instance of a substitute in military service. Scripture has similar instances of it, e.g., the ram for Isaac (Gen. 22:13), Judah for Benjamin (Gen. 44:33), the Levites for the firstborn (Num. 3:11-13), David for Absalom (II Sam. 18:33), and, here, Paul for Onesimus (v. 17). Equivalent substitution is to be distinguished from the foregoing and has been illustrated by a man who rescues another from drowning not by being drowned instead, but by doing in the act of lifesaving what the other is incapable of doing for himself. This is the meaning of the ransom (cf. Lev. 25:47-49) and, applied to the atoning sacrifice of Christ, it is obvious that everything depends upon the power of the substitute and the adequacy of His work. He must be someone capable of rescuing the whole of humanity because He Himself is more than man. The illustration of this in verse 18 is a simple one, but Paul's offer to pay what Onesimus was quite evidently incapable of paying was an entirely adequate equivalent. Miss Frances Ridley Havergal expressed it thus:

> Nothing to pay! ah, nothing to pay!
> Never a word of excuse to say!
> Year after year thou hast filled the score,
> Owing thy Lord still more and more.
> Hear the voice of Jesus say,
> "Verily, thou hast nothing to pay!
> Ruined, lost art thou, and yet
> I forgave thee all that debt."
>
> Nothing to pay! the debt is so great,
> What will you do with the awful weight?

---

1 See the author's *St. Paul's Epistle to the Romans,* pp. 126f.

> How shall the way of escape be made?
> Nothing to pay!—yet it must be paid!
> Hear the voice of Jesus say,
> "Verily, thou hast nothing to pay!
> All has been put to My account,
> I have paid the full amount."

"I Paul have written it with mine own hand" (v. 19), the apostle continues. This sentence was a formal signature, a binding seal (cf. I Cor. 16:21; Col. 4:18; II Thess. 3:17) pledging the writer to repay the debt in question. In those other three passages it is only the "salutation" that is certified as being in the author's own hand, that "which is the token in every epistle" (II Thess. 3:17) of its authenticity. However, in this instance in Philemon it would seem probable that St. Paul meant that for legal reasons he was writing the entire letter himself, which is unusual, just as the subject of the letter is unusual, yea, unique.

2. The Gentle Reminder (v. 19b). "Albeit (notwithstanding this) I do not say to thee how thou owest unto me even thine own self besides." Here is another paradox, namely, Paul's expression of a hitherto suppressed thought: "Though indeed, Philemon, you cannot fairly claim repayment of this debt from me, seeing you owe me a greater one—your own spiritual self, the very being of a son." True love never recounts services rendered nor presses claims, and yet there is a sense in which there can and should be a voluntary recognition and reward. In like manner, while we are told of "the great God, the mighty, and the terrible, who regardeth not persons, nor taketh reward" (Deut. 10:17, *A.S.V.*), we know from such a New Testament passage as Ephesians 1:12 that we as sons of God "should be to the praise of his glory, who first [or, had previously, Gr.] trusted in Christ." Well may Miss Havergal conclude her poem as follows:

> Nothing to pay! yes, nothing to pay!
> Jesus has cleared all the debt away,
> Blotted it out with His bleeding hand!
> Free, and forgiven, and loved, you stand.
> Hear the voice of Jesus say,
> "Verily, thou hast nothing to pay!
> Paid is the debt, and the debtor free!
> Now I ask thee, lovest thou Me?"

3. The Loving Entreaty (v. 20). "Yea, brother, let me have joy of thee in the Lord: refresh my heart in Christ" (*A.S.V.*). Again the apostle addresses Philemon in a tone of affectionate appeal—"Ah, my brother, let me rejoice because of you"—and in still another paradox Paul's son in

Christ (cf. v. 19) is also his brother in Christ (cf. v. 7), for the one born and nurtured and led is blessedly on an equal basis in Christ with the one who begets, feeds, and guides (cf. "brethren," Gal. 3:15; 6:1, 18). The use of the separate Greek word for the pronoun "I" is for emphasis—"I am pleading as though for myself, not just for another" (cf. v. 17). The verb translated "let me have joy" would be more accurately rendered "let me receive help" (cf. *A.S.V.* marg.), or, "satisfaction, comfort, profit," such as a father looks for in a son, or one brother in another. It is another play on the meaning of the name Onesimus, "profitable" (cf. vv. 10, 11): "May I have satisfaction from you such as you will now have from your repentant slave." Then the apostle uses the same word as in verse 7: Refresh, relieve, encourage me, as you have others, and do it, for me as for them, in the Lord—the great sphere of recompense, of compliance, of fellowship!

HUMAN DESIRES AND DIVINE PROVIDENCE, vv. 21-25

Now that the apostle is concluding his letter to his friend Philemon, there is a noticeable buoyancy of expression:

1. The Confident Expectation (v. 21). "Having confidence in thine obedience I write unto thee, knowing that thou wilt do even beyond what I say" (*A.S.V.*). Love can confidently command because it can count on loving obedience that will "go the second mile" and perform even more than is asked. But what is "more" in this case? It is thought that full emancipation of the slave was in Paul's mind. If so, his self-restraint is most significant. The word seems to hover near as he writes, but it never quite comes. This restraint in secular affairs is a characteristic of the gospel; it attacks no one but, rather, undermines error, whether social or individual, by laying down a principle or by setting an example. A result in this particular sphere of society was the abolition of slavery in the English-speaking world that came through the efforts of Christian men such as William Wilberforce, Abraham Lincoln, and Wendell Phillips.

2. The Cordial Anticipation (v. 22). "But withal (at the same time) prepare me also a lodging (guest room): for I hope that through your prayers I shall be granted (sent) unto you" (*A.S.V.*). The apostle was quite evidently longing for a reunion with his friends in Colosse, and it may well be that this episode in connection with Onesimus caused St. Paul to change his plan to go on to Spain (Rom. 15:24) and first to revisit Greece and Asia Minor (Phil. 2:24). There is a sense of gentle compulsion in this verse—he would like to come and see for himself whether Philemon had indeed complied with his request. The "lodging" (cf. Acts 28:23) may have referred to accommodation either at an inn or in a private house, perhaps Philemon's own, although the apostle does not presume to command hospitality or to specify its exact nature. He may have preferred "his own hired house," as in Rome (cf. Acts 28:30), for similar purposes of preaching and receiving inquirers.

Here is an illustration not only of delicacy of feeling in social contacts, but also of the limits placed on prayer for temporal blessings. St. Paul did "hope" he could visit Colosse but did not yet know how far his plan might coincide with the will of God. How much more does it behoove us to make certain of it! For us the prayer of faith, the Word of God, and the circumstances of life are the three factors whose agreement assists us in divining the will of the Lord, in relation both to ourselves and to our influence on others.

3. **The Christian Fellowship (vv. 23-25).** This final section of the Epistle is in two parts, Salutation and Benediction:

a. Salutation (vv. 23, 24). "Epaphras, my fellow-prisoner in Christ Jesus, saluteth thee; and so do Mark, Aristarchus, Demas, Luke, my fellowworkers" (*A.S.V.*). Doubtless Epaphras was mentioned first because he was a Colossian (Col. 4:12), either by birth or by adoption, and as an evangelist there (Col. 1:7, 8) he must have been well known to Philemon, probably ministering to the church that met in Philemon's home (v. 2). The others mentioned were also known to him, most of them having joined in the general salutations to the Christians in Colosse (Col. 4:10-14). Perhaps Justus (Col. 4:11) is not listed because, besides being a Jewish Christian ("of the circumcision"), he was also, from his name, a Roman one. In both passages Epaphras is described as Paul's "fellow prisoner," either a voluntary one, in order to be with the apostle and minister to him, or else because he had been suspected by the authorities and also detained. The others—Mark, Aristarchus, Demas, and Luke—were almost certainly free to come and go—"fellowworkers" whose value to Paul was great and far-reaching. Belonging to this privileged band was quite evidently the former slave Onesimus, subject of this beautiful and unique letter, for in Colossians 4:9 he is described as "a faithful and beloved brother." What a splendid designation, and what a blessed circle of companionship!

b. Benediction (v. 25). "The grace of our Lord Jesus Christ be with your spirit. Amen." With these familiar words St. Paul ends his letter and lays down his pen. It is the same benediction that he pronounced on the recipients of his Epistle to the Galatians (6:18). Even here, in this personal letter to a Christian friend, it is addressed in the plural—"your spirit"—signifying that it is for all those mentioned in the opening salutation of verses 2 and 3, that is, the local church at Colosse. Thus the Epistle to Philemon is concluded, as it was commenced, in Christ, and the sphere of

His grace is the spirit of His Church. The exercise of His grace is the strongest bond of a Christian family, and the desire for it the purest wish of a Christian friendship. And so there is emphasized afresh the blessed means by which, in those matchless words of *The Book of Common Prayer,* "all those who profess and call themselves Christians may be led into the way of truth, and hold the faith in unity of spirit, in the bond of peace, and in righteousness of life." "Amen!" adds the apostle, "So be it!"

15 SUMMARY

Perhaps the best single word with which to sum up St. Paul's Letter to Philemon is service. The very nature of the subject discussed emphasizes the principles that should govern labor in behalf of others.

1. Service Is the Christian's Duty. The Christian's true attitude as a redeemed believer in Christ is well expressed in the words of Luke 1:74: "That we being delivered . . . might serve." Quite evidently there is room for many and varied types of service, since the Greek New Testament has several words for "servant," suggesting various aspects of work—strenuous service, menial service, temple or church service, medical service, household service, etc. But of whatever type Christian service finds its central source and chief impetus in love—love "toward the Lord Jesus, and toward all saints" (v. 5; see also vv. 7, 9, 16).

2. The Apostle Paul Is the Christian's Model. A wonderful illustration of service is found in Paul's life and character. This is because he so fully realized what God had done for him through Christ and, as a consequence, was constrained by love to work for others (cf. II Cor. 5:14; Gal. 5:13). Thus was he able to show in a friendly letter to Philemon a perfect example of Christian service, with its fine qualities of devotion, consecration, faithfulness, and tact.

3. Christ Is the Christian's Power. One of the greatest titles of Christ is Servant of Jehovah, "my servant" (Isa. 42:1; 49:6; 52:13); and one of the greatest descriptions of Him in the flesh is that He took "the form of a

173

servant" (Phil. 2:7). Through His incarnation and His substitution He stooped, and served, and suffered that we might be saved, and sanctified, and satisfied. Everything He did and said showed Him to be an instrument in the Father's hand for man's redemption, and the very grace wrought at Calvary is the compelling secret of our own acceptable service for God. In this letter we hear a tender echo of the divine influence—beseeching, claiming, conceding, identifying, rejoicing, and expecting more than is actually asked. Thus it presents a clear example of ideal Christian living and proves itself to be a true epistle of Christ Himself, wherein even dim eyes may read His marvelous love and catch a glimpse of His very image, who "humbled himself, and became obedient unto death, even the death of the cross" (Phil. 2:8).

"As Christ doth for us with God the Father," wrote Martin Luther, "so doth St. Paul with Philemon for Onesimus. We are all God's Onesimi, to my thinking." "And to mine, Dr. Luther," corroborates Alexander Smellie, adding: "Fugitives, outcasts, who have stolen our Master's property and fled from His house, 'aforetime unprofitable' to Him. Ah, but God's Onesimi too because He welcomes us back, and then at last we begin to be profitable; not now slaves, but children beloved." . . . "You and I may well be glad to be God's Onesimi. For, when the name is ours, we come to our true self, to our proper home, and to our satisfying future" (Smellie, *In the Hour of Silence,* p. 396, and in *The Sunday School Times,* Nov. 26, 1921).

> The trembling sinner feareth
> That God can ne'er forget;
> But one full payment cleareth
> His memory of all debt.
> When nought beside could free us,
> Or set our souls at large,
> Thy holy work, Lord Jesus,
> Secured a full discharge.

The late Bishop Moule of Durham was best known as a great scholar and commentator, but he was also a poet. Under the title "The Bondslave" he has given us these lines, inspired by the example of the medieval vassal who knelt with folded hands to swear allegiance to his feudal lord:

> My glorious Victor, Prince Divine,
> Clasp these surrendered hands in Thine;
> At length my will is all Thine own,
> Glad vassal of a Saviour's throne.
>
> My Master, lead me to Thy door;
> Pierce this now willing ear once more;

Thy bonds are freedom; let me stay
With Thee, to toil, endure, obey.

Yes, ear and hand, and thought, and will,
Use all in Thy dear slavery still!
Self's weary liberties I cast
Beneath Thy feet; there keep them fast!

Tread them still down; and then I know
These hands shall with Thy gifts o'erflow;
And piercèd ears shall hear the tone
Which tells me Thou and I are one.

                    —H. C. G. Moule

APPENDIX 1   THE LIFE AND WORK OF ST. PAUL[1]

Among the leaders in the early Church, the apostle Paul is indubitably unique. By race a Jew, by culture a Greek, by citizenship a Roman, and subsequently by grace a Christian, he is characterized by a combination of elements whose completeness is admittedly lacking in the other apostles. His importance in the Church, and as the writer of the Epistles, two of which are the subject of this volume, is so great that it would seem useful now to have before us in outline form the main features of St. Paul's life and work, with their New Testament sources. From this brief summary the reader may proceed to more detailed study.

1. *Paul's History*
    a. His antecedents: Phil. 3:4-6; Acts 21:39; 22:3, 28; 23:16; 7:58; 8:3; 26:4-10; II Tim. 1:3; Gal. 1:13, 14
    b. His conversion: Acts 9:1-18; 22:4-16; 26:9-18
    c. His early discipleship: Acts 9:19-30; Gal. 1:15-24
    d. His work at Antioch: Acts 11:19-30; 13:1, 2
    e. His missionary journeys:
        (1) The first: Acts 13:3 to 14:28
        (2) The second: Acts 15:1 to 18:22
        (3) The third: Acts 18:23 to 21:17

---

[1] Adapted from the author's article "Saul Who Is Also Called Paul: An Outline Study," in *The Sunday School Times*, June 18, 1921.

    f.   His experiences at Jerusalem: Acts 21:18 to 23:30

    g.   His imprisonment at Caesarea: Acts 23:31 to 26:32

    h.   His journey to Rome: Acts 27:1 to 28:16

    i.   His imprisonment at Rome: Acts 28:17-31

    j.   His probable release and second imprisonment, and his death: Phil. 1:24-26; Philem. v. 22; I Tim.; Titus; II Tim.

2. *Paul's Preaching*

    a.   The messages; note the audiences

        (1) To the Jews: Acts 13:16-41. Based on the Old Testament, God in His revelation to Israel

        (2) To uneducated Gentiles: Acts 14:15-17. Based on natural theology, God in Nature

        (3) To educated Gentiles: Acts 17:22-31. Based on philosophy, God's immanence (His presence in and oneness with the life of man), and God's transcendence (His distinctness from and supremacy over the life of man).

    b.   The methods; note the words used to describe the preaching.

        (1) Proclaiming: Acts 13:5, *A.S.V.*

        (2) Reasoning: Acts 17:2, 3, 17, *A.S.V.*

        (3) Testifying: Acts 18:5

        (4) Teaching: Acts 18:11

        (5) Exhorting: Acts 13:43

        (6) Warning: Acts 18:6; 28:25-28

3. *Paul's Epistles*[2] Paraphrasing Bishop Lightfoot,[3] we may distinguish these, the apostle's finest contribution to Christianity, substantially as follows:

    a.   The Epistles of the coming of Christ: I and II Thessalonians

    b.   The Epistles of the cross of Christ: I and II Corinthians; Galatians; Romans

    c.   The Epistles of the person of Christ: Philippians; Ephesians; Colossians; Philemon

    d.   The Epistles of the Church of Christ: I Timothy; Titus; II Timothy

4. *Paul's Character* Four elements of greatness blend in him and can be fully illustrated from the story of his life:

    a.   Intellectual force

    b.   Emotional fervor

    c.   Moral sincerity

    d.   Spiritual power

---

[2]For a fuller study of these, see Appendix 2.

[3]See Bibliography.

When mind, heart, conscience, and will are thus united, a Christian man attains a strength, nobility, and reality of character that, by divine grace, can accomplish great things for God.

5. *Paul's Influence*
    a. In his own day; note the influential features of his life as seen in the ten stages of Paul's history listed under "1"
    b. In subsequent ages; note the powerful influences of his teaching and writing in general, and also at particular periods of history, e.g., in the lives of Augustine, Luther, Calvin

6. *Paul's Versatility*. Few men have combined so many different and even diverse characteristics. Each of the following designations of the apostle is equally apt and (with others) may be fully documented from The Acts and the Epistles:
    a. The Missionary
    b. The Theologian
    c. The Pastor
    d. The Thinker
    e. The Saint
    f. The Man of Practical Affairs

7. *Paul's Secret*
    What is the explanation of this marvelous life?
    a. In general. His relation to Jesus Christ: e.g., Gal. 2:20; Phil. 1:21; 3:10
    b. In particular. This relation expressed itself in
        (1) Conversion
        (2) Communion
        (3) Consecration
        (4) Commission

APPENDIX 2   A GENERAL SURVEY OF ST. PAUL'S EPISTLES

One of the most amazing characteristics of the life of St. Paul is the extent and magnitude of his public work. Yet he found time and strength with which to accomplish a considerable amount of writing, in the form of a series of remarkable letters that early in the Church's history gained the undisputed status of books to be included in the New Testament canon (cf. II Peter 3:15, 16). We are not only amazed, but also thankful as Christians for these most precious, next to the four Gospels, of the sacred writings. It is clear, however, that the personal value of letter writing was as great then as now, for the bridging of distances and the resolving of difficulties.

1. The Origin of the Pauline Epistles. This was very simple. As long as the apostle was near Antioch, then the center of Christianity, there was no need to write letters; but when he had crossed over into Europe he could no longer superintend the churches of Asia. Therefore, moved by personal anxiety for them, he wrote for their guidance and encouragement directives, exhortations, and expositions of doctrine.

The writing of the Epistles was very necessary also to the completion and confirmation of St. Paul's ministry. In Thessalonica, for example, his stay had an abrupt ending—hence a letter to the Church there. In some cities, as in Corinth, his own character or his doctrines had been attacked. With the Christians in Philippi, he had a personal matter to discuss, and, as we have seen, of Philemon, a Christian friend, an individual favor to ask.

Realizing, as we have also noted, the spread of a Judaizing philosophy in Colosse, St. Paul wrote to the Church there in order to combat the error. To Rome and Ephesus, moreover, he sent perhaps his greatest doctrinal statements for the edification of the Churches in these two important cities.

The dispatching of the letters was a natural procedure, due to the Jewish custom of maintaining connections between their communities by sending letters from synagogue to synagogue. This custom had originated at the time of the Captivity and had continued afterward, in order to announce important events or to consult in matters of mutual interest. This may be noted in the Apocrypha (cf. Baruch, chap. 6 and II Maccabees 1). It is probable that neither St. Paul nor the recipients of his letters can have had any idea of their widespread influence or their far-reaching results, even during apostolic times.

2. The Character of the Pauline Epistles. Since these writings were letters, and not treatises, they were intensely personal, an element well suited to reveal Paul's individuality. They were not fettered by form, but free, spontaneous—warm and tender, or serious and firm, but all written from his heart. As to method, Paul's letters were probably on parchment (cf. II Tim. 4:13), and inscribed with pen and ink (cf. II John 12), and doubtless many were transmitted by dictation to some scribe (cf. Rom. 16:22). This is implied also in most of the other Epistles by means of an autographic salutation as a mark of genuineness (cf. II Thess. 3:17). These "conversations in shorthand," as they have been called, vivid, fresh, heartfelt, gave to the readers Paul as he was, the one who had led them to Christ or whose witness to others had influenced them to accept his gospel. Paul's letters evidently were conveyed either by some friend who chanced to be traveling or by special messenger for the purpose. It is just possible that II Thessalonians 2:1-12 avoids speaking explicitly lest that letter should fall into hands not intended to receive it. In I Thessalonians 5:27 we find an order that this letter should be read publicly, and perhaps that was the usual procedure with the others.

3. The Reception and Circulation of the Letters. There is good reason to think that some of Paul's Epistles were not preserved. There was almost certainly one such addressed to Corinth (I Cor. 5:9), and perhaps two (II Cor. 10:10), and possibly another sent to Thessalonica (II Thess. 3:17). Some scholars think an Epistle to Laodicea (Col. 4:16) was also lost, but it is more probable that this is our Epistle to the Ephesians (see p. 142). Doubtless each church would carefully preserve its autographed copy. Clement, an early bishop of Rome, in writing to the Christians in Corinth, assumes that they still possess St. Paul's Epistle (Clement, *Romans,* chap. 47). St. Peter, in referring to the apostle Paul, speaks of "all his epistles"

(II Peter 3:16), implying that a number of Paul's letters were known throughout the Churches by that early date (c. *A.D.* 66), and suggesting a considerable correspondence and exchange of general knowledge among them. In the second century all the Epistles but Hebrews, about which there was much doubt, were accepted, although the Pastoral Epistles were early rejected by the Gnostic heretics Basilides and Marcion. From the time of Origen, the entire fourteen (including Hebrews) gained practically universal acceptance as Paul's.

The manuscripts included all the Epistles but with certain differences of order. Hebrews was placed before the Pastoral Epistles in the most important manuscripts, and in one of them Colossians was placed next to Ephesians. The order of the King James Version is said to date back to Jerome and seems to be arranged as follows: The Epistles to the Churches come first and within this category the longest are first and the shortest last, except for Hebrews because of the doubts as to its authorship (see the author's volume, *Hebrews: A Devotional Commentary,* pp. 7-19). Then come the Epistles to individuals, also in order of length. The notes at the end of the Epistles are of no authority since they date only from the 5th century, being ascribed to Euthalius, a deacon of Alexandria in about 458.

4. The Grouping of the Pauline Epistles. As we have briefly noted these Epistles in their generally accepted chronological order are divided into four great groups, written at different periods separated in each case by about four years.

a. Group 1 includes I and II Thessalonians, written from Corinth during Paul's second missionary journey, in about 52 or 53 *A.D.* The great theme is hope, with its consolations on the one hand and its obligations on the other.

b. Group 2 includes I and II Corinthians, Galatians, and Romans, written during the third missionary journey in 57 or 58 *A.D.,* the first three probably from Ephesus and the fourth from Corinth. They all deal with practical problems in the light of eternal principles; they present Paul's personal defense against his enemies; and they emphasize freedom from bondage and fulness of redemption.

c. Group 3 includes Philippians, Colossians, Philemon, and Ephesians, all of them written probably during the apostle's first imprisonment in Rome, in the years 62 to 64, although it is just possible, according to some authorities, that these Epistles were written from the prison in Caesarea, two or three years earlier. They discuss respectively fellowship with Christ, the Lordship of Christ, love in Christ, and the possession of all things in Christ; and they point to the Christian means of defense against difficulties, error, hardness, and heresy.

d. Group 4 includes I Timothy, Titus, and II Timothy, written during the interval of Paul's release and in his second captivity in Rome in the years 66 to 68. They are called the Pastoral Epistles and deal with three elements of the Christian ministry: soundness of faith, sobriety of conduct, and strength of life.

5. **The Form of the Pauline Epistles.** St. Paul may be called Christianity's first thinker, the one who made the initial attempt to state doctrines in writing, an achievement that involved immense care and strenuous labor. His style differs from letter to letter, becoming more or less personal as required by the circumstances of composition.

a. The Apostle's Style in General. This is more classical than that of the other writers of the New Testament, except perhaps Luke and the writer of the Epistle to the Hebrews (if, indeed, this latter be not Paul himself). Paul was called by Eusebius "the most skilful of all in the arrangement of sentences" (Eusebius, 3:24). His writings are characterized by the following:

(1) Personal vividness. The probability that the letters were largely dictated, not hand-written by the author, produces a style that suggests conversation rather than literature. Renan called the Pauline method of transmission "a rapid conversation taken down and reproduced without correction." Along with this was direct appeal by name or designation (cf. II Cor. 6:4; Gal. 3:1; Rom. 2:1); frequent assertion of the author's own personal feelings (cf. Rom. 9:1-3; I Cor. 8:13 to 9:6; II Cor. 1:23); and sudden outbursts of doxology (cf. Rom. 7:25; I Cor. 1:14; 15:56). There is noticeable also a frequent adaptation of the language of other people, such as the apostle's opponents, so that it is not immediately apparent that he is quoting (cf. I Cor. 8:1 f; II Cor. 10:1 f; 12:16 f); and there is often a personification of abstract ideas, such as that of sin, as in Romans 7.

(2) Dramatic intensity. This is seen in passages where St. Paul argues on one side of a truth as though it were the whole (e.g., his sweeping condemnation of the Gentile world in Romans 1, and his discussion of predestination in Romans 9 and 10). Such intensity is enhanced by his use of style and structure, such as the piling up of substantive after substantive, adjective after adjective, verb after verb, in order to create a full impression of meaning. Hence, sections of Paul's Epistles are almost like lyrical poems (e.g., his praise of God's love in Rom. 8:31-39 and of man's in I Cor. 13). Note his metaphorical use of the Greek word *ploutos,* riches, peculiar to him, for the wealth of God's mercy (cf. *inter alia,* Rom. 9:23; Eph. 1:7; Col. 1:27), and also his singular use of the preposition *huper,* beyond, above. Compare the compound words *huper-perissenein* in Romans 5:20; II Corinthians 7:4; *huperballein* in II Corinthians 9:14; Ephesians 1:19; 2:7; *huperechein* in Philippians 2:3; 4:7.

(3) Structural irregularity. This is caused by very swift change of

thought on the apostle's part. For example, there are long parentheses (Eph. 3:1-4); inverted constructions where the emphatic word is found out of the usual order (II Thess. 2:7); instances showing a love of paradox and play upon words (I Thess. 4:11; II Cor. 6:9, 10; 8:2; Phil. 4:7; Eph. 6:20; I Tim. 5:6; Philem. 10, 11); and antitheses of thought rather than merely of words (cf. Gal. 6:2-5; Phil. 2:13; II Cor. 12:9, 10).

(4) Old Testament influence. St. Paul's Epistles are permeated by the Old Testament in the form of frequent quotations. Where not directly quoted its language is adapted, so that the clue to the apostle's meaning is often found only along these lines. Thus we recognize that II Corinthians 3:12-18 is steeped in the language of Exodus 34; I Corinthians 2:10-16 in that of Malachi 3 and 4; II Timothy 4:16-18 in that of Psalm 22. In writing Ephesians 1, Paul may well have been adverting to Leviticus 20 or 25.

In addition to these considerations, note the characteristics of the Pauline Epistles listed by G. B. Stevens (*The Pauline Theology,* chap. II, pp. 27-51): (1) Mystical realism, with a conception of religious truth under forms which are determined by personal relationship, e.g., that close connection between the unregenerate and Adam and between the regenerate and Christ (I Cor. 15:45-47). (2) Objectification—almost personification—of religious truth, e.g., the righteousness that comes from God, and the principle of sin as a tyrant. (3) A predominantly legal method of treating certain themes, e.g., deliverance from law (Rom. 7:1-6), adoption (Rom. 8:14-17), justification (Rom. 3:21 to 5:11). (4) The use of parallels, e.g., faith and works (Rom. 3:27 to 4:5), law and grace (Rom. 3:20-26), Adam and Christ (Rom. 5:12-21).

b. The Style and Substance of the Four Groups.
(1) Group 1. 1 Thessalonians and II Thessalonians.

In point of time, these Epistles are nearest to St. Paul's missionary period and therefore more analogous to his speeches recorded in the Book of Acts. They are also called the Eschatological Group from their main subject.

Their style is among the simplest and least impassioned. They were written in the absence of controversy, with a simple salutation and a simple benediction. They are personal and affectionate in subject matter and, because so little argumentative, contain no quotations from the Old Testament. The thought about Christ's work is mainly of Him as future Judge, and the Christian life is described as a waiting for God's Son from heaven (I Thess. 1:10), with believers as servants expecting their Lord's appraisal of themselves and looking forward to His coming as a time of recompense for their sufferings and of punishment for their persecutors. The only point at issue is the date of Christ's coming, and the moral difficulties discussed are those caused by mistaken ideas about it. Faith in Christ is accepted without controversy and the only warnings are against misunderstandings of that faith. Paul's opponents now are hostile Jews on the outside, who try to prevent him from witnessing to Gentiles (cf. I Thess. 2:16), and possibly the great passage in II Thessalonians 2 was provoked by them. This group of Epistles thus embodies Paul's protest against national exclusiveness, the attitude of those who believed that only one nation, the Jewish, would be saved.

There are characteristic words in this group: *ataktein,* to be disorderly, and derivatives, appear only here; *sterizein,* to be established, appears twice in Romans, but otherwise only in this group; *parousia,* for Christ's coming, occurs in I Corinthians 15:23 but otherwise only in this group and here frequently.

This group corresponds to the grace of hope as it looks forward to the coming of Christ.

(2)   Group 2. I Corinthians, II Corinthians, Galatians, and Romans.

This is often called the Anti-Judaic Group of Epistles and is by far the most argumentative, impassioned, and authoritative. Now that the central doctrines of Paul's teaching have been attacked and his authority as an apostle has been undermined, he is face to face with opposition in all his churches. Therefore these Epistles of his are full of arguments in support of those central doctrines. They show much greater self-consciousness and strength of emotion, far more display of his own feelings, a far stronger contrast between external sufferings and internal exaltation, far more of personal entreaty and attachment, and yet more of irony and sarcasm.

The Old Testament is quoted directly eighty or ninety times, and there is frequent use of rhetorical questions and strong assertions: e.g., *me genoito,* "God forbid!"; *ti oun lego de,* "what I mean is this"; *idou,* "behold!" (found only in this group). There is frequent use of double compounds, as *prosanatithemi,* literally, to put anything both up and toward one, or to confer, consult, communicate, impart, words seeming to grow under Paul's intense excitement.

As the former group of Epistles dealt with the future of Christ's relation to the believer, so this group answers a twofold question as to the present: (a) What is Christ's present relation to the believer? (b) How does man's present relation to God differ from what it was under either Judaism or heathenism before the coming of Christ? The answer is given by presenting Christ under the aspect of past Atonement and present Redeemer, the Second Adam who has given man a fresh start. His righteousness is communicated to man now by faith, so that man's relation to

God is presently one of conscious sonship and his standing one of freedom.

Words and phrases peculiar to this group of Epistles include the following: *katalassein,* to reconcile; *katallarge,* reconciliation; *dikaioma* and *dikaiosia,* justification; *eleutheria,* freedom, liberty; *ho deuteros Adam,* the second Adam; *sperma Abraam,* the seed of Abraham.

In the cities to which these Epistles were written, the antagonism to St. Paul was different from that connected with the first group. It was expressed not by Jews, but by Judaizing Christians, those who were trying to keep Christianity narrowly Jewish and make Judaism a worldwide religion by its means. They were not excluding Gentiles but regarding them as on a lower level; and, being on the inside, these Judaizers were the more hurtful to the cause in emphasizing works as a substitute for faith. This group of Epistles, therefore, embodies Paul's protest against legal exclusiveness, against those people who say that only they can be saved who keep the Mosaic law.

(a) I Corinthians. This is the most varied of the group. It has no one subject but provides answers to various questions. It deals with irregularities of practice rather than of doctrine. The most historical of all Epistles, it gives more insight into the beginnings of the early Church, its assemblies, its relation to heathenism, its sacraments, than all the others put together. For example, there is no certain reference in the Epistles to the Lord's Supper except in First Corinthians. It has been called the Epistle of Christian casuistry, in the word's primary sense of dealing with questions of right and wrong conduct in cases of conscience. Thus it discusses difficulties that arose from the relation of the believer to the heathen around him, e.g., as to intermarriage, feasting on idol food, etc. The keynote of the whole Epistle is *agápe,* because both Christian liberty and knowledge, according to Paul, are to be controlled by love.

(b) II Corinthians. This is a very clearly marked Epistle because it is the most personal and polemical of all. In one way, however, it is the most obscure because of the difficulty of understanding the conditions in the Church of Corinth with which the writer is dealing. It gives the strongest defense of himself as an apostle and the fullest expression of his own feelings and of the motivation of his work. It is the guide *par excellence* in the true exercise of a spiritual ministry, a veritable mine of pastoral wisdom, for, as I Corinthians is the most historical, II Corinthians is the most biographical of the Pauline Epistles. The former deals with Church life, the latter with individual life. Three great words in II Corinthians are *paraklesis,* entreaty, exhortation, consolation; *charis,* grace; *kauchesis,* glorying.

(c) Galatians. This Epistle has much more unity of purpose than the

others. It is almost blunt, with its beginning characterized by neither thanksgiving nor praise. It has a more severe tone of condemnation for error. Its primary purpose is to support justification by faith as against the Jewish law as the final guide for life; and its subordinate purpose is a defense of Paul's own apostolic independence. A phrase that summarizes it is *pistis di' agápes energoumenè, "faith working through love" (5:6, A.S.V.)*, a reminder of John's antithesis of "law" and "grace" (John 1:17).

(d) Romans. [1] This of all the Epistles of Paul is most like a complete treatise. It is comprised of an argumentative statement of his central doctrines combined with a conciliatory plan for drawing together Jewish and Gentile Christians; hence his debating in a twofold way, first with the Jew and then with the Gentile. Romans deals on a wider basis than Galatians with the whole question of the relation of Christianity to the world, including very much more prominently the thought of the Gentile nations. It dwells very fully on the eternal purpose of God, and its keynote is *pas,* all, everyone, emphasizing the universality of sin, of the need of redemption, and of the message of salvation in Christ. This Epistle has been called "the Christian philosophy of history," and this is summed up in Romans 1:16, 17.

This second group of Epistles corresponds to the Christian grace of faith.

(3)   Group 3.   Philemon, Philippians, Colossians, Ephesians.

The subject of these Prison Epistles, as they are usually called, is, on the positive side, Christology, or the study of the person of Christ, and, negatively speaking, Anti-Gnosticism. The style of this third group is more like that of the first than of the second. With all marks of excited controversy gone, it is quieter than Group 2, and yet more majestic and dignified than Group 1. The years are passing, and there is the fulness of matured thought coupled with the more elaborate style of experience. In quotations the group is very like the first, only two being directly from the Old Testament (Eph. 4:8 and 6:3), but for the first time there is included an apparent quotation from a Christian hymn (Eph. 5:14), based possibly upon the words of Isaiah 60:1, 2.

The aspect of Christ's work contained in this group of Epistles answers another twofold question: (1) What is Christ now to the whole Church and also to the whole universe? This leads up to (2) What is He essentially in His relation to God the Father? The answer to this latter question may be considered first because of its transcendent importance.

As to God, Jesus Christ is *pleroma tou theou,* the fulness of

---

[1] See the author's *Romans: A Devotional Commentary*

God; He shares and embodies all the divine attributes. Note *en morphe theou,* in the form of God; *isa theou,* equal with God. Thus He is both the instrument of creation and also the agent by whom God now sustains the world.

As to the Church, Jesus Christ is the ascended Lord who is the head of the body, *kephalè.* He is sending out His gifts to the Church and filling it with the *pleroma,* fulness, of His life, so as to enable it in turn to become His complete witness to the world.

Hence this group of Epistles reveals the eternal and universal purpose of redemption as predestined by God, as embodied in Christ, and as effected in the Church. Consequently it gives us the fullest teaching about the person of Christ, together with the highest concept of the Church of Christ. Note that the Prologue to St. John's Gospel (John 1:1-14) is the non-Pauline passage of the New Testament nearest in substance to this group of Epistles.

The antagonists of the time were those who combined Judaism with an Oriental belief in the essentially evil nature of matter, and so were akin to the later Gnostics and also to the Essenes among the Jews. This theory led to (1) a denial of God as Creator of the world, separating Him therefrom by the interposition of angels and the worship of them; (2) a rigid asceticism arising out of a belief in the need of abstinence as far as possible from everything material; and (3) an emphasis on the importance of knowledge as the only means of salvation because of the imagined worthlessness of material things. This was formalism in a new guise—no longer the antithesis of faith and works, but the promulgation of sanctification by the keeping of the Mosaic law, and a climbing up and out of the flesh and to God through the worship of heavenly beings, angels, as an intermediate order. Against all this Paul reacts strongly by magnifying Christ as the instrument of creation, and he emphasizes faith in Him, the central figure in the work of salvation, as the necessary preparation for *epignosis,* full knowledge—a characteristic word. Thus does the apostle protest against an intellectual exclusiveness that would confine Christianity to informed, educated, even learned persons, and at the same time he declares that Christ as Lord and Mediator is all-sufficient.

A. M. Fairbairn reminds us that in these Epistles the antitheses of Judaism are transcended and become universal. Christ occupies not simply an historical, but a cosmical place; and at the touch of evil the cosmology becomes a soteriology. The old antithesis of Adam and Christ has disappeared in the higher one between Satan and Christ (Fairbairn, *The Place of Christ in Modern Theology,* pp. 318f.).

(a) Philemon. This is a short, personal letter, with no doctrinal teaching but, as we have seen, it exemplifies the love of Christ in relation

to fellow-Christians and is full of useful suggestions for practical Christian living (see pp. 145ff.).

(b) Philippians. This also is one of the simplest and most personal of all the Epistles. Its expression of gratitude for kindness and its bright, joyous tone are combined with a great moral appeal to preserve unity in the Philippian Church by mutual forbearance. Thus it leads up almost incidentally to the grand description of Christ's nature and the conditions of His incarnation (see chap. 2). Philippians has also been called the Epistle of holy joy in suffering. Written from prison, it affords abundant proof of the saying that, while happiness depends on what is happening, true joy, the joy of faith that exults in the Unseen, is gloriously free of circumstances. Incidentally, the Christian should never employ the common phrase "under the circumstances" (literally things that stand around), but rather, and more grammatically, "*in* the circumstances," for though he may well be circumscribed by difficulties and sorrows he must never allow them to gain the ascendancy over him.

There is also, in this Epistle to the Philippians, a great emphasis on thanksgiving to God and on a longing for the Christian fellowship so well remembered and appreciated. We find, accordingly, little that is official in nature, and there is no expression of censure. The Epistle does not correct doctrinal errors as does Galatians, nor irregular practices, as does I Corinthians. No dogmatic system is outlined and no method of church government is advocated. Philippians is simply a spontaneous, fervid utterance of Christian love and gratitude, and in this it resembles I Thessalonians, written to another Macedonian church to which the writer was greatly attached.

There was in Philippi only one serious internal flaw. A spirit of strife had sprung up, leading to disputes on some social questions, with each party in the church claiming Paul's sympathy. The apostle attempts to check this tendency and does it gently but firmly, even though indirectly, taking no sides. Note the repetition of the word *pantes,* all, in 1:1-8, and his appeal for unity in 1:27 to 2:4; the example of Christ (2:5-11), and his own example in the verses that follow. He does utter a warning against errors of several kinds, but they seem to be external ones.

(c) Colossians and Ephesians. These two Epistles may be bracketed because, as we have seen, they cover much the same ground. Their subject is the same, Christ and the Church, but it is considered from different standpoints. Colossians is argumentative and controversial in tone. Ephesians is dogmatic and doctrinal, but also devotional and full of thanksgiving to God for the truth proclaimed. Colossians emphasizes Christ's work in relation to the whole world, while Ephesians is concerned with it more specifically as it relates to the Church in the world. It follows that,

of the two, Colossians is occupied more with Christ Himself and Ephesians more with the Church and, in opposition to Jewish arrogance and in reassurance of Gentile fears, it sets forth the Church's unity. Hence the two Epistles are complementary and suitable to be read together (cf. Col. 4:16). Compare with this the relation between Luke and Acts, John's Gospel and his Apocalypse. Moreover, Colossians is full of personal allusions and messages for individuals, while Ephesians is the most general of all the Epistles, with scarcely any personal references.

Here there are more striking verbal coincidences than elsewhere (e.g., Eph. 5:5 and Col. 3:5), but also many differences. Colossians has the *pleroma,* fulness, of Christ only (Col. 1:19; 2:9), while Ephesians uses the word of the Church also (Eph. 1:23; 3:19); the one mentions the Holy Spirit but once (Col. 1:8), the other eleven or twelve times.

This third group of Paul's Epistles, as compared with the others, manifests the grace of love.

(4) Group 4. I Timothy, Titus, II Timothy.

These three, known as St. Paul's Pastoral Epistles, may be considered together in so far as all contain pastoral directions. II Timothy, however, is a more personal, affectionate message, sent at the close of the writer's life to a young colleague, while I Timothy and Titus are primarily manuals for those in authority. These are more abrupt than the earlier Epistles, but the abruptness is of subject rather than of style. There is no continuing theme in any of the three but, rather, as we should say, a number of jottings as to questions of church life. This group contains a wide variety of words not found elsewhere in Paul's Epistles, and hence the difficulty some scholars have raised as to their authorship. There are only two direct quotations from the Old Testament, but there are five of what are called "faithful sayings." There is a possibility in one case (I Tim. 5:18b) that it is Luke's record of Christ's words (cf. Luke 10:7) that is quoted and authenticated as Scripture.

In these Epistles there is no new aspect of Christ's work insisted upon, since they deal rather with church organization and with moral life than with doctrine. Stress is laid on sobriety of conduct as the result of soundness in the faith. The antagonists implied here are very much the same as in the previous group, but appear more complicated in their dogma and more subtle in their approach. They were evidently the kind of Gnostics who combined insistence on Jewish law with a denial of the resurrection, and who differed from heretics only in a tendency to a more immoral life and thus to license rather than to the other extreme of asceticism. Paul no longer argues; he simply urges his young colleagues to "hold fast" (II Tim. 1:13; Titus 1:9) and to live as they profess.

Characteristic words include *kosmios,* well-behaved, *sophron,* discreet, and compounds; *hugies,* sound or wholesome, and the related verb, *hugiainein,* in relation to teaching; *paratheke,* something committed; *mataiologia,* vain words, *kenophonia,* empty talking, babbling, and *logomachein,* to strive about words. The sentence most characteristic of this fourth group of Epistles is found in I Timothy 3:15:—*hina eides pros dei en oiku theou anastrephesthai*—"that thou mayest know how thou oughtest to behave thyself in the house of God."

This fourth group of Epistles may be said to combine all three Christian graces—faith, hope, and love. Note, for example, such a noteworthy passage on salvation as Titus 3:4-7.

6. **The Teaching of the Pauline Epistles.** We may now attempt to sum up the apostle's teaching under the same four headings:

a. Group 1. In Thessalonica the Church's object of keen desire and of joyful hope was to such a degree the Second Coming of Christ that a spirit of impatience had crept in. This led to some mistaken ideas, and so the whole subject was referred to St. Paul. He reminded the Thessalonians, therefore, of his teaching on the subject of the future, outlining in his First Epistle to them the bright side of the Advent and in his Second the dark side. But in his own thinking this subject soon gave place to what Christianity is in itself, as opposed to both Judaism and paganism, a subject vital to any church in the period of its growth.

b. Group 2. Thus there now came a strong emphasis on the work of Christ as it related (1) in I Corinthians to Church order, (2) in II Corinthians to the Christian ministry, and (3) in Galatians and Romans to the whole gospel message.

c. Group 3. Those who were ready to appropriate salvation would want to know more about the One who had purchased and was bestowing it; and so there is a central emphasis upon the person of Christ: (1) In Philippians Christ is in the universe both exalted as God and humbled as a servant; (2) in Colossians and Philemon He is in the believer's heart as Lord; and (3) in Ephesians He is in the Church as life. Thus in this group of Epistles as a whole, there is to be found Paul's explicit teaching on the subject of Christology. Not only so but he expands his views of Christ into a philosophy of history and of the entire universe. It is remarkable that the antithesis presented is of Hellenic and Hellenistic elements with the discussion of cosmical and ethical subjects, and this less than a generation after the Crucifixion.

d. Group 4. After dealing with the great fact of Christ, His work and His person, St. Paul's chief end has been attained, and so he is now writing to two Church leaders, and through them to all others, in view of his departure. There must be the manifestation of Christ by means of the Christian ministry, including the spiritual work of those who are pastors, expressed in their preaching and teaching, and the temporal work of those who are deacons, expressed in their practical leadership and witness. Thus Christian faith and mutual love are to be exercised until the Lord appears again. And so the apostle comes full cycle to the great subject of his earliest writings (cf. II Tim. 4:8 with I Thess. 5:23 and II Thess. 3:5), the Second Advent of the Church's Lord.

7. The Influence of the Pauline Epistles on the Development of the Church. Again under these four chronological groupings, we note briefly:

a. At the time of the writing of *Group 1,* there was a strong emphasis on spiritual gifts, with church organization apparently quite elementary (I Thess. 5:12).

b. During the period in which *Group 2* was written, church offices were listed but were declared secondary to spiritual gifts (cf. I Cor. 12 to 14; Rom. 12:3-8).

c. When the apostle Paul sent out his Epistles included in *Group 3,* the matter of church offices was evidently in the ascendant. Although there is no mention of them in Colossians, their importance is obvious from Ephesians 4:11, 12, and it is implied in Philippians 2:25-30 and Philemon 1, 2.

d. In *Group 4* pastoral work only is under discussion, indicating the gradual development in Church life toward full-time leadership (I and II Tim. and Titus).

8. The Importance of the Study of the Pauline Epistles. A careful consideration of these writings is essential when we note the important part played by St. Paul in the Christian Church from its earliest days. Origen says of him: "He it was who, after Jesus, laid firm the foundation of the Churches that are in Christ" (Origen, *Contra Celsum,* i. 63). The position of Paul, however, was undeniably exaggerated in the nineteenth century by the critics, some of them German, of the Tübingen School, and others French, the Positivists, who tried to make Paul the founder of Christianity as a catholic or universal religion. At the same time, these men treated Jesus Christ merely as a Jew whose teaching, if left by itself, would have remained exclusively Jewish. But to those who today attempt a balanced survey the importance of Paul's Epistles is twofold: (1) for their theological teaching as sources of systematized Christian doctrine; and (2) for their historical value as literary documents concerning early Christianity.

a. The theological teaching. As Bishop Westcott points out, the contribution of St. Paul's Epistles is to provide the logical construction of the gospel as compared with the historical foundation given in the Gospels and in Acts, and with the spiritual completion found in St. John's writings. More than any other writer, St. Paul has indicated the logical connection between doctrines. As regards individual Christians, he shows the significance of Christ's life and death for those who have never seen Him. Clement of Rome calls this *dikaiosunen didaxas holon ton kosmon,* "a doctrine of righteousness for the whole world" (Clement of Rome, *Epistle to Corinth,* i. 5). St. Paul has also outlined the logical connection of Christianity as a system with the previous systems of Judaism and the Gentile religions. Christianity, according to him, speaks in the full language of the gospel as contrasted with systems that were but the alphabet (*tastiochera*) of the world.

Is this a legitimate outcome, or is it purely arbitrary? Can we not take the Gospels and set Paul's Epistles aside? No; this position is seen to be completely untenable when we remember that the Gospels themselves profess to be incomplete and definitely contemplate further teaching (cf. John 15:26, 27; 16:13; Luke 24:48, 49). This is how Dr. Alexander Whyte states the connection:

> The true glory of Paul's Epistles stands in this: He takes of the deepest things of God and of Christ and reveals them to us as no one else ever reveals them. "The Gospels," says an Egyptian Father, "supply the wool, but the Epistles weave the dress." That is to say, it is Paul's Epistles that set forth, in all its fulness, the complete and the final purpose of God in all that we see taking place in Matthew, and in Mark, and in Luke, and in John. In the four Gospels we see Jesus Christ born, and baptised, and tempted; we hear Him preaching also, so far as His hearers were able to bear it; and then we see Him taken by His enemies, and bound, and tried, and condemned and crucified. But it is Paul alone who comes and takes us into the divine heart of all that, and down into the divine root of all that. It is Paul alone who fully preaches out of all that the pardon of all our sin, and our peace with God, and our holiness of heart and life, and the life everlasting. That was all wrapped up, but was not as yet aright revealed, in the four Gospels. Yes; the four Evangelists supply him abundantly with the wool; but it is Paul alone who places the warp and the woof in his apostolic loom, till both he, and all his believing readers, can say, "I put on His righteousness, and it clothed me: it was to me for a robe, and for a diadem."

But even if the acceptance of his Epistles be granted, it may be asked whether Paul's interpretation of Christianity is the right one. This leads us to a fact that is of immense importance, one that cannot be too strongly or frequently emphasized, viz., that the interpretation of Paul was accepted by the other apostles. There is no doubt, of course, that this acceptance came after differences were stated and following discussion and even conflict, but the Pauline teaching *was* accepted, as is proved by noting Paul's own statement in Galatians 1:8 to 2:21. It is also indicated by a careful examination of the other apostles' writings.

In the case of Peter, his first Epistle agrees so fully with all the central doctrines of Paul that critics generally suppose Peter to have been influenced by Paul, and they believe that he knew Romans and Ephesians. Certainly, in II Peter there is a direct testimony to this agreement and a clause that includes the Pauline Epistles in the "scriptures" (II Peter 3:16).

In the case of James there is, of course, a much less obvious agreement with Paul. The Epistle of James portrays a very early and typically Judaic Christianity and is not concerned with controversy. Its keynotes are reality in daily living and endurance under temptation. It has suggested an apparent discrepancy as to the value of faith (cf. Jas. 2:14-26 with Rom. 3:21 to 5:11). But the discrepancy vanishes on a deeper examination into which we cannot now go.[2] Suffice it here to say that the faith by which Paul says we are justified (cf. Rom. 5:1) can be demonstrated only by means of works of a kind to vindicate it in the eyes of the world (James 2:24). In general, however, any seeming contradictions between James and Paul are explained by their differing purposes in writing. These naturally result in differing methods of presentation. Paul enunciates principles; James emphasizes practice. Paul lays the foundation; James builds on it. For example, the fundamental premise of Paul's gospel may be found summed up in James 1:18. After having referred in verse 17 to "every" divine gift, James gives a fine statement of the best gift of all, namely, the new birth. This is not human, but superhuman ("of his own will"), not natural, but supernatural ("he brought us forth by the word of truth" *A.S.V.*), not physical, but spiritual ("a kind of firstfruits"). Then James goes on to give some explicit directions as to the Christian life (vv. 19ff.). Compare this with what Paul writes in Galatians 4:21-31. But even in the realm of practice, there is no conflict between Paul and James. There are, instead, complementary statements. If, for instance, there is moral doubt as to a questionable course of action and yet the course is followed, that, Paul declares, is sin (Rom. 14:23). On the other hand, if there is knowledge as to a good deed and yet a failure to perform it, that, declares James, is sin (James 4:17).

In the case of John, there is an obvious independence of thought on the part of both John and Paul. Yet there is a striking agreement on all essential points. Note that in both love is the chief Christian virtue and faith in Christ's person the primary method of access to Christianity. A frequent word of both writers is *charis*, the special grace of Christianity

---

[2] See the *St. Paul's Epistle to the Romans,* pp. 131 ff.

which has been defined as the free gift of an implanted power of a holy life. There is in the Epistles of both a strong emphasis on the pre-incarnate life of Christ, God's predestination of believers, and the universality of the gospel. Yet nearly always there is a difference in the method of treatment. Both John and Paul contrast sharply law and grace, but Paul treats law as a burden thrown off, John as something incomplete that has been fulfilled. Both emphasize grace, but Paul connects it with the death of Christ as the means, John with His life as the source. Both refer frequently to Christ's death, but Paul treats of it Godward, laying stress on the atoning work of the blood. John, on the other hand, treats of it manward and lays stress on the cleansing power of the blood.[3]

While Paul did the work of adjusting Christianity to the thought of the Jewish race out of which it came, to John was allotted the task of adjusting it to the thought of the age into which it was entering. Paul vindicates the independence and sufficiency of the gospel by freeing it from the yoke of the past; John vindicates its completeness and adequacy for all the future by proclaiming its perpetual, living, present, and powerful Savior and Lord. Paul teaches us that Christianity is a new creation; John shows us that it can never grow old. This difference in viewpoint is inherent in the circumstances of the two apostles.

Paul preached the risen and glorified Christ who had appeared to him on the way to Damascus while John wrote of the human Christ whom he had seen and known. One way of expressing this distinction is to state that the message of St. Paul was that the man Jesus had become the glorified Lord, and St. John's message was that the divine Logos had become the human Jesus. Paul lifts up the ideal of faith by fixing it upon a divine Lord; John makes that faith real by fixing it on One who is as human as He is divine.

Further, St. Paul always claims to be building his teaching on that of Christ but not adding thereto (cf. I Tim. 6:3). In two places, at any rate, he definitely quotes our Lord's teaching and His authority as final: on divorce (I Cor. 7:10, 11); and on the payment of ministers (I Cor. 9:14). In many places the apostle's language is reminiscent of Christ's teaching in the Gospels, especially that of the Sermon on the Mount (Matt. 5 to 7) and of the eschatological discourses in Matthew 24 and 25. Even when not directly quoting from our Lord, he claims to be speaking "in the Lord" (Eph. 4:17), or "in the word of the Lord" (I Thess. 4:2; cf. I Cor. 7:40).

Inversely, we certainly find the germ of Pauline doctrine in our Gospels, such as the universality of Christianity and the catholicity of the Church

---

3 See B. F. Westcott, *The Historic Faith,* pp. 250-54; Wm. Sanday, *The Authorship and Historical Character of the Fourth Gospel,* pp. 36, 37, 80, 81, 232, 278, 280; and G. B. Stevens, *The Johannine Theology,* chap. XV, pp. 355-71.

(cf. Matt. 28:19, 20). We also note the virtual abrogation of the Mosaic Law in all that is specifically Jewish, e.g., Christ's claim to control the sabbath (Mark 2:28); His declaration "making all meats clean" (Mark 7:19, *A.S.V.*); His contemplation of the destruction of Jerusalem and of the Temple (Matt. 24:2); and His announcement of the discontinuance of Jerusalem as the center of Jehovah's worship (John 4:21).

Then there is the New Testament teaching about the Atonement, the presentation of Christ's death as an *apolutrosis,* redemption by ransom. Note the following germs of this: (1) the necessity of it (cf., *inter alia,* Matt. 26:54; Mark 8:31; Luke 24:7; John 3:14 with Rom. 6:6-11; 8:3; Gal. 4:4, 5; Phil. 2:5-8); (2) the nature of it (cf. Matt. 20:28 with I Cor. 1:30); and (3) the object of it (cf. Matt. 26:28 with Eph. 1:7).

On Paul's great subject of justification by faith (cf. Rom. 3 to 5), note the demand of Jesus for faith before miracle (cf. Luke 7:50; 18:42; John 11:26). Paul's doctrine is only an application of that principle to belief in the risen Christ. Note also the parable of the Pharisee and the publican in Luke 18 with its contrast between those who "trusted in themselves that they were righteous" (v. 9) and the man who "went down to his house justified"—by faith in the propitiation of the mercy-seat (vv. 13, 14, Gr., *ilastheti*).

All this bears out the words of Athanasius concerning Paul—he was *ho christopheros aner,* the Christ-bearing man—a veritable "St. Christopher" (cf. II Cor. 4:10)!

b. The historical value. As far as can be determined, the Pauline Epistles are our earliest Christian documents, unless perhaps James and possibly I Peter appeared earlier. The latter possibility, however, is very doubtful. Probably some Gospels in written form appeared prior to Paul's Epistles, although not our present ones.

(1) The Pauline Epistles are documents especially valuable for their form. They are letters, and so any evidence as to history is incidental. Not only do they bear the stamp of sincerity, but since some were written in the face of much opposition the writer obviously could not have ventured on doubtful statements. Two of them, Romans and Colossians, are addressed to churches in places where Paul had not been, and so they assume knowledge and experience independent of his own teaching.

(2) The Pauline Epistles prove a familiarity with the outline of facts of Christ's life. Our Lord is said to have been a Jew (Gal. 4:4), of the seed of Abraham (Rom. 1:3; 9:5-7); He had at least one brother (Gal. 1:19); He instituted the Holy Communion on the last day of His earthly life (I Cor. 11:23-25); he was crucified by His own people (I Thess. 2:14, 15) under Pontius Pilate the Roman governor (I Tim. 6:15); He arose from the dead on the third day afterward and appeared to Simon Peter, to James, and to all of the apostles (I Cor. 15:4-7); and He ascended into

heaven (cf. I Tim. 3:16), where He is seated on the right hand of God (cf. Col. 3:1).

(3) The Pauline Epistles show a definite conception of the character of Christ. In particular, it was marked by meekness and gentleness (II Cor. 10:1) and by self-sacrifice (Rom. 15:3). The general outlines of that matchless character are assumed as well known in frequent appeals to imitate Christ (cf. I Cor. 10:31 with 11:1; see also Rom. 13:11; Gal. 3:27; Phil. 2:5).

(4) Hence these Epistles give strong confirmation to the historical character of the Synoptic Gospels. Almost entirely the recorded facts agree, a noticeable exception being the resurrection appearances to the five hundred brethren and to James (cf. I Cor. 15:6, 7); and also, like the Synoptic writers, Paul lays most stress on the death of Christ.

(5) A more notable exception to this agreement is that Paul never alludes to the miracles of Christ. He is thought, therefore, by certain critics to cast some discredit on the miracles recorded in the Gospels. But note that this argument is only *e silentio,* which is always precarious. We can hardly point to any place in the Epistles where there would be a natural reference to miracles. St. Paul does appeal to miracles that he himself was presently working (II Cor. 12:11, 12); and it is obvious that, as far as evidence went, contemporary "signs and wonders" would be stronger proof of Christianity than the miracles of the past. But the apostle undoubtedly regards Jesus Christ as a superhuman person, as One who had come to earth from heaven, as One risen from the dead, and as One who was presently enabling him, Paul, to live his life and carry on his activities. As this experience of his included miraculous work, there can be no moral doubt that Paul regarded Christ as One who could work miracles.

(6) This leads us inevitably to the strength of Paul's witness to the Resurrection. This was a manifold witness:

(a) It was an evidence of Paul's own belief. Galatians and the two Corinthian Epistles were written in the year 57. In the former there is proof that Paul had held the same views at least fourteen or seventeen years before that Epistle was written (Gal. 1:18; 2:1). This brings his expressed belief in the Resurrection down to within seven or ten years of the death of Christ.

(b) By combining I Corinthians 15:1-8 and Galatians 2:6-9, we see that Paul bears witness to the belief of all the other apostles in the validity of the Resurrection.

(c) Paul's Epistles bear witness also to certain public acts of the Church as a whole which, as he interprets them, point to a general belief in the Resurrection. These are the partaking of the Lord's Supper "till he come" (I Cor. 11:26), and the observance of the first day of the week for giving (I Cor. 16:2), implying assembly for worship. Since there was no reason at that time in either Jewish or Gentile history for this observance, the implication is that the day had already been chosen by the Church to commemorate the Resurrection of our Lord (Acts 20:7).

(7) Furthermore, the Pauline Epistles bear strong witness to the conceptions of the early Church about Christ. They contain such phrases descriptive of Christ as *eikon to theo,* "image of God" (II Cor. 4:4; cf. Col. 1:15), and *isa theo,* "equal with God" (Phil. 2:6). They show that the Church believed that Christ had indeed come from heaven to earth and, possibly, that He was even called God (cf. I Tim. 1:1; Titus 1:3; 2:10, 13; 3:4). Hence St. Paul's Epistles lend very strong confirmation to the teaching of St. John's Gospel, which lays particular stress upon the divine nature of Christ. Thus it becomes impossible to say that the deep teaching of John about Christ is a late addition to Christian doctrine.

(8) St. Paul's Epistles, in addition, bear the earliest witness to the organization of the early Church, especially as to its ministry. As such, they supply very strong corroboration for the Acts of the Apostles and its teaching, e.g., on the usage of the words *prophetai,* "prophets" (cf. I Cor. 15:37 with Acts 11:27; 13:1; 15:32; 21:10) and *episcopoi,* "bishops" (cf. I Tim. 3:1-7 with Acts 20:28; see also 1:20). In this connection it is important to remember that the Greek equivalent for the Hebrew word meaning priest or sacrificer, *hiereus,* is never used by St. Paul (or found elsewhere in the New Testament) to denote the Christian minister as distinct from a layman. (Note that Romans 15:16 is clearly symbolic and spiritual in meaning as the terms and the context show.) Furthermore, the word in the singular number is used only of our Lord (cf. Heb. 3:1, *i.a.*). In its plural form it indicates all believers, i.e., "priests unto God" (Rev. 1:6; cf. 5:10; 20:6). Thus Christianity may be described as a religion that *is* a priesthood, and not one that *has* a priesthood (cf. I Peter 2:5, 9). The Christian ministry is a medium, not a mediation, since believers have unrestricted access to God.

9. Conclusion. Our study of the Pauline Epistles may be summed up under two important elements. These letters are characterized at once by their essential unity and by their infinite variety.

a. Unity. St. Paul's Epistles have one dominant theme which may be expressed in two words—"my gospel" (cf. Rom. 2:16; 16:25; II Tim. 2:8). This "good news" of his is under the three great subjects of justification, sanctification, and glorification, fulfilling the three needs of mankind for faith, love, and hope, even as we have seen that the Epistles themselves do. At the same time, these vitally consistent writings of the apostle Paul display:

b. Variety. Not only is their subject matter characterized by a wonderful depth and breadth, but their author is revealed by their means as a tremendously versatile person. Through his writings St. Paul is seen as apostle, preacher, pastor, teacher, and dialectician, and also as a true father in God, an affectionate friend, a firm disciplinarian, and a methodical organizer. With such versatility, and possessed of so remarkable an intellect and so tender a heart, he could justifiably exhort the early Christians to whom he wrote his great letters: "Be ye followers of me, even as I also am of Christ" (I Cor. 11:1).

Addressing divinity students in 1906, Dr. Alexander Whyte declared:

> Students of divinity! Happiest and most enviable of all our young men! Paul's Epistles are the true divinity for you. They contain God's finest wheat for you. They are full of honey and the honeycomb out of His Rock for you. "Study down," therefore, Paul's Epistles, as we are told Thomas Goodwin studied them down. And as no man with a Pauline eye in his head needs to be told. And your love for Paul's Epistles, and for such expositions of Paul's Epistles as Luther on the Galatians, and Goodwin on the Ephesians, will be a sure prophecy to you of the power and the fruitfulness of your future preaching. Be you—if you will take a word of advice from me—be you sleepless students day and night of Paul's Epistles, and of his only true successors: the first Reformers, and the Puritans of England, and the Covenanted Presbyterians of Scotland. Take the deep substance of Paul's Epistles, and put all that deep substance into Newman's English; or at least into Spurgeon's English, and that will make you perfect preachers to the best of your future people. For do not doubt but that God who watches what books you read in your student days, and what divinity you delight in, will both own and bless the provision you are already beginning to make for His poor in Zion. . . . If they are ordained to eternal life, they will yet be heard repeating Bunyan's great apostrophe, and saying, O blessed Paul! O ever dear and ever blessed Paul! Aye, and to your amazement they will add this: O dear and blessed minister who first taught us to read Paul's Epistles, and to understand them, and to enjoy them, and to enjoy nothing else like them in all the world! Amen.

EDITOR'S NOTE

There is no bibliography for the section on Philemon because, as noted in the Preface, this was expanded from unpublished notes.